THE SAVVY MUSIC TEACHER

Practical, inspirational, and incredibly thorough, *The Savvy Music Teacher* is a book that no independent music teacher should be without!

Brandon Pearce
Founder, *Music Teacher's Helper*
www.musicteachershelper.com

Thank you to David Cutler for creating the "Ben Franklin's Almanac" for independent music teachers, with an engaging combination of practical information and street-smart advice.

Sam Pilafian, tubist
Author, *The Breathing Gym*

David Cutler hits another musical home run with *The Savvy Music Teacher*! Presented with infectious prose that illuminates and inspires in equal parts, SMT hits literally every mark for both aspiring and veteran pedagogues. The blueprints, disseminations of complex "real life" data made charmingly accessible, interviews with countless successful educators, and the author's own rich experience as a world-class performer, teacher, and entrepreneur should be required reading for every musician.

John W. Parks IV, percussionist
Associate Professor of Percussion
The Florida State University

How refreshing to read a book that demonstrates how financial success and passionate dedication to a student's success are not mutually exclusive, but are in fact inexorably intertwined! David Cutler's *The Savvy Music Teacher* discusses ways educators can stay true to their core values and, at the same time, build a viable, sustainable business.

Nina Perlove, flutist
The Internet Flutist
www.realfluteproject.com

As a brand new "SMT," *The Savvy Music Teacher* helped me pave the way to a solid start-up studio. With countless blueprints, artistic initiatives, and financial models, this book has become one of my most valuable resources.

Estela Aragon, trumpeter
Trumpeter and founder, *MusicFit Academy*
www.musicfitacademy.com

This book is an enormous resource for teachers and administrators. Emboldened by the information within, teachers may ascend to "Savvy" early in their careers rather than climbing a slow learning curve over the course of time. If teachers want to be respected as professionals they must continue to grow and to present themselves professionally.

Ronda Cole, violinist
Suzuki Association of the Americas, Teacher Trainer

If success leaves clues, then David Cutler leaves footprints for readers to follow in pursuit of their own goals and dreams. Any musician committed to using the tools provided in *The Savvy Music Teacher* is sure to make a successful living teaching music.

Mike McAdam, guitarist
School Director, North Main Music
Author, *The Private Guitar Studio Handbook*
www.northmainmusic.com

David Cutler provides answers and solutions sorely needed by teachers, while encouraging us to value ourselves and the work we do. Are you worth it or not? Take the first step by saying "yes" and read this book!

Christian Howes, jazz violinist
Performer/educator/producer
www.christianhowes.com

THE SAVVY MUSIC TEACHER

Blueprint for Maximizing Income and Impact

David Cutler

OXFORD
UNIVERSITY PRESS

OXFORD
UNIVERSITY PRESS

Oxford University Press is a department of the University of
Oxford. It furthers the University's objective of excellence in research,
scholarship, and education by publishing worldwide.

Oxford   New York
Auckland   Cape Town   Dar es Salaam   Hong Kong   Karachi
Kuala Lumpur   Madrid   Melbourne   Mexico City   Nairobi
New Delhi   Shanghai   Taipei   Toronto

With offices in
Argentina   Austria   Brazil   Chile   Czech Republic   France   Greece
Guatemala   Hungary   Italy   Japan   Poland   Portugal   Singapore
South Korea   Switzerland   Thailand   Turkey   Ukraine   Vietnam

Oxford is a registered trademark of Oxford University Press
in the UK and certain other countries.

Published in the United States of America by
Oxford University Press
198 Madison Avenue, New York, NY 10016

Library of Congress Cataloging-in-Publication Data
Cutler, David, 1971– author.
The savvy music teacher : blueprint for maximizing income & impact / by David Cutler.
  pages cm
ISBN 978–0–19–020081–7 (hardcover : alk. paper) — ISBN 978–0–19–020082–4 (pbk. : alk. paper)
1. Music—Instruction and study.   2. Music teachers.   3. Music—Economic aspects.
4. Music—Vocational guidance   I. Title.
ML3795.C88 2015
780.71—dc23
2014050059

CONTENTS

FOREWORD

Music education is an apprenticeship with an unfortunate quirk: it frequently delivers graduates with elite artistic skills who are clueless about how to set up their own workshops.

The short-term consequence is that when recent college music graduates stagger blinking into the sunlight, they're likely to be authorities on Dorian mode but not demographics, melisma but not marketing. They can analyze a fugue, troubleshoot intonation, and correctly identify tenor clef but are unable to build a website, craft a business plan, or manage their own taxes.

The longer-term consequence of such blinkered preparation?

Nothing.

Not "nothing" in the reassuring sense of the word, but quite literally *nothing*, in all its horrifying abyssal absence-of-anything voidness. Opportunities are not created. Performances don't take place. The musician's name doesn't come up in conversation. Events are not patronized. Parents seeking lessons don't call. It is a nothing that is frequently the catalyst for an insidious, bleak, anonymizing slide into "this whole music thing didn't work out," which all too many musicians try to cure simply by practicing harder, until one day they decide not to practice at all.

Independent music teachers are a product of that same guild, too often struggling with this basic disconnect between the skills with which they've been equipped and the practical realities with which they're routinely confronted. They can play to an expert level, certainly; they're well versed in pedagogical theory and have an encyclopedic knowledge of teaching repertoire and learning systems. But they don't have training in how to plan for, set up, run, resource, promote, expand, leverage, and diversify the small business that is a teaching studio.

Why would they? Most of *those* skills have nothing to do with musicianship, which is precisely why too many musicians treat them with disdain or fear. I am an *artiste*, is the protest. I do not need to concern myself with such things.

Yes you do. Here's why:

Musicians with successful teaching studios are financially secure enough to continue chasing their dream of being a musician. Secure enough, whether their actual music making generates reliable income or not. Secure enough, not just for the rest of this year or the next, but for the rest of their working lives. In a profession where excellence normally takes decades to incubate, and success therefore belongs only to the prodigy or the patient, time is the only currency that truly matters. Being able to *extend* the time you have for developing your own musical powers and opportunities is a priceless, life-transforming gift.

Music teaching is therefore much more than just the clichéd and convenient manifestation of that day job musicians are told to go out and get; it's a ticket that permits them to continue their own artistic adventure. Teachers with an extensive studio can afford the better instrument, the up-to-date recording equipment, the well-stocked music library, the study trip overseas, the photographer to shoot their CD cover, the time to spend the summer holidays practicing. Whenever they're not actually scheduled to be in the teaching chair, they can afford to rehearse, to perform, to variously fail or succeed, and to treat each imposter the same without concern for viability.

Of course, the reality for most music teachers isn't quite as glossy as that brochure. Their studios are small, their income is meager, and their experience consists of limping uncertainly from utility bill to rent payment while living in constant fear of students abandoning them. But such struggle is not an indictment of music teaching as a profession, or a confirmation of its limitations. It's simply evidence—powerful, impossible-to-ignore, punitive, gray-cloud evidence—that something is missing from that teacher's skill set.

This missing something almost certainly has nothing to do with voicing chords, writing authoritatively about minimalism, or rendering historically informed ornamentation. It often has little to do with the individual's own performance skills or ability to teach.

What, then? What should apprentice music teachers be aware of that the masters of their guild choose not—or are unable—to whisper to them? What lessons are there from studios that spectacularly get this right and from the thousands of small, service-based, people-centered businesses whose own core activities rhyme with what music teachers routinely confront?

The list is so extensive that . . . well, you could fill a book. With *The Savvy Music Teacher*, Dr. Cutler has done exactly that, and music teachers everywhere should be grateful.

A warning though. This book is not a giddy prospectus for quick success. It's a hardheaded, detailed, and meticulously thorough tour of the invisibles that make the difference between a studio that thrives and one that constantly has water at nose level. Readers need to approach the topic with the same work ethic and hunger for improvement that fueled their practice in music studies. There is a lot to digest, and your muses might not always approve of the necessarily practical (to say nothing of frequently arithmetical!) nature of much of the advice. However, when teachers emerge from reading this book, they will do so with the mindset of not just musicians, but business owners. They will be, aptly enough, a good deal more savvy and much more likely to succeed because of it.

Grab a coffee or three. Keep a notepad handy. Return to this book regularly. Take pride in your growing skills and expanding studio, and then take advantage of the remarkable opportunities made possible by both.

With every best wish for the deliciously unpredictable and fertile adventures that lie ahead.

Philip Johnston
Author of *The Dynamic Studio,*
The Practice Revolution, and *Practiceopedia*.
www.insidemusicteaching.com

ACKNOWLEDGMENTS

One of the great things about writing a book on music teachers is that it encouraged me to reflect on the many mentors who have impacted my life. Beyond cultivating passions and abilities, these individuals played major roles in shaping my worldview. I was always the weird one who didn't quite fit in, yet these advisors gave generously, providing guidance and space for me to discover my voice as an artist and human being.

Interviewing literally hundreds of educators when writing *The Savvy Music Teacher*—many of whom are featured throughout these pages—was a sheer joy. Knowing that these instructors are hard at work day after day fills me with great optimism for the future. In particular, it was inspiring to interact regularly with Kristin Yost. More than an innovative educator and savvy businesswoman, she has become a friend.

I am grateful to the individuals who shared their time and feedback during the preparation phases of this text: Estela Aragon, Kristin Yost, Melissa Blasek, students in my Business of Independent Music Teaching class, Rick Ackerman, Richard D'Ippolito, and Oxford editor Norm Hirschy. A special thanks to my mother, Tina Cantrell, and my wife, Erika Cutler, who spent countless hours proofreading and indulging my crazy ideas.

Things have come full circle now that my children, Ashton and Alaina, both take music lessons. I witness on a daily basis how music study transforms their lives. At age 6, my son recently gave his first full-length solo recital, featuring 17 tunes, two jokes, and three magic tricks.

Finally, I'd like to express gratitude to all the music instructors out there. You could do so many things with your life, yet you choose the important work of teaching music. Thanks for all you do to impact students, families, and communities. Your work truly makes a difference.

ABOUT THE COMPANION WEBSITE

www.oup.com/us/thesavvymusicteacher

Oxford has created a website to accompany *The Savvy Music Teacher*. Material that cannot be made available in a book is provided here. The reader is encouraged to consult this resource in conjunction with the chapters. Among other things, it contains links to websites for all featured artists throughout the text, and fillable forms from Appendices A–C.

THE SAVVY MUSIC TEACHER

SO YOU WANT TO BE A MUSIC TEACHER?

Independent music teacher. Now there's a job title that makes sense. After all, you are passionate about music and teaching, and gifted in both. This vocation offers the promise of a dependable income, meaningful work, and a fulfilling existence.

But is it *really* a good career choice?

How Much Can a Music Teacher Reasonably Expect to Earn?

Getting rich quickly certainly isn't your top motivator. If it were, you would have selected an occupation in the business, legal, or medical sector, where six-figure salaries are the norm. Truth be told, you chose music teaching to pursue a profession you love, and for that you should be commended.

But you probably don't aspire to live in poverty either. An existence on food stamps and welfare—with the inability to retire, afford a family, or repair ailing instruments—is also not your life plan.

As crass as it sounds, let's talk money. How much can an independent music teacher reasonably expect to earn?

It's a fair question. After receiving a traditional job offer, one of the first items workers discuss with their potential employer is, undoubtedly, salary. Knowing how much will be generated (per hour, project, or year) helps workers determine whether that employment is a good fit and what lifestyle it enables. Similarly, entrepreneurs and small business owners typically start with a detailed plan that projects income. Though forecasts are rarely 100% accurate, they at least provide a basic financial strategy.

But too many independent music teachers operate differently. They cobble together a few students, and then some more. A barebones poster-and-website marketing campaign is enacted. Some gigs are scheduled on the side. How much do they make? That mystery is solved each April as various income sources are tallied to produce the illusive yearly total filed on their tax return. Or worse yet, poor record keepers guesstimate, never learning the true remuneration exchanged for their time, training, and talents.

My numerous interviews with full-time independent music teachers from around the United States revealed that most generated $25,000 to 40,000 annually. (Of course, the most important total is yours. How much did *you* earn?) How do these wages stack up? According to the US Bureau of Labor Statistics, the 2013 median personal incomes for full-time workers over age 25 were as follows:

- $43,004 for all employees
- $57,616 for individuals with a bachelor's degree
- $69,108 for individuals with a master's degree
- $84,396 for individuals with a doctoral degree

Yikes! As a group, independent music teachers make a fairly weak showing, especially considering that most have undergraduate and often graduate diplomas proudly adorning their studio walls.

There is good news. The *Savvy Music Teacher* (SMT) can reasonably build a career earning $50,000 to $100,000 annually. This book shows you how to generate a respectable, better-than-average middle-class living doing what you love. How many people are fortunate enough to find that balance?

Impact

Achieving financial aims through independent music teaching does not automatically qualify someone as an SMT. SMTs are also driven by a burning and uncompromising desire to make a positive difference in the world around them. Though money matters are taken seriously, maximizing *impact* is valued at least as much, and often more.

What that means exactly varies from teacher to teacher. Some augment influence by sharing their message with a consistently expanding audience. Others modify instructional approaches, inventing ever-evolving activities that offer significant lessons on music and life. All are catalysts for transformation, leaving a legacy that is deep and long-lasting.

The Savvy Music Teacher is not a treatise on music pedagogy. It provides no diagrams of hand positions, explanations of breathing techniques, or strategies for helping students memorize quickly. Nor does it endorse a singular "correct" model of education to which all SMTs should and must aspire. While tools and methodology absolutely matter, there is no omnipotent, board-approved formula for making a difference.

It does, however, begin with a fundamental belief that music teaching is more than a great job—it is *important* work. And though music education certainly has inherent benefits, true treasure emerges when inspired teachers touch the lives of students, families, and communities.

The Impact-to-Income Ratio

This book balances two overriding concerns necessary for a successful music teaching enterprise. An SMT creates a viable business model while making a profound difference in the lives of students and communities. One without the other is not enough.

Are these two very different aspects related? On the surface, connecting them seems absurd. No obvious, mathematical correlation can be drawn between fiscal and pedagogical success. We have all encountered incredible educators who struggle to make ends meet, as well as financially comfortable ones who are mediocre instructors at best.

Yet this book argues that there is indeed a parallel. When done right, impact and income are closely related bedfellows. SMTs find ways to make them both go up, in harmony.

How is this claim supported? It is difficult to devote 100% of one's attention to teaching excellence when simultaneously tormented by problematic personal finances. Economic woes trigger a host of problems, inducing stress, strained relationships, and zapped enthusiasm. Individuals forced to take supplementary "day jobs" they despise just to get by or those with unmanageable schedules and an unbalanced life are unlikely to have the time or energy to go the extra mile for students.

On the flip side, a sound financial model increases the likelihood that teachers will find the psychological space to offer their best. It provides a foundation for maintaining a studio, organizing meaningful activities, pursuing professional development, and tackling passion projects, in addition to fulfilling personal desires such as buying a house or raising a family.

Is there a more direct correlation? There is if you do things right. To increase impact, SMTs employ teaching tools and strategies that expand beyond those of the average teacher. As a result, their offerings are differentiated, which translates to more students and higher fees. In addition, SMTs offer a variety of meaningful products and services beyond lessons that enhance learning and revenue. Independent music teachers looking for a raise have an opportunity: Imagine new, valuable musical experiences. Connect those initiatives to an economic model and, *voila*, both earnings and value rise.

Income and impact; money and meaning. These terms may not be synonymous, but for SMTs, they are closely related.

Math

Many career books make extraordinary claims. They describe "miracle techniques," suggesting that by following their general advice, you will somehow earn six figures or $1,000 per week without even leaving the couch. Whatever the proclaimed outcome, they often fail to show exactly how to get there. Just do what we say, snap your fingers, and things will somehow work out.

The Savvy Music Teacher is specific. It provides a detailed, dollar-for-dollar blueprint demonstrating how SMTs can generate $50,000 to $100,000 annually while increasing impact. There will be math! (To readers who are not mathematically inclined, worry not. Formulas are broken down and explained in plain, easy-to-understand English. Success does not require calculus or trigonometry, just addition, subtraction, multiplication, and division. Calculators are allowed, even encouraged.)

This book distinguishes itself by citing dollar amounts at every turn. It demonstrates how a particular business decision can generate $25 or $5,648 or whatever the number happens to be. By integrating this level of specificity, financial claims are substantiated. No guesswork, no prayer, no genie—just real numbers in real equations, supported by real-life examples.

The problem with this approach is that even concrete numbers are relative. For example, in some regions, $50,000 feels like winning the jackpot. In others, it's practically poverty. And these are year 2015 numbers. In 2, 10, or 50 years, $100,000 may sound laughable. With that in mind, will inflation or other fluctuations in the economic landscape deem this book obsolete before it's even published?

Absolutely not. While every attempt has been made to be honest, realistic, and current with the figures cited, the point is not for you to marry every financial decision with my numbers. Readers emerge with tools for designing a profitable, sustainable music teaching business. Over time, variables for success may change, but the process will not.

Meet the Three *Savvy Music Teacher* Characters

The Savvy Music Teacher is packed with strategies for maximizing impact and income. To illustrate these points, three crucial "characters" play a vital role.

#1: Real-Life Savvy Music Teachers

Over 150 vignettes showcasing actual SMTs appear throughout this book. Their stories are inspirational and instructive, demonstrating how creative, entrepreneurial individuals approach various aspects of their work. Featured artists hail from across the United States and the globe, representing a wide variety of instruments, styles, pedagogies, perspectives, and backgrounds.

#2: One Very Savvy Teacher

Among these are thirty *Lessons from the Trenches*: first-hand accounts of pianist Kristin Yost. Her stories demonstrate how a single instructor can integrate savvy concepts across a career. Yost is the executive director and cofounder of the Centre for Musical Minds in Frisco, Texas (www.centreformusicalminds. org). Earning $100,000+ annually since entering the workforce and continually experimenting with innovative teaching, Yost epitomizes the SMT profile.

#3: You

Without a doubt, the most important character here is *you*, the reader. Ideas in a book are just that. Only you can personalize them into reality.

What I Learned about Savvy Music Teachers

While writing *The Savvy Music Teacher*, I had the pleasure of interviewing some 200 instructors in my search for innovative teaching and business models. Beyond being really fun, this process taught me several things about the art of *savvy*.

First, I was struck that few SMTs are just a little savvy. Though individuals were limited to one story apiece in my book, most featured artists easily had 5, 10, or 50 equally fascinating approaches. Where some see few opportunities in work and life, SMTs seem to find potential everywhere.

Second, I saw that savvy develops over time. Few SMTs begin with perfectly refined business or teaching models. Instead, they get better and bolder with each passing season. I learned that just about any open-minded person can develop these aptitudes when adopting an entrepreneurial mindset and taking action.

Third, it became clear that *savvy* is a transferable skill. SMTs with inventive business models are likely to match them with creative teaching approaches, and vice versa. For example, instructors who generate substantial incomes are more likely to teach improvisation and multiple musical genres than those who don't. That was a fascinating lesson.

Finally, I was moved by the depth and breadth of incredible education that occurs on a daily basis. SMTs of all stripes do more than teach music well. They change the world in positive ways, big and small.

Great Music Teaching Is Great Business

Inspiring and challenging students through music is not simply a sweet but superfluous frill. It is vital work. Our society benefits from music education on multiple levels, yet much of this potential is accessed only when extraordinary teachers make it happen.

Great music teaching is great business. Beyond providing a dynamic and prosperous career path, it transforms students, families, and communities. At least it does in the hands of a Savvy Music Teacher.

1 THE VERY, VERY, *VERY* IMPORTANT WORK OF SAVVY MUSIC TEACHERS

Savvy Music Teachers (SMTs) do not fulfill basic human needs such as food, water, or clean air. They don't shelter the homeless, defend the innocent, or cure the ailing (except, perhaps, spiritually). In the scheme of things, just how crucial are these professionals?

At this point, you may be tempted to reach for the music advocacy handbook, citing arguments such as the following:

- **Music has intrinsic value.** Like reading, writing, and arithmetic, there is inherent value to music study.
- **Music makes you smarter.** A slew of studies suggest that musical participation positively increases IQ, affecting spatial-temporal reasoning, memory function, hand-eye coordination, observational skills, and more.
- **Music makes you more successful.** Music study is often linked to higher academic achievement, standardized test scores, high school graduation rates, and college attendance.
- **Music is good for the soul.** Soothing the heart and mind, music channels emotions and promotes healthy living. Playing music can be therapeutic.
- **Music is an international language.** Every culture and time period has championed music as a form of expression and communication.

These rationales, backed by numerous studies, have been espoused extensively. They often appear on websites of independent teachers, and most claims have indisputable merit.

However, such declarations apply to music learning in general, regardless of teacher. Inherent benefits are bestowed upon any individual wise and fortunate enough to investigate this special topic.

"Why is music study beneficial?" is indeed a meaningful inquiry, but it asks something far different from the question posed here: "Why are independent music teachers important?" Or more significantly, "Why does *your* music teaching matter?"

While the list of rationales is undoubtedly robust, consider this: SMTs are unique characters in the lives of students, particularly children. With one-on-one weekly meetings that span years, SMTs are a constant force with a front-row seat for many of life's milestones: learning to read, pursuing hobbies, junior high dances, and the hunt for college. Beyond a parent, what other adult figure has this kind of continuous access and influence? Not the classroom teacher, sport coach, or band director. Playing this role is a privilege and honor, accompanied by significant responsibility. The ultimate impact and consequence of your work has everything to do with how these interactions are approached.

Priorities

The Power of Music (Teachers)

Music has the power to build community. It can engage critical thought, fuel the pursuit of excellence, and spawn creativity. Music possesses the capacity to impact large-scale social change while cultivating leaders and facilitating collaboration, or to touch the soul of an individual in highly personal ways. With its potential to foster curiosity, innovation, discipline, humility, spirituality, empathy, or monstrously wild dreams, it is no wonder that music has played a vital role in every society since the dawn of time. Music can change the world, and it has many times over!

But here's the catch: music does not do all these things inherently. It is inanimate after all, just notes, rhythms, harmonies, and textures. Music only builds something meaningful when placed in the hands of creators, observers, and educators.

SMTs are vessels to a vast and majestic kingdom. Every student—every lesson—presents an opportunity and a challenge. The framing of these experiences plays a vast role in determining which musical powers students ultimately embrace and what they come to value.

Wearing the job title of "music teacher" is not enough. What you emphasize matters. Imagine that your job is among the most significant professions in the world and it just might become that.

What's Wrong with the Way We Were Taught?

In the introduction to his book *The Dynamic Studio*, Philip Johnston argues, "If a music student from 1950 were to teleport into a music studio of this decade, they'd feel oddly at home. Various technological curiosities notwithstanding, the structure, content, pacing, and expectations of the lessons themselves really wouldn't be so different from what they would have been used to." He then goes on to propose literally hundreds of uncommon, innovative solutions for the twenty-first-century music studio, suggesting even radical changes to the traditional paradigm.

But what's so wrong with the way we were taught? This formula works. Efficient, effective, and proven, it has served countless learners admirably. Just look at you and me. We had affirming experiences, remained committed, and even made music our profession. Our training models were case studies in success.

It is natural for people to teach the way they were taught, and truth be told, most of us encountered more or less comparable music lesson programs. True, some teachers were better than others. Sessions addressed different instruments employing different pedagogies with different levels of intensity. But on a basic structural level, most of our experiences were similar, as follows:

1. **Lesson format.** Lessons were consistent, weekly, one-on-one meetings of 30 to 60 minutes.
2. **Summers.** There was no set summer curriculum. Students scheduled lessons when and if they wanted.
3. **Values.** The top priorities were generally improving technical ability while learning new repertoire.
4. **Atmosphere.** Most environments were fairly serious. Teachers were the primary talkers; students listened and diligently followed instructions.
5. **Lesson activities.** Most teachers developed a fairly consistent lesson regimen.
6. **Time between lessons.** The student practiced music or technique according to instructions provided by the teacher.
7. **Repertoire.** This was typically one genre (i.e., classical), often linked to a single method book or approach.
8. **Events.** Many studios scheduled one or two recitals per year (though too many skipped this activity altogether). A marathon of students performed polished solo pieces during this serious event.

9. **Incentive systems.** These consisted of praise, moving to the next piece, and perhaps stickers.
10. **Listening.** For some studios, listening to music was not part of the curriculum. Others encouraged students to study recordings of assigned pieces.
11. **Music theory/history.** Some studios integrated theory into lessons, others incorporated workbooks, and others did not emphasize this value. Written theory was given priority over ear training. Music history played little to no role.
12. **Creativity.** In most classical lessons, intentional creativity was not emphasized. In jazz and popular lessons, this value was stressed primarily through improvisation.
13. **Technology.** Beyond a metronome, there was not much technology involved. (Many fewer tools were available!)
14. **Community.** There was not much sense of studio community.
15. **Collaboration.** Team projects typically played no role.

The previous points are clearly incomplete, overgeneralized, and not applicable to every teacher of the past. Even when they are the case, such observations are not at all condemnations. Just because something is traditional does not make it problematic; different or new is not inherently better.

Conversely, typical or historic approaches should not be viewed as sacrosanct, petrified solutions untouchable until the end of time. We are not educating clones of ourselves in a world mirroring the one that existed years or decades before. In this new era defined by postmodern globalism and disruptive technological change, learners have different expectations, curiosities, and learning modes. Understanding this, SMTs intuitively follow the code outlined in Marshal Goldsmith's book *What Got You Here Won't Get You There: How Successful People Become Even More Successful.*

With any of the previously listed aspects, consider the potential of expanding upon or departing from the status quo. For example, might fresh incentive systems promote student progress and commitment? Would a greater variety of musical genres, lesson activities, or listening assignments promote a more relevant, comprehensive music education? How can technological power tools (that simply did not exist years ago) transform learning today? What role might a greater emphasis on community building or collaboration have on a host of issues?

The best innovations amplify student impact, engagement, enjoyment, and achievement. They increase retention and differentiate your studio while serving as effective marketing.

SMTs, indebted to legacies that helped groom them into musicians, teachers, and human beings, have no qualms drawing from time-tested traditions. But they are also careful not to become enslaved to "the way things are supposed to be done." After all, the primary responsibility of a music teacher is not to maintain any particular tradition, composer, structure, genre, or methodology. Nor is it to innovate for the sake of innovation. *First and foremost, SMTs serve students, families, and communities.*

As fearless explorers, SMTs are constantly on the lookout for new repertoire, exercises, tools, games, processes, technologies, activities, and studio traditions that enhance student learning and impact (as well as their own personal growth). As the world changes, so do SMT teaching, studio, and business models. This unshakable insistence on relevance is one reason SMTs will never be deemed obsolete.

An Essential Question

Let's get specific. Why do *you* teach music?

Because it's something you enjoy, of course, and because it pays the bills. But what is truly of consequence to you?

In his book *Start with Why*, Simon Sinek suggests that "people don't buy what you do, they buy why you do it." He goes on to explain that most businesses, organizations, and individuals know what they do (e.g., teach violin) and how they do it (weekly lessons using a methodology X). Yet relatively few have a deep understanding of larger purpose. Great and successful leaders, on the other hand, start by asking "why." The specifics of "how" and "what" are necessary to achieving that overarching mission but are lower-level details rather than the main point.

The best and most impactful SMTs start with *why*, utilizing their discipline as a spectacular forum for solving some kind of problem. They are driven to answer an *essential question*, or top-level priority to be addressed by a lesson, class, curriculum, or even business.

In the past, the essential question of most independent music teachers looked something like this (whether stated or not): "How can I help students improve as performers through repertoire and exercises?" Based on that priority, a host of curricular decisions were made. Master music teachers developed extremely efficient and effective strategies for solving the problem at hand.

Outstanding musical performance is clearly a valid goal. Why wouldn't you want to play well? I, for one, have incredibly high expectations for students and myself. But this is just one framing question drawn from an ocean of possibility. Luckily, there is both room and demand for teachers with a great variety of emphases.

What is the driving force behind your instruction? Twenty years from now, when current students reflect back on your time together, which benefits do you hope they cite above all others? Identifying an essential question is an imperative step toward developing a potent teaching philosophy true to your core values. Examples include:

- How can I help students improve in their area of study (flute, violin, songwriting)?
- How can I help students experience a well-rounded musical/artistic existence?
- How can I help students develop self-esteem through music and creative exploration?
- How can I help students find joy through the music-making process?
- How can I help students become lifelong music patrons/lovers?
- How can I help students become lifelong amateur performers, even if (especially when) their profession has nothing to do with music?
- How can I help students create community through musical interactions?
- How can I help students use music as a tool for success in other areas of life?
- How can I help students find more meaning in life?
- How can I help students become successful professional musicians?
- How can I help students develop excellence as a musician while becoming lifelong music patrons, lovers, and performers?

With the potential to influence just about every studio-related decision, changing the question changes the answers. Spend some time crafting your essential question, considering the implications of every word. This is not merely an academic pursuit or hollow marketing propaganda to be prominently displayed on studio websites. What kind of students and world are you hoping to build?

An Essential Question	
Provides CLARITY	A reminder of *why* you chose this profession, and what is truly important about your work, it forms the cornerstone of a teaching philosophy.
Impacts CURRICULUM	When planning lessons, events, and other activities, determine "how does this help solve my essential question?"
Offers a METRIC	Essential questions provide criteria for measuring teaching effectiveness. If your question is "How can I foster lifelong performers?" but most students quit by middle school, something needs to change.
Helps with RECRUITMENT	Teachers with strong essential questions often have competitive advantages, with a differentiated program and philosophy that is easily explained and compelling to a certain kind of student.

While contemporary SMTs share many goals with traditional music teachers of the past, their essential questions and resulting programs tend to be somewhat broader weighing the following types of issues:

1. In today's world of near-infinite access to a vast array of activities, the number of individuals enrolling in formal music study has declined. Which approaches might reverse that trend, increasing music's perceived value?

2. Equally worrisome are the number of individuals who begin music lessons but ultimately quit, growing disenchanted with this pursuit. Why do so many more 7-year-olds take music lessons than 15-year-olds? When we have their attention, what are the keys to igniting a lifelong addiction (in the best sense of the term)?

3. An independent teacher is typically the most musically literate person to interface with students and their families (perhaps tied with a classroom music teacher). What role might music instruction play in architecting a comprehensive musical existence? How might such an approach positively impact long-term sustainability of the arts?

4. How can we create a more musical society? What role should music lessons play in impacting larger societal values?

5. A common theme today stressed by members of all political persuasions is that our school system is largely outdated and ineffective. What might music instruction offer to help solve greater educational challenges of the twenty-first century?

6. At this point in history, we have a "jobs" problem. Unemployment is too high, advertised positions often lack qualified applicants, and the need for creative entrepreneurs is staggering. What valuable, transferable twenty-first century skills might music instruction instill in students, regardless of career path?

7. Beyond jobs, what life aptitudes should music instruction nurture? How can it help solve challenges that face students and their communities both today and tomorrow?

SMTs don't simply teach lessons on a given instrument with a particular pedagogical approach. Instead, they start with *why*, driven to solve a burning essential question. On a mission to effect change in meaningful ways, this obsession drives their life's work.

Lessons from the Trenches

"Lessons from the Trenches" throughout this book profile pianist Kristin Yost, director of Centre for Musical Minds (www.centreformusi-calminds.org).

Far outweighing any methodology, stylistic emphasis, or trick of the trade, my teaching is driven by the desire to guide learners through a joyous, meaningful personal journey. The essential question: "How can I make your musical dream(s) come true?"

Kids don't always have an immediate answer. Honestly, some are initially there due to parental pressure rather than internal drive. But with digging, just about everyone discovers purpose in this magical tool called *music*.

Once a year, I host a Pop Showcase, where studio members select, learn, and perform songs in collaboration with a hired rhythm section. Though most choose popular music, any piece goes as long as they *love* the selection. The point of this event is to begin with students' passion rather than my preferences as a teacher.

Tragically, one student was losing her father to terminal cancer. More than anything, she yearned to give him one final gift. We worked overtime learning a tune with personal significance to the family and shot a video. Sharing it with her father one Monday afternoon brought a moment of joy despite heartbreaking circumstances. By Tuesday he was unresponsive; he passed away Thursday.

It recently became clear that a high school boy in my studio was destined to major in music. Wanting to give him every possible advantage, I sent him to another teacher more suited for professional training. Granted, I miss this student's hard work and great attitude, but sometimes empowering people means letting go.

I begin most lessons with another question: "How can I help you today?" Instead of imposing the teacher's will, it is essential to listen to students' desires, aspirations, and interests on a regular basis. This way, they take ownership and lead the way.

Learning Objectives

For SMTs, fulfilling an essential question requires tapping into relevant *learning objectives*. Think of them as second-level goals that contribute to your primary purpose or mission. In fact, sometimes these desirable outcomes are embedded in the essential question itself.

With a little imagination, music education is capable of emphasizing a great many learning objectives. The chart that follows provides just a taste.

Potential Music Learning Objectives	
• Academic skills	• Curiosity
• Adaptability	• Discipline and focus
• Advocacy	• Diverse musical experiences
• Artistic excellence	• Diverse skills
• Attention to detail	• Empathy
• Career skills (transferable)	• Engaged citizen
• Collaboration	• Entrepreneurship
• Communication	• Expression
• Community building	• Goal setting
• Community engagement	• Healthy living
• Comprehensive artistic existence	• Imagination
• Creativity	• Innovation
• Critical thinking/problem solving	• Instrumental technique
• Cultural engagement	• Leadership

(*continued*)

Potential Music Learning Objectives	
• Lifelong music lovers	• Pursuit of excellence
• Listening skills	• Self-esteem/identity
• Memory development	• Self-expression
• Multicultural understanding	• Social change
• Multitasking	• Social skills
• Musical excellence	• Spirituality
• Musical identity	• Stage presence
• Musical literacy	• Strategic planning
• Opportunity creation	• Teaching skills
• Organizational skills	• Technological fluency
• Performance skills	• Values
• Positive attitude	• Versatility
• Professionalism	• Work ethic/drive

Many learning objectives overlap, enabling "educational multitasking." For example, improvisational exercises can cultivate creativity, self-expression, self-esteem, critical thinking, diverse skills, innovation, and imagination.

Other objectives contradict. There is a danger that the pursuit of excellence comes at the expense of creativity, or vice versa. If both are important to solving your essential question, develop a diverse and balanced curriculum accordingly.

Though the entire list may sound desirable, it is impossible to do justice to all these things. Attention in one direction often comes at the expense of another. Rather than trying to be all things to all people (and failing), *identify and prioritize the five or so learning objectives most important to your studio.* Which values are most vital to solving your essential question?

While whittling the list down to just five can be a challenge, prioritizing is even harder. What is more important to you, instrumental technique or a positive attitude? Theory skills or active listening? Committing to an order helps you make tough decisions about what to emphasize.

Only once you have defined an essential question and ranked top learning objectives are you fully equipped to begin designing a unique, personalized, meaningful SMT curriculum. **What specific activities/environments are most likely to cultivate your stated goals?** Build educational platforms that actively stress essential values.

Though some aims occur naturally as the result of a pedagogical approach, imagine what creative solutions might accentuate and amplify these priorities. A great question is, "How can I multiply progress toward this particular objective by 10?" Expand beyond the intrinsic to devise an approach that is intentional and uniquely your own.

The remainder of this chapter examines several learning objectives that music training can emphasize when framed appropriately, along with suggestions for magnifying these values. Similar logic can be applied to any ed ucational priority.

Team Dynamics

Learning to play piano can be a lonely journey. Yet *community building* is a core value for Janna Carlson (www.hellopianostudio.com).

She and a colleague periodically organize *Music Days*. These one-hour seminars, which replace lessons that week, spotlight a composer, period, or topic such as "The History of Recorded Music." In most cases, students have little prior knowledge of or appreciation for the subject, but that changes by the end of each engaging session. Open to students and their families, these popular events provide an opportunity to socialize and learn as a group.

Rather than scheduling formal recitals, Carlson does the opposite. Her spring and (costumed) Halloween *un-recitals* build team spirit. In the week before each event, small group rehearsals have up to six participants play for one another, practice bowing, discuss nerves, and "rehearse cheering. We do a lot of that. I emphasize that we are a team, and a great performance is one where everyone has fun."

Immediately preceding each un-recital, performers bond at a pep rally. After the audience enters, parents test their cheering abilities, but they usually pale in comparison to the animated student artists. With encouragement, the whole crowd begins hooting and hollering. Performers feel like rock stars in front of an adoring crowd.

A *practice-a-thon* challenges studio members to track work throughout February. Carlson posts weekly performance videos of five to six students who made great strides, as well as a summary of collective accomplishments. "This week, we practiced over _ _,000 minutes! That averages ___ minutes per person!" Most kids work diligently to be featured and win awards: prizes (e.g., headphones), tickets to a candy bar party, and the opportunity to enlist parents as performers on an upcoming un-recital. Though a "competition" of sorts, everyone wins something, and they celebrate collective progress.

"Kids in my studio become great friends. They feel like valued members of a community, which encourages them to work hard and root for the whole team!"

Diverse Musical Experiences

All private music students encounter at least two modes of engagement: interactions with a teacher and (let's hope!) practice. But this represents a tiny portion of what is possible. Music is also performed, heard, watched, shared, composed, improvised, collaborated, recorded, memorized, interpreted, and studied. Furthermore, each and every one of these activities can be approached from numerous perspectives. The options are literally infinite.

Consider the enormous canon of literature, encompassing numerous time periods and styles. Most instruments, or their close relatives, have played a role in multiple genres. Take violin, for example, central to Baroque through contemporary Western classical, Indian classical, modern jazz, Irish fiddling, bluegrass, country and western, Celtic, tango, Middle Eastern, pop—and we're just getting started. It is also possible to play adaptations, reproducing content originally conceived for other instruments.

Starting from standard notation is just one of many strategies for learning new music. Lead sheets, teacher imitation, transcription, dictation, harmonic analysis, stylistic composition, and Solfège study all offer valuable and distinct musical literacies. Students challenged to approach repertoire through a variety of processes often enjoy a richer artistic existence than those exposed to just one or two.

Beyond solitary practice and work with a mentor, chamber and large ensemble playing provides invaluable experience. Performance opportunities include formal concerts, interactive shows, side-by-side events, competitions, jam sessions, community engagement, and *busking* (street performance). Technology opens a world of possibility through recording, sequencing, video gaming, and other avenues.

Music is not only played but also experienced. A holistic musical existence involves attending concerts, listening to recordings, watching videos, taking classes, observing rehearsals, reading blogs, going to camps, researching history, advocating causes, and sharing experiences with "friends" both online and offline.

If this learning objective is important to you, imagine the possibilities for providing an assortment of challenges and encounters to all who enter your doors. After all, your title is not "instrument," "technique," or "literature" teacher. You are the "music" teacher.

Diversity

Lynnette Barney's (www.creativekeysmusic.com) approach to teaching music is as diverse and comprehensive as they come. Students learn some pieces from notation and others through improvisation or by ear. They may be asked to transpose songs into all 12 keys and regularly discuss works from historical/analytical perspectives.

Beyond music from method books, master classical composers, and the pop/world music canon, students improvise at least once a month during lessons. This tradition begins on day one, well before note names or complex instrumental techniques are introduced.

Barney recently encouraged all students to enter a competition where original compositions were based on outer space themes. Studio members explore technology such as computer notation, sequencing, and drum programming via digital keyboards and iPads.

In an ideal world, Barney would require individual and group lessons each week. But with the challenge of scheduling, she developed another system. Typical months include three private meetings plus a week devoted to groups. She also encourages *overlapping lessons*, perhaps working with student A from 3 to 3:45 and student B from 3:15 to 4, providing each with 15 minutes of personal attention and a half hour of collaborative engagement.

Studio members perform in a variety of events each year, including a traditional studio recital, a monster piano concert hosted by a local piano association, six to eight outreach events, and *family nights* where four to six families meet, play for one another, and engage in musical dialogue.

Each summer, Barney offers multiple camps with varied themes: animals in music, drumming, electronic music. She prefers that new clients enter music study with her "Beginning Piano Camp," providing an exciting and effective framing musical experience.

What is Barney's primary purpose? "I want students to experience the lifetime joy that comes from collaborating, creating, and re-creating through music."

Discipline, Focus, and Time Management

Music is an extraordinary vehicle for developing discipline and attention span. When young students practice for 15 minutes straight, or older ones for hours on end, the ability to focus is honed in ways with which few other disciplines can compete, particularly in our society plagued by attention deficit hyperactivity disorder.

Despite this training, however, many budding musicians struggle with time management. They procrastinate, miss deadlines, work inefficiently in and out of the practice room, and fail to "get it all done." Even music teachers find handling the scarce resource of time a challenge. (In fact, this is such a pertinent SMT issue that chapter 12 is devoted to the topic.) If this learning objective is prioritized, how might you increase impact?

Though music lessons often focus on what—rather than how—students should practice, devote energy to helping them develop the transferable skill of efficient work habits. Teach them to identify challenges, set concrete measurable goals, and assess growth. Have them make audio/video recordings of practice sessions, to be examined during lessons.

To ensure progress, some teachers require a certain amount of practice each day, documented in a log. But not all 30-minute periods are equivalent. Some are incredibly productive, while others are essentially a waste, even harmful. Rather than simply noting start and end times, practice journals become exponentially more helpful when indicating what was reviewed, how it was approached, and which improvements occurred. During lessons, review journal entries with students, discussing successes, challenges, and opportunities. Stress the significance of making minutes count rather than simply adding them up.

Efficient practice is just one issue. Beyond that, discussions on time management prove instrumental, since this challenge never goes away. Educate students about strategies such as formally scheduling just about all important activities (practice times, meal times, homework times, socializing times), articulating and prioritizing goals through written lists, and distinguishing between urgent versus important activities.

The Practice Matrix

Flutist Alexis Del Palazzo (www.sensibleflutist.com), author of *The Practice Matrix*, teaches primarily adult amateurs. While performance excellence is clearly desirable, "I focus on practicing better." Beyond musical and technical issues, her holistic approach stresses time management, wellness, and additional process-oriented issues.

Flute students, and human beings in general, are notorious for "end gaining." This Alexander Technique term signifies an obsession with large-scale objectives while discounting the means of getting there. For example, a musician might push so hard to play a challenging passage up to tempo that an injury develops. Del Palazzo emphasizes the necessity of cultivating healthy habits, acknowledging setbacks, and enjoying the journey.

She helps students articulate and prioritize goals, working backward from long-term aspirations. Creating exercises that pinpoint one challenge at a time, studio members define attainable tasks, asking, "What actionable step can I take now that has the most immediate impact?"

We've all heard that "practice makes perfect," suggesting that long hours are the key to success. Yet a mountain of research suggests that extended, uninterrupted focus actually *decreases* productivity. Del Palazzo teaches a time management tool called the "Pomodoro Technique," where 25-minute periods of work are followed by 5-minute breaks to allow for stretching and reflection. Students learn to eliminate distractions, estimate effort required for each issue, and set clear timetables. This approach can be transferred to all areas of life.

Many challenges are psychological rather than physical: stage fright paralyzes; the ego judges ruthlessly; we become our own worst enemy. When life gets stressful or overwhelming, Del Palazzo encourages students to quell mental chatter and "let go." They might visualize their terrifying to-do list, wrinkle it up, and throw it away, freeing them to cherish the moment. "The value of holistic flute lessons expands beyond playing a hollow metal tube. It teaches us how to live a more productive, peaceful, and fulfilling life."

Self-Esteem and Identity

Without a doubt, music can build self-esteem, boost confidence, and instill pride.

But it can also damage these things, paralyzing some with fear while bringing others to tears. Too often, nerves plague. Public music sharing feels far more terrifying than seeing the dentist. Less accomplished players judge themselves inadequate and ultimately quit. Memory slips or note mistakes inflict depression. Even some of the best musicians on the planet exhibit destructive behaviors, fixating on every minor blunder while constantly doubting their gifts.

For many musicians, personal identity is tied closely to artistic achievement—it feels great to reach high performance standards. But when identity connects primarily to perfectionistic tendencies, performers experience a roller coaster of emotion: great one day, unworthy the next. The ego is constantly judging, looking for any excuse to disapprove and doubt talent. Even slightly flawed renditions have caused folks to question their very value as human beings. This perspective does not represent music engagement at its finest.

When this learning objective is important, recognize that the values emphasized by a teacher make a huge difference in the self-esteem trajectory of students. Attaching "success" only to ability and performance accuracy is often counterproductive.

There are at least three musical values that more reliably build self-worth. The first is *ownership*. This occurs when students are empowered to place personal stamps on musical projects. Often tied to creative pursuits such as composition, improvisation, or unique interpretations, ownership is also linked to participation, such as helping to plan an event or choosing repertoire.

The second is *meaning*. When teachers stress that a successful performance requires moving or connecting with an audience as opposed to flawless execution, students shift focus and are likely to discover greater joy, despite the inevitable flaws that emerge. Activities like Christmas caroling or interactive nursing home shows are great vehicles for showcasing fun and meaningful music sharing.

The third is *community*. Self-esteem tends to rise when people feel they are a valued part of something bigger. Classes, camps, ensemble work, field trips, studio blogs, and other group activities can be extremely positive in this sense.

Ironically, when values like ownership, meaning, and community are placed over the relentless pursuit of perfection, students often play better. Nervousness diminishes, the condemnatory ego is suppressed, and confidence rises. As a result, students increase engagement, practice harder, and improve more rapidly. Reasons behind this counterintuitive reality are explored in books like Barry Green's *The Inner Game of Music* and Kenny Werner's *Effortless Mastery*.

Whole-Person Development

"Music lessons are not just for learning songs," explains cellist and singer Emily Ann Peterson (www.emilyannpeterson.com). "They become the sandbox in which we learn life lessons." The challenges and triumphs that emerge through playing often mirror other aspects of existence, making music an ideal tool for what she calls *whole-person development*.

Consider one adult amateur who exhibited annoyance or even outright self-disdain when cello challenges arose. No matter how large or small the blunder, his ego was merciless. "Put it all in perspective," pleaded Peterson. "It's just a piece of wood you play!"

Three years later, his life began spiraling out of control: family, love life, work. Yet this man remained surprisingly calm, one day admitting, "Cello lessons taught me to roll with the punches. This too will pass."

A high school student began lessons to catch up with peers. Adopted from Ethiopia two years prior, she needed to find her voice, and English was difficult. Perhaps music could help.

As lessons progressed, Peterson deduced that this girl suffered from post-traumatic stress disorder. After making a mistake or forgetting something, she would brace herself, as if anticipating a beating. Peterson responded with kindness and empathy. They practiced breathing, yoga, and even laughing. What began as a quest to advance in orchestra transformed into therapy on responding to life.

A third student had landed a great-paying job at Microsoft. Unfortunately, this woman detested every moment of work. Hoping to add spice to her life, she began studying cello. Music not only brought enjoyment but also helped her discover something far more profound. She didn't just have a doozy of a job; her life was a disaster.

In meetings, they played tunes and discussed the ways of the world. Ultimately, this student worked up the courage and wisdom to take action. In fact, she decided to break from her old life completely: moving across the country, starting her own business, even quitting cello.

"Goodbye lessons" with Peterson are something of a ritual. She and the departing student play everything they've worked on together in duet. Celebrating their unique and collective journey, the two reflect on memories and imagine the future. In this case, things got emotional, and tears flowed freely. At lesson's end, Peterson watched this one-time-disgruntled employee leave empowered, determined, and as her friend.

And *that* is the power of music.

Creativity

In our uncertain and constantly evolving world, many thought leaders argue that creativity ranks among the most valuable twenty-first-century skills. This transferable aptitude allows individuals to problem solve, discover fresh solutions, differentiate work, innovate, and get ahead. It is beneficial to just about every career and life situation.

Though standardized tests, strict rule following, and homogenized thinking may have a place in education, they have clearly negatively impacted the creative development of too many learners. Music education can help remedy this situation. In fact, creativity is often used as a primary justification for this study. But does music automatically nurture inventive impulses?

A common claim suggests that every musical rendition demonstrates creativity, since it features slightly different dynamics, articulations, and note lengths (even when students precisely follow teacher demands to the best of their abilities). But then again, everyone walks a little differently each journey, varying path, step size, and travel time. Is strolling also inherently creative? Are accidental interpretations truly demonstrative of right-brain thinking?

Music learning that is focused on the "correct" notes the "correct" way, as dictated by teacher preference and "authentic" performance practice, offers many benefits. Active creativity, however, is not one of them. In fact, this approach is known to punish imaginative impulses, encouraging correctness, uniformity, and faithfully following instructions at the expense of chance taking, experimentation, and personalized decision making.

If this learning objective is important to you, look for activities that promote active inventiveness and imaginative solutions: composing, arranging, improvising, writing lyrics, reorchestrating, selecting literature, designing events, practicing innovative performance, developing exercises, creating music videos. Empower learners to make personal decisions, including those that differ from your own inclinations. Push students outside their comfort zone at times, presenting problems solvable only with engaged ingenuity.

Genius

"The definition of genius is being well versed in the practice of a given field, plus creativity," explains cellist Sera Smolen (www.serasmolen. com). Determined to ignite brilliance, her pedagogical approach balances discipline with freedom, combining elements from the Waldorf and Suzuki philosophies. All creative exercises are done in parallel with repertoire training.

Not everything is creative: holding a bow, fingering, playing without tension. Yet improvisation, vital to musical and personal growth, plays a celebrated role in almost every meeting. "The number one rule of creativity is that there are no mistakes. Like ice cream flavors, all notes are delicious. Pick one at a time and savor the taste."

Even beginners have creative capacity. Smolen challenges "pre-twinklers" to play a variety of white and black key games on piano. As cello facility develops, students improvise within a given mode (D major for starters). Backup recordings provide harmonic progressions and textures where any scalar note works well. This fun, engaging approach allows students of wide-ranging abilities to explore a flexible musical canvas.

Improvisation is often a communal activity. Smolen guides string quartets and other ensembles as they explore in real time. In addition to developing ears and imagination, this provides an ideal forum for learning theory experientially, whether examining bass lines, countermelodies, harmonic function, or interlocking rhythms.

One popular recital event has her entire studio play and improvise over dance melodies from around the globe. The performers are joined by a professional band, and parents dance to the beat.

Each year, Smolen's students compose one piece based on a theme (e.g., nature). Beginning as improvisations, these works are refined, rehearsed, memorized, and notated. A *Composer's Concert* invites participants to present one standard repertoire piece followed by an original work.

"Children feel valuable and valued when asked to share *their* music. Giving permission to explore not only increases artistic devotion but alters how they approach a number of life issues. We often argue that creativity is necessary but underdeveloped in twenty-first-century citizens. I can't imagine a better platform for cultivating this aptitude than music!"

Twenty-First-Century Skills

The Partnership for 21st Century Skills (P21), a national organization composed of business and education leaders, came to the following conclusion: "There is a profound gap between the knowledge and skills most students learn in school and the knowledge and skills they need in typical twenty-first-century communities and workplaces." P21 argues the most underdeveloped competencies crucial to contemporary workplaces are the "4 Cs": (1) critical thinking and problem solving, (2) communication, (3) collaboration, and (4) creativity.

If these learning objectives make your priority list, what activities might the curriculum emphasize? The previous section examined creativity. To follow are helpful activities for the other objectives.

Critical Thinking	Communication	Collaboration
• Aesthetic response • Analyses with multiple solutions • Anything creative • Considering music's impact on society • Interpretative analogy (imagery, narrative) • Interpretive decisions • Open-ended questions • Recording comparisons • Reflecting • Self-assessment	• Audience mingling • Blogging about music • Music advocacy • Music as communication • Music video scripting and production • Peer teaching • Presentations on music • Program note creation • Reflection journaling • Spoken recital introductions • Student marketing	• Chamber ensembles • Group composition • Group improvisation • Group lessons • Joint studio recitals • Large ensembles • Leadership roles • Lesson overlap interactions • Student-organized activities • Studio blog • Studio initiatives • Team projects

How to Be Human

"My music lessons are not about presenting the great work of composers," explains Australian pianist Elissa Milne (www.elissamilne.wordpress.com), "but the great work of *students*." Repertoire represents the beginning of an educational journey, rather than the end. Offering far more value than the opportunity to duplicate pretty sounds, music is a vehicle for learning what it means to be human.

A full life requires discovery, engagement, critical thinking, and informed choices. Similarly, music literature represents an enormous field of potential. Emphasizing these values, she often plays the "what if?" game. What if you change the octave? How about the rhythm? What happens when you play every other bar as written and make up what goes in between? For one exercise, students transform *Old MacDonald* into several modes. If just one note can change life from sad to happy, imagine how you might transform the world.

To begin each lesson, students are asked to share a weekly "Eureka" moment. Perhaps they experimented with the sustain pedal or tried a tune in retrograde.

Milne views her role as that of guide, not referee. She might direct students to a proverbial waterfall, but young explorers have the right and responsibility to decide how to approach this miracle of nature. Her job is to listen carefully, be responsive, and not get in the way of learning.

Milne's retention rate is close to 100%. Most students insist on continuing after high school, and she often receives notes from alumni reflecting on how music study empowered them to take chances and become leaders.

"Music teaching should be the opposite of telling students to shut up and do the 'right thing' through mindless repetition for accuracy. *The right thing* is making personalized, informed judgments and having faith in your abilities as a human being. Granting permission to explore is not simply a perk of lessons. It's the main point!"

Impact First

While no standardized teaching approach or bias is endorsed here, most SMTs seem to follow a similar process. They begin by examining large-scale objectives and then work backward to determine the details. This powerhouse formula can lead to extraordinary results:

1. Start by defining *your essential question*, or primary purpose.
2. Then identify and prioritize *learning objectives* that support this mission.
3. Finally, design *activities* and *initiatives* that promote desired outcomes.

The next chapter introduces savvy rules for teaching prosperity. However, the desire to run a profitable music teaching business by no means implies selling out core values. On the contrary, the most successful SMTs are driven by a sense of purpose. Their commitment to financial viability is matched with a near-fanatical devotion to creating value at every turn.

Music teaching is more than a means for paying the bills, after all. It is very, very, *very* important work that can change the world. At least it can be, in the hands of an SMT.

2 NINE SAVVY RULES TO TEACHING PROSPERITY

Savvy Music Teachers (SMTs) are driven by a deep sense of purpose, but they match that impulse with a clear business strategy. Our journey continues with nine savvy rules that lead to teaching prosperity. All are critical on the roadway to success.

Rule #1: Get Over Your Fear of Money

Conventional wisdom warns against discussing the controversial topics of politics or religion. These issues, thorny and explosive, are best left untouched. Yet there seems to be a subject far more taboo, at least among musicians: *money*.

As artists, we are conditioned to believe that talking—or even thinking—about money means selling out. Starving artistry is our destiny, almost a badge of honor. Musicians who even contemplate financial stability have obviously sold their souls to the devil. Even if you secretly don't want to be poor, it would be wise to keep that selfish detail to yourself while in polite company.

This cultural value is unfortunate, because money *is* important. It is not everything, but it is not something to ignore or neglect either.

Of course, you are pursuing independent music teaching to do something you love while making a positive difference on the world. But doctors may also share that goal. The difference is that medical practitioners expect to be compensated for their time, expertise, and service. Few people question their integrity. Doctors are the good guys (well, doctors and SMTs!).

The work of a dynamic, vibrant instructor can truly change lives. Yet you will be far less attentive to students' needs if falling deeper into debt by the minute, working for far less than you are worth, fearing the collection agency at your door. Conversely, when life (and finances are a part of life) is going well, it is probable that you will go the extra mile to better serve learners.

Failing to address issues of personal finance and well-being isn't heroic. In fact, it can be dangerous, even detrimental. Acting responsibly about money does not signify a lack of commitment to students or art. It does indicate that you care for yourself while helping others.

The SMT is not greedy by any stretch of the imagination. However, he or she is financially literate, comfortable contemplating, discussing, and managing money.

Rule #2: Music Teaching is a Business

Many people pursuing this line of work possess outstanding artistic and pedagogical "chops," with degrees galore from world-famous music schools, yet they have an incomplete understanding of the job description. As a result, financial—and possibly educational—success is limited. Unfortunately, this incomplete approach often leads to diminished quality of life, dreams, and impact.

SMTs implement business models, market services, address logistics, oversee accounting, supervise financing, direct operations, manage customer service, control human resources, and develop products. They are founders, CEOs, managers, and employees of their own enterprise.

The good news is that professional success requires the same kinds of aptitudes you teach on a daily basis. SMTs understand the transferable nature of skills and perspectives like discipline, time management, creative problem solving, long-term strategies, and being passion driven. There is an art and a science to achieving artistic excellence. The same can be said of professional success.

Skill	Music Learning	Career Success
Discipline	Success requires time, energy, and focused commitment directed toward artistic goals.	Success requires time, energy, and focused commitment directed toward business/career goals.
Time management	The best musicians effectively and efficiently use minutes, devoting ample time to improving their art even when juggling a busy schedule.	The best businesspeople effectively and efficiently use minutes, devoting ample time to improving their business model even when juggling a busy schedule.

(continued)

Skill	Music Learning	Career Success
Creative problem solving	Addressing musical challenges requires critical thinking, problem solving, developing creative solutions, and risk taking.	Addressing career challenges requires critical thinking, problem solving, developing creative solutions, and risk taking.
Long-term strategies	The goal is not just to learn a piece of music, but also to grow as a musician over time.	The goal is not just to maximize one paycheck, but also to create a sustainable business model that thrives over time.
Passion driven	As music teachers, we are passionate about cultivating great art and motivated students.	Business models are an art form. SMTs directing passion toward career success find these pursuits exhilarating and fulfilling as well.

Music teaching bursts with career potential for those skilled and creative enough to seize it. No MBA required: you are perfectly capable of developing requisite aptitudes! This book provides a roadmap, but first you need to start thinking like an entrepreneur.

Rule #3: Charge the Right Amount

When charging for lessons or any other service, you trade life energy for cash. How valuable is your time?

The price tag on anything is relative to its time and place, and somewhat arbitrary. In the 1920s, the average $265 car could be filled with 22¢-per-gallon gasoline and parked in the garage of a luxurious new $8,000 home. In today's market, $8,000 is unlikely to get you either a beat-up minivan or a questionably decorated half-bathroom.

Even when using contemporary pricing, values are relative. You can find a great home in rural Indiana for $100,000 that would easily sell for $1 million in Manhattan. The corner Italian restaurant might charge twice as much as the one two blocks away, even though their meatballs and service are as cold as they are lousy.

Some independent music teachers severely undercut the competition. While that approach might attract customers in the short term, beware. First, it is not the best ethical decision for our profession, devaluing the contributions of an entire workforce. Second, it may scare off clients who assume that meager pricing suggests inferior quality. Third, it makes it difficult to reach your earning goals.

Other teachers steer in the opposite direction, attaching a bloated price tag. If you can identify willing buyers, this no doubt helps your economic model. But beyond a tipping point, most people simply cannot or will not pay exorbitant amounts, even if you have ten college degrees, a great personality, and the best hair in town.

The ideal price for anything is where the buyer and seller both feel they get a great deal. Because of this metric, SMTs generally command above-average rates, thanks to a differentiated curriculum and superior service.

Rule #4: Teach for Yourself

To maximize earnings, teach for yourself.

True, there are appealing aspects to working through a music store, academy, or other program. Primary benefits are that your employer:

1. Recruits students
2. Organizes logistics
3. Provides a space (and possibly a piano or sound system)

Because of these and other justifications, young and seasoned teachers alike choose to work as an employee in someone else's business. Such positions may be a good fit for college students, instructors seeking to impact distant communities, and those who recently relocated or will move in the near future. With all the nitty-gritty addressed externally, instructors simply show up and work their teaching magic.

From a strictly financial point of view, however, the price tag is steep. For every lesson taught, you earn less than the student is willing to pay, as the supervising institution takes their cut. That commission—as much as 50%—is often justifiable, since they provide the services previously described.

The economic cost to you is more than a lower hourly salary. Music students and their families spend more on music-related studies than the price of lessons—a concept explored in later chapters. When teaching for someone else, you are ineligible to access that income. Instead, employers receive the benefit. You earn a reduced hourly wage, and no more.

In addition, many music teaching centers require employees to sign a "noncompete agreement." This means that you can't legally balance some work there with students of your own, as it causes a conflict of interest.

As we will see, marketing and logistics are not difficult but rather a matter of strategy and determination. If a store can do it, so can you. Teaching space may be a legitimate concern, but savvy solutions exist here as well.

If you are able to teach for someone else while reaching your financial goals, wonderful! For those hoping to earn more, read on.

Rule #5: Teach From Home

Teaching out of your home offers many benefits. It:

- Avoids the expense of renting a separate studio space (the BIG one)
- Avoids the time, expense, and frustration associated with commuting to work
- Reduces additional expenses, such as the temptation to eat out
- Minimizes inconvenience when a lesson is cancelled at the last minute
- Allows you to relax at home during teaching breaks
- Provides maximum scheduling flexibility compared to non-full-time rentals
- Gives you full control over how the physical studio is organized and decorated
- Provides homeowners a tax break

From a strictly financial point of view, you can earn a lot more without the expense of renting a separate space. It is often economically advantageous to shell out a little more in rent or mortgage payments for an appropriate primary residence rather than making separate payments to an external location.

Please note, there are disadvantages to home studios as well. It may be tricky to separate work and personal life if they both occur in the same physical location. Teaching from home can inconvenience family members and roommates. If walls are thin and lessons are loud, neighbors may not be enthusiastic about your contributions. Some dwellings are simply not appropriate: too small, bad neighborhood, no room for a piano. Of all the rules, this is the most flexible. It does not work for everyone.

However, seriously consider the benefits of teaching from home. The financial model detailed in the next chapter assumes that no additional rental fee is required. If leasing a separate location, account for this expense in your income blueprint.

Rule #6: Work Hard, but Work Smart

Here is one path to earning an annual salary of $80,000 as an independent music teacher. Suppose your hourly lesson rate is $45, and the average student takes 40 lessons per year. All you need is to teach 44½ hours per week.

$45 per hour × 40 lessons per year × 44.5 hours per week = $80,100

This model is possible, but are you crazy? Supervising 40+ hours per week of private lessons is ludicrous. In fact, few teachers can reasonably handle 30 without burning out in a matter of a few short years.

Most music teachers I've met are avid workers, and the blueprint outlined here requires hard and consistent effort. On average, SMTs spend 30 to 45 hours per week focused on career issues, a significant time investment. Some periods or models necessitate more.

However, this workload is all-inclusive, incorporating preparation time, ironing out logistics, marketing, organizing events, and even taking the occasional bathroom break. Hopefully it includes enough teaching to earn a good living without suffering such exhaustive labor requirements that your joy of education and music gets zapped.

All work and no play makes Jack a dull and sad trombone teacher, or however the saying goes. Make no mistake, income is indeed important! But so are other things in life: family, friends, lifelong learning, hobbies, passion projects. A sustainable career must be balanced with a gratifying and meaningful life to be worth a hill of beans.

The SMT is a doer, unmistakably dedicated to art, craft, and students. However, earning a decent income mustn't require humanly unreasonable demands. It does necessitate working smarter and investing energy strategically.

Rule #7: Balance Multiple Streams

With unreasonable teaching loads off limits, how is it possible to reach $50,000 to $100,000, or whatever your goal salary? Another option is raising the hourly rate. For example, when charging $100 per hour to students averaging 40 lessons per year, it is possible to reach $80,000 with just 20 teaching hours.

$100 per hour × 40 lessons per year × 20 hours per week = $80,000

While this sounds great, the challenge is obvious. Few teachers can secure 20 hours' worth of students willing or able to pay this fee on a regular basis, even if they've recorded with Wynton Marsalis, toured with Joshua Bell, and share Lady Gaga's fashion designer.

While charging the right price is critical, another secret to a prosperous and vibrant career as an SMT is balancing multiple income streams. Private lessons are just one of several professional activities. This kind of professional profile is known as a *portfolio career*.

A portfolio career keeps your work interesting, varied, and energized. The SMT blueprint details seven large-scale streams, each offering multiple substreams.

SMT Income Streams		
1. Lessons	4. Events	7. Additional
2. Classes	5. Technology	
3. Camps	6. Products	

Rule #8: Earn More from Less

Seasoned businesspeople understand that selling more to established customers is easier than attracting new ones. For example, it is often simpler, cheaper, and less time consuming for clothing stores to retail an extra $3,000 to existing customers than persuading new ones.

Once a positive relationship has been established, clients become more open to sales messages. In fact, if the connection is strong enough, they anticipate this marketing. Just look at the unshakable enthusiasm of Apple's customers when a new iPad (iPhone, iPod, or other iProduct) is released. People who like and trust a business are frequently happy to part with hard-earned cash in exchange for enhanced quality of life. SMTs embrace the concept of earning more from less, prioritizing relationship building and outstanding service.

As an SMT, you have far fewer customers than a clothing store or Apple. Your studio consists of just 20, 40, or maybe 60 students. But personal bonds created with these learners (and their families) are tight. They trust and value you immensely, often to the point of exchanging holiday gifts. So when you—the cherished music teacher—recommend buying a new book, instrument, or experience, it is likely that they will comply. As long as you don't abuse these relationships, most students and their families are grateful for any musical and/or educational guidance you provide.

Like a travel agent, you facilitate fascinating adventures into the world of music. When leading the way toward meaningful encounters, there is potential to be compensated.

As you will see, SMTs earn more from students than lesson fees, one reason it is crucial to work for yourself. (Otherwise, the governing institution is entitled to these financial perks.) For example, if you teach fiddle lessons and rent violins, it is probable that students will lease an instrument from you, contributing to two separate income streams. Clients are destined to spend this capital either way, but working directly with the trusted teacher provides a win-win.

Obviously, do not nickel-and-dime students. Never make recommendations that provide you income but fail to benefit them significantly. That only irritates clients, breaks down trust, and erodes your reputation. Don't bill to attend students' youth symphony concerts or make the occasional phone calls on their behalf. These actions strengthen relationships, demonstrating your devotion.

However, you should not feel guilty being compensated for helpful, time-consuming work. There is no ethical dilemma here. Every penny received is in exchange for a valuable experience, service, or product. Create powerful bonds with clients and reap the rewards.

Rule #9: Make a Plan and Make it Happen

Too many independent music teachers earn far less than they desire, and far less than their capacity. In the long run, they fail to achieve financial independence, instead existing paycheck to paycheck. When that occurs, one of the following is typically to blame:

1. They don't understand the economic potential available to music teachers.
2. They don't know how to create a viable business plan.

3. They do understand these things but don't take action (a warning to people who read this book but fail to follow through), instead leaving finances to fate.
4. They aren't steadfast in their devotion to bringing that blueprint to fruition.

Careful planning, and a commitment to that plan, is the surest path to success. While it is impossible to accurately predict the future, professionals with a map are much more likely to reach a desirable destination than those relying on serendipity alone. This book provides the knowledge, tools, and structure for creating a viable business strategy. The rest is in your hands. Are you ready to get down to business?

3 LESSONS: STREAM 1

In this era of financial uncertainty and disruptive technological change, the music industry is in crisis. Funding sources are drying up. Record labels are going extinct. Symphony orchestras are declaring bankruptcy. And in a world of infinite choice, attracting a following for your music is cutthroat.

Yet one path that continues to hold great promise is independent music teaching. Demand exists in just about every corner, making it one of the most stable, promising career options available to musicians regardless of instrument, genre, or background. For a host of reasons, people are seduced by the mystical power and challenge of creating sound in the first person. Even with the wide range of technological tools available today, music learning is so personal and nuanced that countless individuals employ a mentor to lead them on this journey. Private lessons are the medicine of choice.

And that is very good news for Savvy Music Teachers (SMTs).

Lessons from the Trenches

Here are the top 10 surprising things I've learned as an independent music teacher since graduating with a master's degree in piano pedagogy:

1. Financial success is dependent on my knowledge and management of finances, not how much money I make.
2. Teaching "formulas" in pedagogy classes applies to the top 15% of my student base. Approaches for the other 85% are up to me.
3. Familiar music (e.g., famous classical arrangements, popular hits) is not dessert—it's protein!

4. Time management in graduate school is practice for life as a professional music teacher. If you're good, things never slow down.
5. Downloadable sheet music is one of the most transformative inventions of my lifetime. I'm still in awe of what an iPad does for my back and for shelf clutter.
6. Large-scale goal setting should happen not once, but three times each year: in May for the summer, August for the fall, and January for the spring.
7. I used to think being a musician was the hard part and the rest was cake. As it turns out, business communication and management account for 50% of my time. The other half is divided 40% for teaching and 10% for organizing/facilitating performances.
8. Appearance matters across the board, whether dealing with print materials, online presence, or in-person meetings.
9. Life without regularly interacting with colleagues gets lonely. Be deliberate about scheduling time to build relationships.
10. My network of true friends has grown exponentially based on relationships with clients. I am continually amazed by the wonderful people who find me.

Your Unique Studio Identity
What You Teach

Fourteen Instruments

Musical potential is everywhere. At least that is the philosophy of Cheryl Suwardi (www.suwardimusic.com). Originally a clarinetist, a high school music director challenged her to play almost every instrument the program owned. As a college music education major, she specialized in woodwinds and strings and continued to explore further.

Today, Suwardi offers instruction in 14 instruments: violin, viola, cello, bass, mandolin, guitar, clarinet, flute, saxophone, oboe, trumpet, baritone, euphonium, and piano. Some are taught only to beginners, while others expand to intermediate and advanced levels. Her *Instrument Introduction Sessions* allow kids to experiment with three to five instruments, discovering which instrument best suits their personality.

Performance skills (technique, repertoire, and practicing) are just one of five competencies addressed in her curriculum. Music theory, composition/improvisation, music history, and world music also play key roles.

In addition to lessons, Suwardi organizes the *Junior Orchestra* (grades one to four) and two *Advanced Orchestras* (grades five to eight and the occasional high school student). These classes, each open to 4 to 10 studio members, expose participants to a supplemental learning environment.

Teaching such a wide range of topics ensures there are always more than enough students. But it does something else as well. "This kind of variety makes things really interesting and fun for me. I always have something to learn."

Complete the phrase: "Open for business, _____ lessons!" So reads the proverbial neon sign on your website, business card, and front door.

At first glance, solving this puzzle appears easy. Most independent music teachers offer lessons on their primary instrument. But you are certainly qualified to do more than just that. Even if you aren't the world's leading authority, basic fluency may be enough to offer meaningful instruction to beginning or even intermediate students.

Lesson Topics	
Primary instrument	This is where most teachers start (and many end).
Secondary instruments	You do not need to be a virtuoso to teach secondary instruments.
Same-family instruments	A trumpet player might offer instruction in horn, trombone, euphonium, and/or tuba.
Styles	Specialize in jazz? Baroque? Bluegrass? Salsa? Golden Oldies? Offer "style" lessons to musicians of all instruments or voice types.
Non-instrument-based performance	A bass player with incredible musicality, rhythmic chops, or stage presence might teach those aptitudes to students of all instruments.

(*continued*)

Lesson Topics	
Nonperformance skills	These include composition, film scoring, improvisation, arranging, classical theory, pop theory, jazz theory, ear training, sequencing, computer notation, practicing techniques.
Wellness	There is a market for teachers who address physical (e.g., tension) and cognitive (e.g., nerves) wellness.
Career issues	These include coaching on marketing, branding, fundraising, entrepreneurship, music business, and other practical issues.

SMTs utilize their range of skills in different ways. Multiple aptitudes allow you to offer instruction in several areas, making it easier to fill the roster while providing variety to your schedule. They can also broaden the scope of meetings. For example, perhaps viola lessons are infused with a focus on stylistic composition. Doing this differentiates your studio, increases competitive advantage, and enhances the student experience.

They Teach What?

Here are some interesting offerings by independent music teachers:

- Sahffi Lynne (www.sahffi.com), who trained as a classical French horn-ist, offers lessons in voice, beginner guitar, horn, songwriting, and "performance coaching" (overcoming stage fright).
- Carolyn Downie (www.carolyndownie.com) teaches "Holistic Music Lessons," combining basic piano and vocal performance, theory, ear training, songwriting, world music, therapeutic sound, and additional subjects.
- Tom Nothnagle (www.allthingsguitartom.com) provides instruction on 13 plucked-string instruments including classical guitar, new flamenco, rock and blues guitar, 12-string guitar, bass guitar, mandolin, banjo, and ukulele.
- Nicky Tierra, aka "Nicky T" (www.nickytmusic.com), gives lessons in guitar, vocals, songwriting, production, artist development, recording, and "DJ".

Who You Teach

SMTs clearly define their target audience(s). Who are your ideal students? What are their ages, backgrounds, ability levels, neighborhoods, and aspirations? While few teachers make it a policy to refuse interested students outside this profile, specializing offers several benefits.

1. **Curriculum.** Different categories of students have contrasting aspirations and learning needs. Concentrating allows you to create a program honed to a particular group.
2. **Community.** Group classes, events, and other team-building exercises are often more effective when participants share common interests or backgrounds.
3. **Credibility.** Students prefer teachers with a history of helping people like them.
4. **Reputation.** Specializing builds name recognition within a given community. Perhaps you become known as *the* accordion teacher for medical doctors.
5. **Referrals.** Students are likely to refer friends with a similar profile.
6. **Resources.** Because it requires additional money, time, and energy to reach each segment, the more specific you are, the better. It's simpler to market to elementary students from schools A, B, and C than promoting to every 6- to 18-year-old in the county.

Students with Disabilities

Tubist Philip VanOuse (www.pvostudio.com) has developed a reputation for teaching students with disabilities. Around 30% of his studio has been affected by some type of mental or physical ailment: fetal alcohol syndrome, dyslexia, seizures, off-the-charts attention deficit hyperactivity disorder.

"Many band directors don't think these students are capable of playing melody instruments, so they get moved to the bottom of the brass section." Over the years, he has developed a reputation for effectively addressing these special learners, and as a result, many seek him out actively.

Beyond recruitment potential, each demographic brings a unique perspective and energy to your studio.

Potential Music Student Groups	
• Actors*	• Music lovers with no prior
• Adult beginners	experience
• Adult hobbyists	• Music nerds and Star "Trekkies
• Advanced players	• Music teachers (teacher training)
• Autistic children	• Nannies/au pairs*
• Blind players	• Online students from various
• Business employees	time zones*
• Children of professional musicians	• Preschoolers*
• College music majors*	• Prodigies
• College nonmusic majors*	• Professional musicians
• Dancers	• Recovering music majors
• Doctors*	• Religious individuals
• Elementary school students	• Retirees
• Entrepreneurs*	• Self-trained musicians (up to
• Ethnic group members	this point)
• Exchange students	• Seniors
• Film directors	• Show choir members
• Gays/lesbians	• Singers
• Golfers and bowlers (maybe music	• Singles (Why not? Music is a great
improves your aim?)	social tool!)
• High school students	• Social organizations
• High school students to major	• Special needs individuals
in music	• Teenagers
• Homeschoolers*	• Unemployed*
• Honor band members	• Visual artists
• Honor students	• Wealthy patrons of the arts
• Housewives/househusbands*	• Workers with night shifts*
• Independently wealthy*	• Working class
• Jocks	• Young adults
• Karaoke singers	• Young professionals
• Lawyers	• Your students' parents
• Middle school students	• Youth symphony members
• Minorities	

Often available during typical "off limit" weekday morning and early afternoon times.

While students enroll in music lessons for a variety of reasons, consider typical motivations:

Primary Motivations for Music Study	
Young children	A host of studies suggest that young children exposed to music excel in a number of areas. Parents often enroll kids to give them a head start in life.
Elementary school students	Music is one of many activities, in addition to the likes of soccer, swimming, ballet, horseback riding, and scouts, providing them with a well-rounded array of experiences.
Junior/senior high school students	Most students who continue throughout the teen years view music as a defining part of their personal identity. They often play in school/community ensembles as well.
College music majors	Most hope to earn a living through this field, though some simply choose an enjoyable major before determining their ultimate career direction.
College nonmusic majors	These individuals often continue lessons for an enjoyable activity that provides a break from challenging (and less fun) work required for their degree program.
Music professionals	Lessons facilitate continued growth or the development of new skill sets that help secure additional work and fulfillment.
Adult amateurs	Music is a passion, often a relaxing respite from the "day job." Some begin from scratch, while others are quite accomplished.
Senior citizens	Senior citizens may begin or rediscover music after retirement, with hopes of staying active, challenged, and engaged in this life chapter.

A Teacher with Tails

British pianist Richard Meyrick (www.thepianostudio.co.uk) had an international touring career when tragedy struck. A diagnosis of neck cancer immediately halted his career. Five years later, he was ready to jump back into the game, this time as a music teacher.

At 7:30 one morning, he dressed in tuxedo with tails. Appearing in a business district, he touted his credentials and passed out flyers. *This renowned artist is now accepting students—even beginners. Nobody will be turned away.* The message and its delivery were so curious that it generated newspaper, radio, and television coverage. Within two weeks, he attracted 15 students. By the two-month mark, his studio was packed.

Most students are highly successful professionals with limited prior performance background: lawyers, judges, entrepreneurs, scientists, and bankers. With passion but limited time for music learning, his 50 adult learners schedule lessons every two to three weeks on average.

In 2004, an investment firm approached Meyrick with a novel proposal. They would pay for him to travel the country, offering workshops to young, underserved pianists without access to top-notch training. Gifted youngsters discovered through the process were then invited to London to take free lessons with this master musician, all expenses paid by the company.

Where You Teach

Because the decision of where to teach is so significant, chapter 10 is devoted exclusively to this topic. For now, consider the world in which your lessons take place—physical or virtual.

Since the very first private music lesson, there has been a single instructional forum available: master and apprentice convene at a mutually convenient time and location to investigate tricks of the trade. Twenty thousand years ago, advanced Paleolithic music makers probably invited disciples to their cave, unveiling innovative grunting techniques and stylistically appropriate methods for striking rocks. Though instruments, styles, and teaching techniques have evolved considerably, this mode of delivery has not.

At least not until the twenty-first century. But now, thanks to the miracle of technology, music teachers have a second platform that deems geographic proximity irrelevant. An oboist in Cambridge can offer online instruction to students in California, Calgary, or Cairo without leaving the comfort of her air-conditioned office. Cyberspace has changed the rules.

Video conferencing has not made in-person music teaching obsolete. Unlike so many other industries, the unique characteristics of music learning make it likely that face-to-face meetings will remain a popular option for the foreseeable future.

It does, however, open new doors. Virtual lessons make music learning accessible to people who otherwise would not have the opportunity. It permits students to select from a wider net of instructors, while SMTs can reach a world of learners never before accessible. Regardless of location or specialty, there have never been more options for filling a studio.

In many ways, online lessons are not so different from in-person encounters. The qualities that make a great teacher have not changed. Regardless of delivery platform, clear learning objectives, powerful pedagogy, effective communication, enthusiastic outlook, and personalized attention are paramount. Each forum, however, is accompanied by unique advantages. Flip the equation to consider the challenges.

In-Person Lesson Advantages	Internet Lesson Advantages
Allows you, as the teacher, full control over the learning environment	Allows you to teach from anywhere
Subtle nuances are best addressed in person	Allows you to accept students from anywhere
Certain people, particularly children, focus better when in the same room as their teacher	Allows you to continue working with students after they move out of the area or if their driver/parent cannot take them
Easier to pinpoint sources of tension or other unhealthy physical habits	Allows lessons to occur even when you or a student is out of town
Students can feel your wrist or abdomen when demonstrating a technique	Eliminates commute time and expenses (also good for the environment)
Easier for student and teacher to play together in terms of timing and balance	Avoids cancellations due to traffic or weather (unless your power goes out!)
Easier to show students where to start playing or to make markings in their music	Sick students can take lessons without infecting the whole studio
More personal bonds are formed with students and families when meeting in person	Lessons can be scheduled during hard-to-fill slots thanks to different time zones

(continued)

In-Person Lesson Advantages	Internet Lesson Advantages
Whipping out a sight-reading example or reward sticker for a job well done is easy	Students can more easily record lessons, view repeatedly, and observe progress over time
No time is wasted with technological hassles	Students can watch themselves in real time
Certain kinds of learning and relationship building are best done in person	Performing for the camera helps students overcome nerve issues

Most music teachers still run primarily local businesses, maintaining a physical address where the lessons take place. However, even if that describes you, there are several reasons to consider online forums:

1. If there aren't enough violists (or whatever specialty) to fill your studio locally, the Internet permits access to students from across the state, country, or globe.
2. Learners from distant time zones may be available during hard-to-fill slots.
3. Internet lessons may command higher fees than locals are willing to pay. For example, perhaps you live in a Midwest town where the going rate is $45 per hour, but students on the East Coast are accustomed to paying $60.
4. When students are physically unable to attend a lesson because they are out of town or sick or transportation difficulties arise, this option prevents a cancellation.
5. Internet lessons offer some superior features. Having local students take the occasional online lesson allows them to experience music learning differently. In fact, these unique qualities may even influence how you approach face-to-face meetings.

Lessons from the Trenches

When students are sick or weather prohibits travel, I love the option of online lessons. This way, the schedule remains uninterrupted, progress stays consistent, and the student and I experience an enjoyable change of routine.

To make sessions more effective, I integrate *Internet MIDI*, by Zenph. com (currently $69). The student and I plug MIDI instruments into interfaces at our respective locations. Rather than hearing warbled sounds over the Internet, notes are transmitted directly to the other keyboard, allowing us to demonstrate and listen in real time as if the two of us were just feet away.

Most students and teachers have access to all they need for online lessons: a computer, tablet, or smartphone with built-in microphone and web camera, decent speakers, Internet connection, and video conferencing program like Skype or iChat (both are free). The biggest technological challenge is often a slow connection, though that gets better each year.

International Impact from Home

Trumpeter Jeff Purtle (www.purtle.com) dreamed of balancing a nice standard of living with an independent teaching career while impacting students from across the globe. As an early adopter of video conferencing technology, he recognized that geography was largely irrelevant to reaching these aspirations. Moving to Greenville, SC, he built a vibrant teaching business while residing in this beautiful, affordable city that is close to family.

Around 75% of Purtle's 50 regular students take weekly online lessons. He also impacts another 40 to 50 people who study sporadically. Residing on every continent besides Antarctica, they connect from Brazil, Jamaica, England, Portugal, Italy, Norway, Greece, the Czech Republic, Iran, India, Nigeria, and across the United States. His roster includes beginners, professional musicians, the Pentagon's head of army budgeting, a capital investment manager, an NSA officer, the music censor for the Islamic Republic of Iran Broadcasting, and the president of a major fast food chain.

Though his teaching method is consistent both online and offline, the two populations engage Purtle for different reasons. "Local students find me because they need a trumpet teacher and I happen to live in town. Online students seek out my unique approach and style, which they discover through word of mouth or online articles."

All teaching is scheduled Tuesday through Thursday. Some days are hyperprogrammed, with nonstop sessions essentially from 9 AM to midnight. With students from a range of time zones, lessons can be conveniently scheduled at virtually any hour. Though such an intense regimen does not suit everyone, this arrangement works well for Purtle. It also opens up four-day weekends to take out-of-town gigs or simply enjoy time with the family.

How You Teach

In chapter 1, we examined *why* you teach. Building on that framework, you can determine what the defining features of your studio are. In developing specifics, weigh the following:

1. How does each item/bias help answer your essential question while advancing prioritized learning objectives?
2. What traditions are distinct to your studio? How do they augment value?
3. Which elements increase student engagement and likeliness that they will embrace a musical life for years to come?

There is no "correct," sanctioned way of organizing a studio. On the contrary, SMTs are careful to develop a high-impact, intentional program unique to their brand and personality. In addition to issues brainstormed in the chart to follow, consider the role events (chapter 6), technology (chapter 7), and physical teaching space (chapter 10) play in defining your studio "brand."

Possible Teaching Elements	
Atmosphere	
• Creative	• Parental involvement
• Friendly	• Perfectionistic
• Fun	• Relaxed
• Intense	• Respectful
• Interactive	• Serious
• Joyous	• Strict
• Laid back	• Student driven
• Mistakes are a healthy part of life	• Teacher driven
Pedagogies	
• Dalcroze	• Other
• Gordon	• Solfège
• Kodaly	• Suzuki
• Method book	• Your own
• Orff	

(continued)

Possible Teaching Elements

Repertoire

- Classical (standard) literature
- Contemporary/new music
- Early music
- Ensemble
- Etudes
- Excerpts (orchestral)
- Folk music
- Holiday music
- Jazz
- Multiple genres
- Original compositions
- Popular music
- Sacred music
- Solo
- Women composers
- World music

Activities/Focal Points

- Arranging
- Authentic performance practice
- Composing
- Creative interpretation
- Critical listening
- Ear training
- Flash cards/learning tools
- Fundamentals
- Games
- Harmonic analysis
- History
- Improvising
- Instrumental/vocal technique
- Mock auditions
- Movement and music
- Musicality
- Orchestrating
- Patterns/exercises
- Physical technique
- Playing by ear
- Practice strategies
- Rhythmic emphasis
- Scales/arpeggios
- Score study
- Sight reading
- Sight singing
- Singing (for nonvocalists)
- Stage presence
- Team projects
- Theory
- Transcription
- Wellness

Studio Traditions

- Awards and prizes
- Certificates
- Competitions (external or studio)
- Composer of the month
- Newsletter
- Parent events
- Practice logs
- Practice rewards and incentives
- Stickers
- Student of the month
- Student profiles/news on website
- Studio fundraisers
- Studio parties
- Team projects

Workload

This book promises to deliver a realistic SMT blueprint for earning $50,000 to $100,000 annually. To make accurate projections, we must carefully calculate totals generated through each income/impact stream.

Hours per Week

In an average week, how many hours should SMTs devote to lessons? Few brave souls can handle 30+ hours for years on end without eventually burning out or checking into rehab. Even if you have the physical stamina, such a swollen workload quickly becomes mentally exhausting, likely to zap enthusiasm and diminish lesson quality.

While music teachers keep all kinds of schedules, the "full-time" SMT blueprint involves 20 lesson hours per week. That's just three to five hours daily when spread over four to six days.

Number of Students

As a rule, younger/beginning students take shorter lessons than older/more advanced ones, thanks to commitment level, attention span, and how much material can reasonably be absorbed.

Typical Lesson Durations	
1 hour	High school, adult, and advanced students
45 minutes	Junior high and less advanced high school students
30 minutes	Elementary students and other beginners

Therefore, the quantity of clients needed to fill a given number of hours depends largely on median age and ability. A 20-hour week may necessitate 40 beginners but just 20 advanced players. Educationally, neither solution is a hands-down SMT favorite. But from a financial perspective, more students means increased income, even with an identical per-minute rate.

Why? This happens thanks to peripheral earning streams. Here's a simple example: suppose your studio requires a $30 annual registration fee. Twenty students generate $600 ($30 × 20 students = $600);

40 students contribute $1,200 ($30 × 40 students = $1,200). A larger client base also makes it easier to fill classes and camps, rent instruments, sell products, and so forth.

In our model, we split the difference. Our 20-hour lesson schedule impacts a roster of 30 (adoring and devoted) students.

Lessons per Year

Most music students enroll in weekly lessons. Meeting regularly allows for educational continuity and consistent momentum. Set lesson times become habit, simplifying logistics for all involved.

Though there are 52 weeks in a year, it is unrealistic to expect that students complete that many sessions. Lessons *will* be missed as the result of holidays, family vacations, illnesses, emergencies, forgetfulness, conflicting activities, last-minute complications, and the occasional need for a break. In fact, you will also cancel for comparable reasons from time to time.

Children maintain their most consistent schedules when school is in session. American public school calendars in most states consist of around 180 school days, or 36 weeks. While some SMTs find ways to pack 36 lessons into this period, 30 to 34 is more realistic. Stated another way, fall and spring terms typically involve 15 to 17 lessons each.

Consistency during the three-month summer is much trickier as families travel, enjoy downtime, and experience less predictable schedules. With this reality, summer terms tend to incorporate 6 to 10 meetings.

15 fall + 15 spring + 6 summer = 36 lessons
17 fall + 17 spring + 10 summer = 44 lessons

Combining these numbers, SMT programs involve 36 to 44 lessons per year. For a fairly dependable average, we assume 40.

Monetization
Base Hourly Rate

"Charge the right amount" was Savvy Rule #3 in the last chapter. But how much is that? And what exactly are clients purchasing? Your time? Expertise? Good humor? The oft-cited article "Where Does My Tuition Go?" by composer Wendy Stevens explains that payments fund much more than just lessons:

- Time spent with students
- Preparation time
- Past teacher training and experience
- Continued teacher education
- Recital costs and preparation
- Professional organization memberships and conference attendance
- Studio expenses
- Instrument purchase and maintenance
- Music books and recordings lent to students
- Property taxes, self-employment taxes, insurance, business licenses, and retirement
- Certification costs
- Book and music club memberships

My survey of independent music teachers from across the United States indicated that most charged $40 to $65 per hour (though clearly there are outliers on both ends). Some readers may salivate at those numbers, while others develop a stress headache. These fees are typical at the time of publication, however, and will be used in our calculations.

Which factors are most important when determining your rate?

Lesson Rate Factors	
Going rate	What do local competitors charge? Research thoroughly.
Experience	How long have you taught?
Credentials	What formal education do you have?
Reputation	How well known are you? A higher rate may be appropriate if you're clearly a local celebrity.
Supply and demand	How much competition for clients exists in your market? If the answer is "not much," charge more.
Value added	What offerings make you different, thus justifying higher rates? SMTs shine in this category, as we will see.

(*continued*)

Lesson Rate Factors	
Financial background	How affluent are students? Some SMTs target wealthier communities with the means to pay more.
Full studio	Here is a strategy for driving lesson rates: (1) fill studio, (2) swap out problematic students with better ones, and (3) raise tuition.

Conventional wisdom suggests that pedigree is among the most important considerations when setting rates. In other words, teachers with a doctorate ought to charge more than those with only a bachelor's degree. While this rationale seems logical, SMTs use a different metric. *Far more important than teacher background are the quality and uniqueness of student engagement.*

Music teachers are not like bottled water, where all available brands are more or less comparable. While families may begin with price comparison shopping, their eventual choice is usually based on other factors. In addition to quality instruction and a likeable personality, SMTs offer highly differentiated curricula, unique tuition packages, and a spectacular array of experiences that are clearly unlike the competition. As a result, their price points are typically above average. Clients pay the difference because the value added is substantial.

Charging What You're Worth

How important are music lessons in the scheme of things? Will families pay top dollar to participate? Am I truly worthy of a middle-class living? These questions weighed on Suzanne Greer (www.sgstudio. musicteachershelper.com) when founding her piano studio. Tempted to undervalue tuition with hopes of quickly attracting students, she fought the urge, instead establishing a price point significantly above average (though not the most expensive).

How was this justified? For starters, "I'm a devoted teacher, committed to outstanding and comprehensive music education." Her specialty is young children, a demographic with limited local competition. Before lessons begin, mothers and fathers are taught to foster a positive learning environment through six weeks of mandatory "parent education." Said another way, her offerings are unique, in demand, and high quality—a winning combination.

Admittedly, the inception of Greer's teaching career was a bit scary financially. Though proactive marketing generated plentiful leads, not all joined her roster. Some were scared by the price tag, others by her overt insistence on hard work and intense commitment. By the end of year one, just 17 lessons were scattered throughout each week. But after a colleague explained that the average entrepreneurial business requires seven years to reach profitability, Greer took the long view, insistent on building the studio she desired. A decade later, her teaching business is thriving, with 43 students and a waitlist to boot.

Beyond personal impact, Greer's fee structure and public advocacy that other teachers charge what they're worth have helped increase mean wages across an entire community.

Variations

How much difference does $1 per hour make? For most students, the answer is "not much"; $53 and $54 feel roughly equivalent. But what does it mean for the SMT?

If you average 20 teaching hours per week and 40 lessons per year, every dollar increase to the hourly rate adds $800 annually. A $5 supplement boosts income by $4,000. Though $1 or $5 might not seem like a big deal in isolation, they really add up!

$1/hour rate increase × 20 hours per week × 40 lessons per year = $800
$5/hour rate increase × 20 hours per week × 40 lessons per year = $4,000

Many SMTs maintain a fixed hourly rate, regardless of lesson duration. Another option is *scaled pricing*. In the example that follows, there is a discount for longer lessons (or added expense for shorter ones). Compare the following pricing schemes:

	Fixed	Scaled	Fixed	Scaled
1 hour	$40 ($40/hour)	$40 ($40/hour)	$60 ($60/hour)	$60 (60/hour)
45 minutes	$30 ($40/hour)	$31 ($41.33/hour)	$45 ($60/hour)	$48.75 ($65/hour)
30 minutes	$20 ($40/hour)	$22 ($44/hour)	$30 ($60/hour)	$35 ($70/hour)

According to these scaled models, longer lessons are incentivized. Your benefit is that extended sessions mean fewer students to supervise, recruit, and fill 20 teaching hours. The opposite strategy is also worth consideration, since more students means more income.

An alternate pricing method involves different rates based on student level, using an objective metric like grade or age.

	30 minutes	45 minutes	Hour
Beginning (grades K–5)	$20 ($40/hour)	$30 ($40/hour)	$40
Intermediate (grades 6–8)	$25 ($50/hour)	$37.50 ($50/hour)	$50
Advanced (grades 9–12 and adult)	$30 ($60/hour)	$45 ($60/hour)	$60

As a rule, beginning students take half-hour lessons, intermediate ones switch to 45 minutes, and advanced players request a full hour. Therefore, longer lessons typically trigger higher rates. This structure resembles restaurants that entice families with discounted children's meals, as they begin developing loyalty that may extend for years after diapers and recess are long forgotten. When SMTs start with younger students, these students are likely to continue even if rates rise as they age.

Tuition

Many independent music teachers collect payment by the lesson, enjoying the constant influx of cash and the reminder that their valuable time is exchanged for valuable money. As with a barbershop, clients pay once the service has been completed.

Despite certain advantages, this is not the SMT solution. Collecting payment and drawing up receipts takes time—particularly intrusive for half-hour sessions—with the administrative hassle compounding daily rather than monthly. Things become complicated when customers forget their checkbook; weaker bookkeepers have even been known to overlook missed payments, affecting the bottom line while devaluing their work.

Another significant challenge is cancellations. End-of-session billing suggests that compensation buys *lessons*, rather than *access*. As a result, individuals who miss are often reluctant to pay. After all, why should they be charged if no meeting took place? (Cancellation policies are discussed in chapter 12.)

SMTs charge tuition by the term. This structure facilitates many benefits:

- **Consistent income.** Students pay a fixed amount per term, making it easier to predict earnings and make sound financial decisions.
- **Bookkeeping.** With consistent payments made less frequently, accounting is simplified.
- **Cancellations.** Tuition makes justifying a strict cancellation policy easy and clear.
- **Retention.** Students questioning their commitment are more likely to continue to the end of a term, since tuition has already been paid.

The most common SMT tuition plans include three semesters, involving 15 to 17 meetings for the fall and spring semesters and 6 to 10 over the summer. Alternatives include a single 9-month school-year term or annual 12-month plan.

To determine base tuition, multiply your lesson rate by the number of meetings. For example, if 16 half-hour sessions are $25 each, base tuition is $400.

$25 lessons × 16 meetings = $400 tuition

Paying this large sum at once is cost prohibitive for many families. A good solution is dividing the full-term rate over equal installments, due by a given date each month. Payments are identical regardless of how many meetings occur during that period.

Lessons from the Trenches

The most effective way I've discovered to keep income stable is invoicing by the semester but allowing the option of monthly installments. Here is how things worked one year:

1. The fall invoice, created on July 1, was for a 16-week semester beginning late August. Half-hour lessons cost $608.
2. People paying full-semester tuition in one large chunk by August 1 triggered a 5% discount ($578). Though this shaved off some earnings, lump-sum payments simplify bookkeeping and guarantee a term's worth of income.

3. People on the installment plan pay one quarter of tuition ($152) by the first of each month (August, September, October, December).
4. The payment cycle for spring begins December 1 with a similar structure.

I like receiving a large amount at the beginning of each term, followed by a steady stream of smaller payments each month. This is as close as it comes to job security for SMTs!

While tuition typically involves one lesson per week, students sometimes request *supplemental* meetings, either consistently or leading up to a performance. This kind of dedication should be encouraged. A la carte sessions at a 10% to 15% discount are a nice idea.

On the other hand, you may encounter people who want only *sporadic* lessons. If you accept this kind of client, add at least a 15% premium. Additionally, insist on scheduling these meetings outside the "prime time" after-school slots.

Getting a Raise without Changing the Fee

Soprano Kathleen Nitz Kasdorf (www.kathleenkasdorf.com) faced a challenge common to independent music teachers. Income was inconsistent, particularly during the summer. Considering a rate increase, she ultimately found a solution far more drastic.

Kasdorf switched to yearly tuition. She set the hourly rate to $240 per month, since the average month has four weeks and her rate was previously $60 (12 months × $240 tuition = $2,880 for the equivalent of 48 lessons). Forty-five- and 30-minute lessons were priced proportionally.

Students pay the same amount 12 times per year regardless of holidays, vacations (by them or the teacher), or meetings missed for other reasons. Some months, learners receive five to six lessons (e.g., five Thursdays in the month, supplemental meetings requested). Other times, they take just one to three. "It's like joining a soccer team. To participate, a certain amount is charged regardless of how many times you show up."

Studio members who miss frequently or want summers off have the option of purchasing individual lessons for the elevated price of $70 per hour (a $10, or 16.5%, increase). In the first season, just three students chose this route.

Beyond financial stability for Kasdorf, this arrangement has educational merit. Learners are less likely to skip lessons or hibernate during the summer, ensuring consistent progress and higher retention. Additionally, students who enroll are typically serious music learners.

Kasdorf introduced her new policy through an email blast. While some families requested time to consider implications, there was essentially no pushback.

Tuition Packages

A great benefit of charging tuition by the term is that it encourages SMTs to design engaging, varied, and comprehensive packages rather than an endless stream of private lessons:

- **Lessons.** How many private lessons are included in each term? Fifteen to 17 is common during fall and spring; 6 to 10 is average for summer.
- **Bonus lesson.** Some SMTs allow the option of one "bonus" lesson per term or year, scheduled within a week or two of a performance event.
- **Supplemental classes.** Classes teach different lessons than solo meetings. Some tuition packages include one or two supplemental classes per term. Others incorporate both private and group lessons on a weekly basis.
- **Substitute classes.** Another possibility is offering interesting group activities in lieu of lessons once or twice per semester. Perhaps the semester involves 14 weeks of individual sessions plus 2 weeks of classes. On group weeks, the teacher's schedule is freer, while students experience variety, new challenges, community, and collaboration.
- **Events and technology.** Recitals, field trips, and other events (chapter 6), as well as technological tools (chapter 7), can transform the learning experience.
- **Other.** What additional assets contribute to the experience of students? A robust library? Interactive teaching space (chapter 10)? Access to your personal network?

If your package includes great features beyond lessons, consider their impact on tuition.

Summer Term

Many music teachers watch their income take a severe hit each summer. Weekly lessons simply don't work for 90% of families, thanks to month-long European vacations, impromptu road trips, changing routines, and the need for a break. Some students schedule lessons sporadically, while others hibernate. Unfortunately, this lack of engagement often leads to attrition.

Though summer presents a challenge, there are also opportunities for the SMT. Think creatively when designing summer tuition packages that are appealing and flexible. Perhaps lessons are longer and less frequent, or normal length but compact (e.g., two to three times per week for an intense period). One-on-one meetings can be bundled with enrichment classes or even a camp. This season provides a wonderful excuse to change focus from the school year, offering a contrasting perspective on music making and sharing.

Some clients use the freer summer months to test the waters. Summer is a fantastic time to recruit, and four- to six-week lesson trial packages at a promotional price can help fill your calendar.

Lessons from the Trenches

Early in my career, I offered only private lessons. As time went on, two supplemental group classes were added per semester: one focused on theory, the other on performance. Parents loved the concept, but logistics were problematic. Due to competing schedules, we often wound up with two 6-year-olds, a 10-year-old, and a 17-year-old (or some other bizarre combination).

My current tuition model includes one (fall) or two (spring) 75-minute performance classes per term, each with 6 to 12 students. Because they are offered in place of private lessons for the week, parents find ways to make them work. Not only do group weeks shrink my workload, but also classes are extremely gratifying, breaking the monotony of lessons for all involved. Fall/spring tuition also covers administrative fees, participation in a variety of (really fun!) events, and all sheet music.

I have "required" summer lessons each year since starting to teach full time, and partly as a result, my annual turnover is less than 5%. Summer provides an opportunity to ease up on the schedule (for me as well!) and encourage creative activities. Last year, I offered just one option: six 45-minute lessons plus two enrichment classes chosen from a menu including African Drumming, Garage Band Basics, and Songwriting for

Beginners. Several sections of each class were offered during two separate weeks (one in June, the other in July). Some students had such a great time that they requested to swap an additional lesson for a group class!

Discounting and Scholarships

Charging different prices for comparable services, though common with the airline industry, is not recommended. When parents discover that their child's half-hour lessons are $7 more than their neighbor's, expect an angry phone call. In some cases, this faux pas can cost you students.

Of course, there may be wonderful students who simply cannot afford the published tuition. Rather than secretly discounting, consider offering a very public "scholarship." Unless you secure external funding, these are essentially teacher-subsidized lessons. However, framing it this way provides several benefits:

1. The student, proud to receive this award, may be motivated to work even harder. If not, the scholarship can be revoked.
2. Other families will be proud to be part of a studio that helps less affluent learners.
3. Scholarships sound impressive, adding credibility and prestige to your brand.
4. Music scholarships are newsworthy. If a local newspaper runs a story about your award, generated publicity may help with recruitment.

Some teachers charge discounted rates for less desirable slots, such as lessons before the school day begins. Evening hours and weekends are prime time, commanding full price.

A final pricing strategy is bartering. Why not exchange discounted lessons with an adult who performs handiwork around your house in return? Or have a high school student babysit for five hours in exchange for each lesson? Remember, money is swapped for life energy. If the exchange is equivalent, what do you have to lose?

Lessons from the Trenches

Everyone felt the 2008 economic crash on some level. My area came out relatively well, but several parents of elementary students lost their jobs. In one sad situation, the family almost withdrew their daughter from lessons, though she was outstanding and I wanted to keep her.

Instead, we set up a spring semester scholarship. She signed a "contract" agreeing to 30 minutes of practice for the duration of the award, six days per week. In exchange, she received 50% off. I required a parent/student/teacher meeting at the halfway point to discuss the job search and assess whether progress and commitment remained high.

The result? Rather than losing a student, she worked her tail off and ultimately went back to full price when her parents obtained new employment.

Additional Fees

Beyond tuition, some studios charge additional fees to mitigate costs and subsidize features beyond lessons. (Alternately, these expenses can be embedded into your tuition package.) Typically, applicable fees are charged at the beginning of the term/year for the following:

- **Recital fees.** Applied toward the cost of hosting recitals (chapter 6)
- **Media fees.** To support technology tools (chapter 7)
- **Registration/administration fee.** Pays for the paperwork of setting up a new account
- **Late fee.** Charged when bills are not paid on time, typically 10% of the amount due
- **Bounced check fee.** Should cover expenses charged by your bank plus a $10 to $20 penalty

Tuition and Fees

Tuition with clarinetist Kristen Grattan Sheridan (www.kristensheridan. com) includes 35 lessons per year. Ten equal installments are due by the first of each month from September through June. A short grace period is allowed, but payments arriving after the 10th trigger a $15 penalty. In cases where students complete all sessions before June, they are still responsible for the final payment. Tuition is prorated for studio members beginning after the first week of school.

In addition to tuition, Sheridan charges a $30 spring recital fee. This amount underwrites the venue rental, an accompanist, and administrative efforts.

She also collects an annual "music and activities deposit." Student expenses that arise for items such as reeds, music, and competition entry fees are deducted from the total. At year's end, the balance is returned. Sheridan, who does her best to keep these incidentals to a minimum, prefers this solution over requesting $5 here and $15 there throughout the year.

Raising Your Salary

Raise your rate annually or biannually, typically 1% to 3% per year, to account for the rate of inflation and average salary increase nationally. Clearly communicate this policy with families.

Lessons from the Trenches

Though my studio handbook clearly states that tuition is raised periodically, it's always a little hard to swallow when prices go up. I typically raise the rate 5% every other year but simultaneously remind parents about the value of my studio, stressing wonderful student achievements, my professional accomplishments, and instrument/equipment additions. This is not justification, mind you, but a proactive communication strategy. The message comes in a beautifully designed newsletter distributed mid-February and explains that the new tuition rate will take effect the upcoming summer semester.

I offer discounts to families who pay for the entire year in one lump sum. They can also secure the "current" tuition rate as long as full payment arrives by March 1. This tactic provides a large sum of capital that I can direct to living expenses, taxes (April 15 is right around the corner . . .), passion projects, and budgetary planning for the upcoming year. In exchange, I save mental energy and time spent on administrative upkeep.

The Savvy Music Teacher Income Blueprint

If lessons are responsible for a good portion of your income, get this piece of the puzzle right!

Following our blueprint, the SMT maintains a studio of 30 students, averaging 20 lesson hours per week. Though tuition is charged by the term, the hourly rate falls between $40 and $65. Between fall, spring, and summer semesters, students purchase the equivalent of 40 lessons.

Hour Per Week	Lessons Per Year	Hourly Rate	Net Annual Income
20	40	$40	$32,000
20	40	$65	$52,000

From lessons (stream 1), the SMT earns $32,000 to $52,000 per year.

4 CLASSES: STREAM 2

Some independent music teachers mistakenly believe their job title is synonymous with "private lesson specialist." This is unfortunate and far from the truth, as Savvy Music Teachers (SMTs) are superbly positioned to offer a wide array of products and services.

Whether providing supplemental experiences for current clients or appealing to new ones, classes are a logical complement, with potential to increase both income and impact. Unlocking an arsenal of activities inaccessible to private learners, group settings allow participants to lead, interact, learn from peers, compete, and work toward collective goals. Effective as a recruitment tool, lessons can feed classes and vice versa. Less expensive for participants yet more lucrative for you, group ventures deliver an economic win-win.

Group Lessons
Why Group Lessons?

In many communities, there seems to be an unwritten rule that serious students best learn the art and craft of music through one-on-one instruction. Private study certainly offers numerous benefits, but this is not the only solution worthy of consideration. In fact, group lessons provide an abundance of advantages that simply cannot be duplicated by their lonelier counterpart.

Learning with a Team

Dellana Cook (www.dcpiano.musicteachershelper.com), who specializes in piano lessons for beginners, has a clear mission. "I want to be the teacher whose students still find great joy playing for family and friends 30 years from now." This priority is more than theoretical, impacting even the lesson format itself.

When Cook began teaching, her curriculum involved two meetings per week: a private half-hour lesson plus a 45-minute theory class. Evolving over time, she now offers only group lessons, once a week for 45 minutes. Bringing three to six students together in a room with five digital pianos, her "Way Cool" keyboarding classes typically keep kids within one grade level of each other. Adult meetings include hobbyists aged 18 to 84.

This is opposite the structure of most independent teachers, who use private lessons as their primary educational platform. But Cook is quick to articulate the many benefits of a collective approach. Combining students eliminates the need to repeat information ad nauseam, allowing her to maintain a higher level of energy and inspiration. Attendees have more fun when playing games with peers, working in ensembles, and functioning as a community. When young studio members begin school band or orchestra, they have no trouble adapting, since playing for and with others has always been their norm. Financially, earnings per hour are considerably higher, making it possible to reach her ambitious income target in less teaching time.

Group lessons typically involve two to six students, resulting in a learning environment quite different from private meetings. Though neither format is inherently superior, both offer distinct benefits.

Individual Lesson Strengths	Group Lesson Strengths
Lessons are more personalized.	Lessons with others can be more fun.
Students work at their own pace.	Students learn from one another.
Students may be more comfortable expressing themselves and being critiqued individually.	Students are challenged to critique and compliment peers, forcing active listening and strong communication skills.
The teacher can take as long as necessary to address technical or musical issues.	Students become accustomed to playing for others, which helps calm nerves and simulates performance settings.

(continued)

Individual Lesson Strengths	Group Lesson Strengths
Individual lessons require a smaller workspace (some studios cannot accommodate multiple students).	Teachers are challenged to use the workspace in creative ways.
The teacher and student build strong relationships, without the fear of judgment from peers.	Peer encouragement, teamwork, and a social environment are promoted.
Individuals can work on unique repertoire.	Group lessons allow for ensemble work and learning how different musical voices interact.
Private lessons are an efficient way to learn skills and techniques, since 100% of energy is focused on an individual.	Group lessons keep the teacher from getting bored introducing the same concepts repeatedly to individuals.
Parents are more likely to engage with individual lessons.	Students become more engaged in group drills and exercises.
Multiple students need not be entertained simultaneously.	Students have an easier time focusing for longer periods in group settings.
Teacher preparation time is usually less.	Cost is less per student, but the teacher earns more.

There are three general categories of group lessons:

1. Those offered in lieu of private lessons
2. Those offered in addition to private lessons (regular or sporadic), reinforcing various performance concepts while adding a communal element
3. Those offered in addition to private lessons, addressing further topics such as ear training, music fundamentals, or improvisation

Some SMT curricula entail private and group lessons each week. Adopting this policy may scare off clients unable or unwilling to make this level of commitment, but perhaps those aren't the students you want anyway. Others incorporate just a few per term.

When group lessons play a role from the beginning, participants simply assume they are a natural part of the music learning process. Most learners quickly recognize the benefits (if you're good at what you do) as they progress faster and gain more enjoyment.

A Class Act

Singer Regina Zona (www.thezonastudio.com) offers three types of lessons to groups of four to six students. The first, typically administered to a collection of friends, is geared toward adults who just want to sing for fun. The second, targeting high school students, focuses on technique and solo competition preparation. The third is built around dramatic coaching for musical theater. Most participants do not take additional private lessons. Instead, they choose the group format as a cost-effective and communal alternative. Zona's offerings span six or eight weeks and conclude with a public showcase. Rather than aligning with the academic calendar, meetings begin as soon as four students enroll.

The Suzuki-inspired program of violinist Timothy Judd (www.timothyjuddviolin.com) illustrates a contrasting model. In addition to weekly private meetings, hour-long group lessons are scheduled two Tuesdays per month. Though open to the entire studio, they are geared toward kids younger than 13 and beginning adults. With 25 to 30 violinists and family members typically in attendance, sessions are focused on technique, ensemble playing, and repertoire. Participation is built into tuition. The lessons are held at a Unitarian church with a nice piano, and Judd has an optimal arrangement, accessing the space for free in exchange for a few volunteer services annually. His only expense is an accompanist.

Trumpeter Lyn Schoch (www.lynschoch.com) pursues a third option, leading group lessons at several elementary, middle, and high schools. In most cases, she is paid a fixed hourly fee (funded by the band boosters) to work with students on trumpets, low brass, or both. Sessions typically address technical issues, though she occasionally rehearses ensemble literature before performances or competitions. Students are pulled out of band, allowing directors to concentrate on the rest of the group. Since most participants do not take private lessons, these meetings are vital. That said, they have become an effective recruitment tool for Schoch. Better yet, sessions take place during the school day, a time when most private students are unavailable.

Challenges

Group lessons require significant preparation, particularly at the beginning. SMTs ultimately invent or discover strategies that can be recycled, but in the short term, they need to allocate adequate planning time.

When students differ widely in age, ability, or maturity, things can get tricky: it is frustrating when just one participant struggles to execute a task; the most advanced/oldest participant might feel bored; a single, discipline-challenged student negatively affects everyone. Though few groups represent utopia, you must carefully consider dynamics when constructing groups.

Agenda

A 45-minute group lesson for young students might be structured like this:

Time	Activity
7 minutes	Calisthenics, standing in a circle or at a table, with many exercises repeated from week to week
3 minutes	Solfège
10 minutes	Performing
15 minutes	Two rotating areas per week: improvisation, harmonization, theory games, sight reading, Italian terms, rhythm, listening, music history, etc.
5 minutes	Sight reading, rhythm, or theory game
Extra 5 minutes	Wiggle room

Play Time Is Learn Time

Julie Knerr (www.pianosafari.com), coauthor of the Piano Safari method, has dedicated years of her life to the art of group lessons. The Piano Safari website is a treasure trove of resources for group activities, featuring instructional videos, miniessays, and teacher guides. Knerr believes that games are a great way to keep children of all ages engaged. They make learning fun and help lessons stick. Some activities from her arsenal follow.

Animal Sound Game

SKILL: IMPROVISATION AND LISTENING

On a whiteboard, the teacher writes animal names or draws pictures suggested by participants.

One student whispers a creature to the teacher, who captures its essence through improvisation. Class members guess the animal. The first to get it right picks another and can either perform the improvisation or ask the teacher to do it. After a few rounds, most students can't wait to play.

Flashcard Hiding Game

SKILL: THEORY

Flashcards hidden around the studio address intervals, chords, key signatures, rhythms, or notes. Students search for cards, run to the piano, and share their solutions. With multilevel groups, different parts of the room can be devoted to varying difficulties. "Having young students run around is much more exciting than forcing them to stand quietly in line."

Music Video Hall of Fame

SKILL: LISTENING AND HISTORY

Though young musicians frequently study influential composers, they rarely learn about great performers. This activity highlights both. Students gather around a laptop to watch YouTube videos of champion artists playing masterworks. After discussing what they saw and heard, graphics of each composer and performer are taped to poster boards with timelines. Nonmusical events are listed as well, and students learn interesting trivia (e.g., Mozart and George Washington lived around the same time), linking musical lineage to history lessons from school.

Enrichment Classes

Topics

SMTs are renowned for imagining unusual, intriguing enrichment classes with captivating titles and content. Tapping into a vast array of fascinating topics, many can be administered at various skill levels (theory 1 to 4, beginning/intermediate/advanced guitar, etc.).

Enrichment Class Topics		
• Accompanying	• Guitar	• Rhythm
• Alexander technique	• Improvisation	• Rock history
• Arts entrepreneurship	• Jazz arranging	• Rock theory
• Career development	• Jazz history	• Score reading
• Chamber music	• Jazz improvisation	• Sight reading
• College preparation	• Jazz theory	• Sight singing
• Composition	• Keyboard	• Songwriting
• Conducting	• Literature class	• Special topics
• Drumming	• Music appreciation	• Style class (fiddling,
• Ear training	• Music business	jazz, rock, etc.)
• Ensemble	• Music fundamentals	• Teacher training
• Eurhythmics	• Music history	• Technique class
• Excerpt class	• Music technology	• Vocal styles
• Fiddling	• Music theory	• Yoga for musicians
• Group class	• Pageant preparation	• World music

Dumpster Jam and Blustery Boomwhackers

While most SMTs teach individual lessons primarily and group classes to supplement, accordionist Rachel Bell (www.rachelbellmusic.com) flips the model. Her offerings include the following:

- **Beginning Ukulele Club** (grades four to five). In addition to learning this four-stringed instrument, participants play a number of singing and clapping games. One club adopted the name "The Fuzzy Mustaches."
- **Dumpster Jam and Instrument Petting Zoo** (grades one to three). Music is made from fly swatters, cardboard boxes, and other recyclables. The petting zoo includes odd instruments like a hurdy gurdy, eight-string banjo, and Indonesian angklung.
- **Music for Babies, Toddlers, and Preschoolers.** This is Bell's original early childhood curriculum, for children and their parents.
- **Snowflake Songs and Blustery Boomwhackers** (age 3 to grade two). These classes are similar to early childhood classes, though parent attendance is optional.

Bell's 40-minute sessions are held at two churches and a library, all of which allow her to use the space for free in exchange for minimal service. Offering seven weekly classes (organized in three 9-week units per academic year), four monthly classes, and a host of independent workshops, she also teaches public school music to students in kindergarten through grade 3 one day per week.

Startup costs for her business Crab Apple Jam Music Studio included 15 ukuleles, a piano, some drums, and 20 dulcimers built from kits. These turned out to be fantastic investments, motivating many clients to return term after term.

Bell challenges herself to continually explore and create new offerings. "There are so many things I find exciting about this work!"

Chamber Music

While every topic offers unique value, chamber music deserves special mention. Small groups of any style or instrumentation—classical quartets, jazz combos, fiddling trios, rock bands, jam bands—are unmatched in their ability to emphasize learning objectives such as the following:

- **Musical literacy.** Experientially examine form, harmonic progressions, melodic construction, texture, register, density, counterpoint, and other concepts.
- **Leadership.** Allow all members to shine, rather than continually featuring the same top player. A young string quartet (often three violins and a cello, since child violists are rare) might rotate first violinists.
- **Teamwork.** Have players discuss interpretation and rehearsal strategy, brainstorming solutions, operating democratically, and working toward a collective vision.
- **Interdependency.** Every voice is essential in chamber music. Teach participants not only their own parts but also how to support and interface with others.
- **Creativity.** Challenge members to choose repertoire, improvise, orchestrate/transcribe, imagine personal interpretations, brand the group, market a concert, and so forth.

Chamber ensembles are most effective when engaging students of similar ages and abilities. Even when individual parts are simple on the surface, there are always lessons to be gleaned about balance, intonation, interpretation, phrasing, rhythmic precision, form, and interaction.

Join the Band

In addition to guitar, bass, and drum lessons, Aaron Denny (www.aarondenny.com) offers a "Rock Band Ensemble Workshop Series" several times per year. Denny handpicks groups of four to six players who are compatible and similarly aged. Though 80% of contributors already work with Denny, nonstudio participants are required to enroll in private instruction for the duration. Dividing focus between cover tunes, originals, and experimentation, they meet one hour per week for two months. "Beyond musicality, playing in a band develops social skills and confidence. It's also really fun."

A culminating public performance is scheduled at a café or other venue geared toward teens and their families. This event "keeps it real," simulating a club environment. Because shows draw customers who order food and drinks, hosts typically thank Denny with a $50 to $100 check or voucher.

Online Classes

Online classes offer intriguing potential. Without the need to rent a large venue, classes big and small can impact participants regardless of geographic proximity. Each year, group video conferencing platforms improve in design and effectiveness. While online chamber music or early childhood classes do not work for obvious reasons, SMTs have invented ingenious virtual solutions for topics such as theory, music appreciation, and beyond.

Ready-SET-Film

Like many SMTs today, drummer Mark Letalien (www.learndrumslive.com) teaches lessons online. He also offers virtual classes through a platform called Powhow (www.powhow.com) with titles like "Essential Latin Grooves," "Drumset for Beginners," and "Jazz Independence."

Letalien films classes from his home studio with a standard webcam. He places four microphones on the drum set (two overhead, one kick, and one snare) and wears a lapel microphone. All sound passes through a preamp and is mixed in ProTools.

The 4 to 12 participants in each class see Letalien and his instrument, but not one another. The instructor's display, on the other hand, has boxes for each student that can be rearranged or enlarged. To question, comment, or demonstrate, attendees click on a "virtual hand raise." When the teacher grants permission, their audio pipes through.

Powhow allows Letalien to set class size parameters. When minimum requirements are not met, the event cancels automatically and enrollees receive a refund. Of the five sessions he offers in an average week, anywhere from one to all five generate enough participants. In exchange for their 20% commission, Powhow accepts payment, displays teacher pages, helps market, and consistently works to improve the interface. Students may purchase stand-alone classes or larger packages.

Audiences

Enrichment classes allow SMTs to interact with several distinct populations:

1. Current students who benefit from additional musical training
2. Students from same-specialty teachers who don't offer classes
3. Students who may join your studio at some point. (If hoping to tap into a new market, classes for that segment are a great way to build reputation and generate interest.)
4. Students who will never study with you privately (perhaps they play an instrument you don't teach) but can nonetheless benefit from your body of knowledge

Clef and Canvas

Hornist Mike Walker and soprano Katie Dukes (www.studioforza.org), a husband-and-wife team, offer a class called "Clef and Canvas." Unlike their lesson rosters, which cater primarily to children, this is geared toward adults aged 55 and up. Most participants have considerable disposable income and seek gratifying personal experiences.

Six consecutive Wednesday evening sessions are scheduled at houses of class members, creating a fun social dynamic. Addressing topics related to music and visual art, one minisemester examined (1) the Beatles, (2) pop art, (3) musical terms and the history of instruments, (4) Mahler Four, (5) Gilbert and Sullivan, and (6) student choice. Rather than academic lecturing, each class is experiential and participatory. "It is inspiring to watch seniors expand their understanding of music and art, getting excited and increasing comprehension in ways they never before imagined," explains Dukes.

Topics frequently correspond to local art events. In fact, two to three optional field trips (with an added cost) are scheduled each term. When appropriate, outings are paired with a food and/or wine experience that somehow connects to the event's theme.

Early Childhood Classes

Premise

Early childhood music classes are geared toward babies, toddlers, young children, and their parents. Though readers probably won't need much convincing, here are rationales provided by Musikgarten (www.musikgarten.org) on why music and movement are vital for youngsters:

- Music is a language, and children's brains are wired for learning language.
- Music evokes movement, and children delight in and require movement for their development and growth.
- Music engages the brain while stimulating neural pathways associated with such higher forms of intelligence as abstract thinking, empathy, and mathematics.
- Music's melodic and rhythmic patterns provide exercise for the brain and help develop memory. Who among us learned the ABCs without the ABC song?
- Music is perfectly designed for training children's listening skills. Good listening skills and school achievement go hand in hand.
- Developmentally appropriate music activities involve the whole child—the child's desire for language, the body's urge to move, the brain's attention to patterns, the ear's lead in initiating communication, the voice's response to sounds, and the eye-hand coordination associated with playing musical instruments.
- Music is a creative experience that involves the expression of feelings. Children often do not have the words to express themselves and need positive ways to release their emotions.

- Music transmits culture and is an avenue by which beloved songs, rhymes, and dances can be passed down from one generation to another.
- Music is a social activity that involves family and community participation. Children love to sing and dance at home, school, and church.

Benefits

In addition to educational and financial benefits, there are many reasons SMTs offer early childhood classes. As long as kids are around, demand for this experience exists. Even parents who would never consider music lessons may be drawn to enroll. From a scheduling perspective, weekday mornings and afternoons—periods off limits to most private students—are ideal. Working with a continuous stream of families expands your network. Toddlers are great connections! If you bond with families, some of these youngsters are likely to join your studio down the road.

Sharing music with young children and their parents is different from teaching an instrument. The process will undoubtedly shape your identity as a teacher and artist, including your approach to older students.

Private School

Following a move across country, violinist Erika Cutler (www.cadenzamusicstudio.org) was challenged to build her teaching business from scratch. In addition to seeking students, she approached several private schools about employment opportunities. Two expressed interest.

The first had an after-school program, with courses like art, science, and Broadway. Though they had never before offered violin, her pitch was intriguing. Their 30% commission seemed high, but instructors were allowed to set the price and class size. In the first term, 11 elementary students enrolled in two consecutive group classes.

The other program had a violinist on staff, but there was an opening to teach early childhood music. This nine-month salaried position involved four half-hour classes each Tuesday morning and a brief service on Wednesdays. Though Cutler had no formal early childhood training, she loved that age group and accepted the position.

Incidentally, when the aforementioned violin teacher moved the following year, most students joined Cutler's studio.

Curriculum

Though possible to develop a unique early childhood curriculum from scratch, doing so requires an exorbitant amount of time, energy, and expertise—no easy task when maintaining a studio and balancing other life demands. Most SMTs affiliate with an existing organization.

Early Childhood Music Programs	
Gymboree Music	www.gymboreeclasses.com
Harmony Road Music	www.harmonyroadmusic.com
Kindermusik	www.kindermusik.com
Melody Hounds	www.melodyhounds.com
Music for Aardvarks	www.musicforaardvarks.com
Music Together	www.musictogether.com
Musikgarten	www.musikgarten.org
The Music Class	www.themusicclass.com

Working with one of these businesses offers several perks. Each provides teacher training, lesson plans, specific repertoire, exercises, recordings, videos, business/marketing models, and a support system. They also allow you to join an international community of like-minded professionals who can answer questions, brainstorm ideas, and become friends.

Each organization listed previously has developed multiple classes targeting various age groups: 0 to 18 months, 18 to 36 months, 3 to 4 years, 5 to 7 years, multiage, and so forth. Sessions typically integrate singing, dance, movement, instruments, games, improvisation, and other activities. The specific structure and emphasis is different with each brand, so research which is best suited for your personality. However, all agree on the following principles:

1. All children are musical.
2. Music should play a central role in every child's life.
3. The most important goal of early music training is active participation.

4. Music making should be fun and joyous.
5. Parents are the best teachers for their children.

Starting a Center

There are two ways to work with umbrella organizations: (1) teach within an existing program or (2) open your own center. Most SMTs choose the latter for the significant financial advantage. An argument can be made, however, for temporary employment within a preexisting program to observe regularly and receive feedback as you learn the ropes.

Starting a center places you as the owner of a franchise.

You Control	They Control
Where classes are held	Brand name
How many classes are offered	Repertoire
Marketing	Lesson plans/activities
Recruiting students	Some policies (maximum number of students per class, etc.)
Price tag	Materials (that you must buy)
Personal teaching style	Organizational dues

The trek to opening a center begins with teacher training. Depending on the organization, this entails a multiday workshop or online course addressing the company's philosophy, structure, repertoire, teaching strategies, approach to classroom management, and sanctioned lesson plans. There is an assessment element, but as long as you have musical skills (let's hope so!), can sing in tune, foster good rapport with kids and parents, and complete work with enthusiasm, passing with flying colors won't be much of a problem.

Following the initial training, most organizations provide a personal business mentor for at least one year. Armed with case studies and experience, this mentor helps you develop a successful venture. Asking the right questions can also benefit other aspects of your SMT career.

Do It for the Children

Australian retired classroom music teacher and clarinetist Julie Seal opened Seal Music Studio (www.sealmusicstudio.com.au), offering private lessons and Kindermusik classes at her home.

Seal teaches four to six 45-minute early childhood classes per week, Wednesday through Friday mornings. The classes are held in a large family room that features large colorful mats and several bookcases with age-appropriate percussion instruments, music educational materials, a piano, and a sound system. Each session involves four to seven enrolled children plus a parent and the occasional sibling.

Her Kindermusik training required a singing audition and four-month online course with 20 classmates worldwide. A mentor assigned specifically to her, as well as the Kindermusik Café social media platform, provided invaluable and ongoing support as she established her business. "This experience helped open my mind to a more child-centered approach. It also impacted how I teach clarinet and piano, in very positive and creative ways."

Seal fell in love with Kindermusik when enrolling her granddaughter in a class. Interestingly, her daughter—who lives abroad as an expatriate—also teaches Kindermusik.

Costs

Though minimal, there are expenses associated with operating this kind of franchise. The initial training typically runs $400 to $500 for individuals looking to found a center, and this includes a business mentor for at least one year. Teacher training without the commercial aspects costs around $200. Each company has a different structure for maintaining your affiliation. Music Together requires a one-time $100 licensing fee and claims $38 for materials from each family's tuition in exchange for two CDs, a songbook, and a parent guide. Kindermusik charges $130 annually, which buys the following:

- Their brand name
- The ability to purchase teaching materials from them
- The ability to purchase parent materials from them
- A listing on their website

- Professional development as needed
- Membership to their teacher association, consisting of 5,000+ instructors in 35 countries

Purchasing an assortment of inexpensive instruments, teaching materials, and marketing items typically costs just $150 to $200. Higher-level workshops, around $100 per session, can be inspiring and energizing while allowing you to expand offerings.

Stand-alone Classes

Stand-alone events such as presentations, workshops, and master classes typically entail 30-minute to three-hour sessions. For our purposes, *presentation* implies a "lecture" where an expert on a given topic leads a discussion. The best presentations offer more than mere information, providing an interactive, engaging, provocative, and inspiring experience. *Workshops* are generally more hands-on, teaching participants a particular skill or approach to art making. While there is a spoken component, events focus on doing. In many cases, attendees are expected to actively participate, bringing instruments or working with supplied materials.

Overcoming Performance Anxiety

As a young flutist, Helen Spielman (www.performconfidently.com) suffered severe performance anxiety. Playing with orchestras was tolerable, but solo opportunities inflicted paralysis. In fact, answering questions in college classes even felt terrifying. Over time, she worked to overcome these extreme phobias and ultimately calmed her nerves.

Years later, Spielman was invited to give a summer camp workshop. She supplied a list of 10 potential topics, and the organizer requested "performance anxiety." To her surprise, the room was packed and attendees hung on to every word. The organization invited her back the following year to deliver a full week of training.

It turned out that the music world was hungry for this information, and word about Spielman began to spread. Soon she was globetrotting across the United States, South Africa, England, Italy, Spain, Honduras, and Canada, offering classes with titles like "Performance Anxiety from Inside Out," "Mental Visualization for Peak Performance," and "Do They Think I'm No Good? Freeing Yourself from Fear of Judgment."

A private coaching business also emerged. Beyond musicians, she helps businesspeople, athletes, physicians, dancers, actors, and beauty queens overcome the fear of presenting publically. Performance anxiety, as it turns out, is a universal problem.

Workshops and consulting have evolved into major income streams for Spielman. They have also influenced her flute teaching, and she is rightfully proud of client success stories in both areas. "When approached with the right attitude, music and performing publically can be tickets to a big world and a joyful, exciting life!"

Presentations and workshops offered by SMTs are most often geared toward music students, professional musicians, amateur musicians, music teachers, or nonmusicians who can benefit from musical engagement. Employment opportunities include:

- College music classes
- Conference presentations
- Graduation speeches
- Keynote conference addresses
- Preconcert talks
- Public school classes
- Self-hosted events
- Summer camps

Learning through Cyberspace

Film composer Mike Verta (www.mikeverta.com) offers a series of virtual presentations on topics such as composition, orchestration, production techniques, and "the business." He attributes their popularity to quality content, friendly delivery style, and high production value. "Many people remark that I share the 'real stuff,' information few others discuss in detail."

Though marketed as 90-minute presentations, they always last longer, typically exceeding 3 hours. Live "attendance" is limited to 50 to 100, and these participants may submit questions. Recordings of events may also be purchased for viewing at a later time. Access to both options runs $30. He typically gets 8 to 10 orders per day of past sessions.

Verta insists on a positive, hiccup-free virtual experience. He alternates between live footage from two HD cameras—one on him, the other on a keyboard—and prerecorded segments created with Wirecast (www.telestream.net, $500). Video is streamed through a Ustream channel (www.ustream.tv), which charges $100 per month to keep presentations ad free. Everything runs through his laptop.

In a *master class*, the guest expert provides critical feedback on performances by individuals or ensembles. An audience observes, gleaning wisdom and direction from the experience.

Student Sharing

Realizing that no single teacher has all the answers, cellist Kristin Palombit (www.monkcellostudio.net) has studio members periodically work with external mentors. These interactions bring new ideas, build relationships, and create a varied learning environment. It also has another benefit: "While independent music teaching is wonderful, it can be lonely." Collaborating creates a sense of professional community, enriching for all involved.

Three times per year, she hosts two-hour *mini-master classes* for five to six kids. The meetings are held in Palombit's house and taught by a surrounding area cellist. Each attendee plays, receives critique, dialogues, and observes. Three times per year, she also coleads larger *joint studio classes* with a colleague, involving students of both teachers. Typically divided into adjacent sessions (less than two years' experience and advanced), the classes consist of short solo numbers followed by ensemble work. Younger students often "audit" the advanced class; older ones receive high school volunteer credit when helping with beginners. To accommodate such large groups, she rents a room. In both cases, participants are charged a fee that covers venue (when applicable), refreshments, and teacher compensation.

Palombit has also experimented with *coteaching* high school cellists. Participating students alternate lessons between her and another instructor. "Away" sessions are videotaped and then discussed during "home" meetings. "Some teachers are threatened by the idea of sharing students, but I find it inspiring."

Monetization

Income Models

There are three ways that SMTs generate income through classes. The first is *participation based*, where attendees pay a set amount to enroll. Obviously, larger classes generate more revenue. My survey showed that most independent music teachers charge $10 to $40 per student per session, with the average being $15 to $25. Higher amounts are typical for group lessons taken in lieu of private meetings, often commanding 50% to 80% of the private lesson rate per person.

The second income model is *all-inclusive*. In this case, supplemental classes and/or group lessons are calculated into a tuition package.

The final structure is *fee based*, where you receive a fixed amount from an employer, regardless of participation numbers. Typically, a school, university, music store, business, library, church, or other business is responsible for the paycheck. Terms are determined before the gig.

The Healing Harp

The harp has been used for its mystical healing properties across cultures for thousands of years. Many people are interested in both its beautiful musical voice and therapeutic value.

In addition to playing at patients' bedsides, Portia Diwa (www.portiadiwa.com) offers a number of "Healing Harp" courses through a hospital. Beginner and advanced beginner (intermediate) classes involve eight weekly meetings, 75 minutes apiece. Adult students include patients, nurses, and community members. She also leads a yearlong certification program, which entails classes, private lessons, and 150 hours of practical experience.

While participants pay to enroll in her classes, Diwa receives a fixed salary from her employer. Beyond dependable income, it offers abundant meaningful encounters.

Stand-alone, fee-based workshops typically generate $75 to $300 for local presenters or $200 to $500 plus expenses for out-of-town engagements. Experienced, in-demand speakers can command $400 to $1,500. When multiple presentations are offered, payment should increase accordingly.

Cost of Goods Sold

If you bring in $150 but earning that money cost $50, how much should be counted as income? In our model, we record just $100.

The phrase *cost of goods sold* (COGS) describes expenses directly related to a service or product. Room rentals, class supplies, and babysitting are all COGS if these fees occur as the direct result of a class. Without the offering, their necessity and price tag evaporate. In the SMT Income Blueprint, COGS are deducted before calculating income.

On the other hand, taxes, insurance, and general overhead like a computer or monthly room rental are not considered COGS since these outflows are identical whether offering one class or a hundred. These expenditures, called *overhead*, must be paid from earned income. Remember this crucial distinction as you read through the following chapters.

Worth the Cost

In a given week, guitarist Michael Ward (www.mikewardguitar.com) offers an average of two classes or workshops. His theory/ear training course was originally organized as a 16-week semester. It worked moderately, but many students were wary of this long-term commitment. A switch to four-week self-contained "minicourses," which allow students to pick and choose topics, yields larger participation. Sessions typically have 4 to 10 enrollees.

Ward's six-week "Group Guitar Lessons for Beginners," capped at six participants, provides an exciting medium for kids to begin. It also frequently leads to new private students (though his roster has exploded, and most are referred to colleagues).

Ward also offers stand-alone workshops. The 3-hour "Basic Guitar Care and Maintenance for Beginners" usually attracts 6 to 10 partakers. In addition to the $50 admittance fee, a "care kit" purchased by around 80% of attendees includes materials used during the class. "Effect Pedals for Beginners" costs $25 for the two-hour session. Audiences of up to 15 include parents.

Because Ward lives in an apartment without appropriate teaching space, his lessons and classes are held at a music school. As an independent contractor, he sets the prices, while the school claims $6 per private lesson ($36 maximum per day) or $3 per class attendee (up to five). Though these COGS reduce income, the trade-off is worthwhile. Other instructors regularly refer students to his sessions, and he loves being surrounded by a musical community.

Making the Numbers Work

Classes typically require more preparation than lessons. To make them finan-cially worthwhile, aim to earn at least 150% to 200% of your private teaching rate. Assuming a $40 to $65 hourly lesson fee, classes should generate $60 to $130+.

$40 per hour × 150% = $60
$65 × 200% = $130

Calculating participation-based class wages entails three variables:

1. Number of students enrolled
2. Tuition per student
3. Expenses directly resulting from the class

While group lessons and small classes may be taught from home, many teach-ers must lease a separate space for larger groups (considered COGS). Suppose this rental costs you $15. If tuition requires $15 per meeting, 5 to 10 partici-pants are needed to reach the wage range noted earlier.

(5 students × $15 per session [$75]) – $15 rental fee = $60 earned per session
(10 students × $15 per session [$150]) – $15 rental fee = $135 earned
    per session

With $25 as the hourly rate, just three to six students are required. Of course, you may want to create a model generating more. A class of a dozen really helps the bottom line!

(3 students × $25 per session [$75]) – $15 rental fee = $60 earned
(6 students × $25 per session [$150]) – $15 rental fee = $135 earned
(12 students × $25 per session [$300]) – $15 rental fee = $285 earned

Additional Considerations

There are a few additional points to consider:

• **Tuition due.** Class tuition covers a term. Fees should be paid in full by a specified date before the first class.

- **Term lengths.** These range from 4 to 16 weeks, with 10- and 15-week sessions being most common. (Programs such as Kindermusik dictate term lengths. Failing to honor these rules results in a revoked license.)
- **Prorating.** If someone wants to join partway through a term, consider prorating rather than deferring enrollment.
- **Early payment discounts.** Consider offering a 5% reduction to clients who pay full tuition before the semester begins, since you receive a large sum upfront, and bookkeeping is simplified.
- **Siblings.** Some SMTs offer a reduced rate to siblings who enroll in the same class.
- **Absences.** Refunds are not given for sessions missed. However, if you happen to offer comparable courses at different times, allow the option of swapping sections.
- **Materials.** When a class requires books, music, recordings, videos, flashcards, or art supplies, there are three ways to cover expenses: (1) roll them into tuition (making this COGS), (2) charge a separate "materials fee," or (3) have students purchase items on their own. Don't get stuck paying out of pocket unless that is part of your economic model.
- **The residual effect.** Consider how class participants might benefit from other streams of your business such as lessons, events, or products.

The Savvy Music Teacher Income Blueprint

Classes have the potential to generate substantial hourly wages. Coupled with enormous educational potential, they present an opportunity too valuable to ignore.

For our blueprint, the SMT offers four to six weekly classes per year (two to three per fall/spring term). Tuition is $300, which breaks down to $20 for each of the 15 hour-long meetings. Each class attracts 6 to 12 students. Sessions are held in a location requiring a $15 rental fee.

4 classes × 15 meetings each × $15 rental = $900 rental fee
6 classes × 15 meetings each × $15 rental = $1,350 rental fee

Remember to deduct this rental fee from earning projections, since it is COGS. On financial documents, parentheses indicate negative values (subtraction).

# of Students	# of Classes per year	Tuition	Gross Income	(COGS)	Net Annual Income
6	4	$300	$7,200	($900)	$6,300
6	6	$300	$10,800	($1,350)	$9,450
12	4	$300	$14,400	($900)	$13,500
12	6	$300	$21,600	($1,350)	$20,250

From classes (stream 2), the SMT earns between $6,300 and $20,250 per year.

CAMPS: STREAM 3

According to the American Camping Association, over 10 million kids attend summer camps in the United States each year. Add adults to the mix, and that number jumps to a whopping 11.5 million. That's a lot of eager campers! Why has this become such a popular pastime?

Camps provide quality, transformational experiences, presenting an opportunity to make new friends while strengthening bonds with old ones. They offer kids educational and engaging activities when school is out of session and allow adults to pursue hobbies, learn new skills, and rejuvenate the soul. For musicians of any age or level, camps offer rich, intense, artistic environments. Most of all, they're fun.

You can certainly supplement income and activities by working at someone else's camp, but why not start your own? Founding and directing this enterprise provides maximum financial benefit and creative control. Camps don't have to require a big upfront investment, yet the return can be significant. Providing variety to your routine, camps allow current students to further their music education while serving as a platform for meeting, impacting, and recruiting new ones. Many Savvy Music Teachers (SMTs) report that running a camp is a highlight of their year.

Camp Design

Savvy Music Teacher Camp Brands

Music super-camps like Aspen and Tanglewood support world-famous faculty, top-notch large ensembles, and hundreds of students each summer. Something of that magnitude requires massive facilities, huge investment, and year-round work by a dedicated staff. As wonderful as they are, don't fall into the trap of trying to model an experience after these mega-organizations. There is no way an independent teacher can possibly emulate their resources and infrastructure. At best, such imitations come across as weak caricatures.

Imagine, instead, what is uniquely possible on a smaller and more local scale. SMT camps most often span a week or less, meeting three to eight hours per day. Between 15 and 30 students enroll (though single-employee models involve fewer campers, while ambitious SMT directors have been known to manage 50+), primarily from a local or regional radius.

Why might someone attend your local camp instead of a national one?

1. Because they seek fun, intriguing local activities to fill the summer
2. Because they're young, and not yet ready to tackle a national camp
3. Because they want to avoid travel, housing, and other expenses
4. Because they want to do something fun during the day and be with family at night
5. Because they are connected to one of your faculty members
6. Because they know former campers who have raved about the experience
7. Because a small camp is more personal than a big one
8. Because the experience is quite different from what they would experience elsewhere
9. Because your camp caters specifically to their interests
10. Because your small camp has a unique identity

Rather than trying to be all things to all people, SMTs typically design camps with intriguing themes geared toward a limited age group, ability level, or demographic: kindergarten to grade three beginners, advanced middle through high school, college music majors, adult hobbyists, professionals.

Examples of Camp Themes	
• Amateur adult chamber music	• Guitar for nonguitarists
• Banjos, mandolins, and harps	• Improvisation for beginners
• Baroque performance practice	• Interdisciplinary exploration (music, dance, art, drama)
• Brass performance	• Jazz performance and arranging
• Career development	
• Chamber music	• Music exploration for kids
• Clarinet	• Music technology
• Composition	• Percussion techniques
• Contemporary music performance	• Rock band performance and recording
• Fiddling	• Songwriting
• Garage band	• Suzuki

SMT camps do more than teach aptitudes. They *transform* campers. Beyond building technical facility (which can only be affected so much in five days), design meaningful events that inspire, build community, offer unique experiences, and generate long-lasting memories.

88 Creative Keys Camp

Jazz artist Bradley Sowash (www.88creativekeys.com) launched the inaugural 88 Creative Keys Camp in Denver, CO. Focused on creativity through improvisation and American musical genres, this intensive week combined overlapping events catering to different audiences:

1. **Main Camp** (Monday–Thursday, 8:30–12), for student pianists ages 8 to 18
2. **Teacher Workshop** (Friday–Saturday, 8:30–12:30), for piano teachers
3. **Adult Piano Clinic** (Friday–Saturday, 1–4:30), for beginning and intermediate adult amateurs
4. **Private Lessons** (Monday–Thursday, 1:30–5), optional, offered for an additional fee

Sowash, who lives across the country, partnered with a prominent local piano teacher. Beyond having complementary skills, 10 of his partner's students ultimately enrolled. They rented a church for the duration, and three sponsors provided in-kind donations: a local music store (20 keyboards for the week), Downbeat (box of magazines), and the software/app iRealPro (eight free downloads, given as prizes).

In year one, 88 Creative Keys Camp attracted 22 participants aged 10 to 18, plus 12 adults (several of whom enrolled in multiple tracks). After expenses, the remainder of the tuition was divided equally between the codirectors. Sowash, who taught at four camps that summer, generated more from his own venture than all the others combined.

Sowash learned many instructive lessons during the inaugural season, which were integrated into the design of year two, including:

• **Length.** Participants wanted more time.
• **Cost.** Campers were willing to pay more than originally assumed.
• **Value.** There is a great interest in creative music making, including individuals who were not originally trained that way. Because there is a shortage of quality instruction in this area, his business has significant growth potential.

Activities

Various activities can fill the hours of a summer camp.

Possible Camp Activities	
Performance Oriented	
Most SMT camps involve individual and/or ensemble performance.	
Lessons	These can be one-on-one or small group lessons.
Master classes	Students perform for a "master" teacher, coached in front of others.
Group/ technique classes	These are typically limited to a single instrument, and teams learn together, develop performance/technical skills, and work on music as a group.
Chamber music	Small groups of three to six players rehearse and receive coaching.
Large ensembles	These typically consist of a composite group involving most or all campers.
Chorus	While chorus is typical for vocal camps, consider the benefits of incorporating singing for instrumentalists as well.
Practice time	Time can be built in for participants to practice independently or with small groups.
Enrichment Classes	
Rather than cramming in highly academic content, provide experiential and engaging classes that participants are unlikely to encounter during the year.	
Theory/history	Many camps integrate theory classes, and a few offer history.
Other	This includes composition, improvisation, literature, aesthetic response, world music, electronic music, sight reading (see chapter 4 for more topic suggestions).
Presentations/ workshops	These include African drumming, movement for musicians, career issues, piano tuning, programming concerts, auditioning, practice strategies, instrument maintenance, and so on.

(continued)

Special Events	
Special events, which typically occur just once during the camp, may be open to participating campers, family members, or the community at large.	
Faculty recital	Featuring you and/or faculty colleagues.
Guest recital	Presenting a visiting artist.
Student recital	Students performing solo literature, perhaps learned before the camp.
Ensemble concert	Student groups performing music rehearsed during camp.
Outreach concert	Performances for hospitals, homeless shelters, or other underserved communities where music is appreciated and meaningful.
Talent show	This may feature both campers and faculty demonstrating primary or secondary talents (other instruments, nonmusical skills, etc.). Or to shake things up, why not host an "un-talent show"?
Field trip	Visit a recording studio, music hall, local concert, or other relevant site.
Recording session	Students experiencing a studio session while creating a memento that will be prized for life.
Tour	A short tour following the camp, giving some or all students the opportunity to perform in external locations.
Other Options	
Additional options provide variety and add to the fun.	
Warm-ups	Sessions on issues like breathing, movement, singing, Alexander technique, Eurhythmics, tai chi, or Pilates.
"Power reading"	Students to read books on relevant topics while calming down and getting focused. A good idea for third to eighth graders after a meal or break.

(continued)

Art	Students build instruments, draw music-related themes, design posters and T-shirts for their ensemble, and so on.
Physical activities	Frisbee, hikes, soccer, volleyball, or anything else that's active.
Reflection sessions	An opportunity to debrief, dialogue, and formulate next steps.
Meals	Don't forget to schedule time for eating!

A Different Kind of Camp

In 2009, cellist Martin Torch-Ishii (www.thecellodoctor.com) cofounded a summer cello camp with a colleague. Though just 10 students attended the first season, this four-day event grew quickly and tripled enrollment by year four. Using similar models, he created the San Diego Cello Camp and Cellovation with another friend and his father, respectively.

While participants work on cello-related issues through private lessons and performance classes, much of the event's appeal is due to less traditional activities: group composition, songwriting, improvisation, Eurhythmics, multiple genres, chamber music, and fun lunchtime activities. In fact, though these camps originally targeted locals, many out-of-towners have flown in claiming, "I haven't seen anything else like this!"

Scheduling

The keys to effective camp scheduling are:

1. **Providing high-quality experiences.** This goes without saying.
2. **Balancing continuity with variety.** Too many activities feels overwhelming. Too much of the same thing gets boring.
3. **Keeping sessions the right length.** No activity should ever last more than two hours. First graders do not have the same attention span as college students, so plan accordingly.
4. **Not overworking participants.** One common mistake is cramming in too much content. Playing requirements should not leave participants with

tendonitis or swollen lymph nodes. Be sure to include breaks through-out the day for relaxing the mind and muscles. Give just enough so that attendees can't wait to return the next year.

When possible, keep daily schedules somewhat consistent, creating a sense of routine. Obviously, adjustments are necessary for special events such as a recital or field trip. The following chart describes a sample itinerary for a chamber music camp.

Time	Activity
9:30–10:00 AM	Arrival
10:00 AM	Eurhythmics
10:30 AM	Chamber rehearsals
11:30 AM	Break/lunch
12:30 PM	Chamber rehearsals
1:30 PM	Faculty recital
1:50 PM	Break
2:00 PM	Large ensemble
3:00 PM	Pick-up

Here is the outline for a shorter three-hour camp. Notice how students are broken into groups early on but then join forces for the large ensemble.

Time	Group A	Group B
9:00 AM	Chamber rehearsals	Guest presentation
10:00 AM	Guest presentation	Chamber rehearsals
11:00 AM	Snack	
11:15 AM	Large ensemble rehearsal	
12:00 PM	Pick-Up	

A sample itinerary for a high school camp involving 25 to 30 participants follows. Some activities involve two groups, while others bring the entire community together. There are three faculty members, denoted as "1," "2," and "3," along with a counselor called "C" who keeps things running smoothly and supervises breaks.

Time	Faculty	Activity A	Activity B	Faculty
9:00 AM	1	Tai Chi		
9:30 AM	1	Technique class	Individual practice	3
10:15 AM	3	Individual practice	Theory	2
11:00 AM	1, 2, 3	Group class		
12:00 PM	C	Lunch/break		
1:00 PM	2	Musical exploration		
1:30 PM	3	Individual practice	Technique class	1
2:15 PM	2	Theory	Individual practice	3
3:00 PM	C	Break/snack		
3:20 PM	3	Large ensemble		
4:30 PM	2	Reflection		
5:00 PM	C	Pick-up		

It is imperative that scheduling be well designed and documented before students arrive. Disorganization quickly leads to frustration. Crafting the ideal itinerary requires thoughtful planning and tweaking. Particularly if it's your first year, run the proposal by more experienced camp directors (possibly from outside the music world) for feedback.

Camp Scheduling

Here is a typical daily schedule for Flute-a-rama, a week-long camp cofounded by Carrie Rose (www.rosearts.org) and a friend, for flute players in grades five through nine:

9:00	Warm-ups and fundamentals	9:30	Coached ensembles
10:30	Rhythm band	11:15	Music history
11:30	Lunch break *(lunch not provided)*	12:30	Coached ensembles
1:30	Yoga for flutists	2:15	Music jeopardy
3:00	Depart		

On paper, Monday through Friday of the Bert Truax School of Trumpet Summer Camp (www.berttruaxbasicbrass.com) look similar. But in reality, each day provides unique adventures, featuring a different superstar of this instrument. Guest artists, responsible for two master classes and a concert, have included some of the biggest names in the industry.

9:00	Group warm-up	10:00	Masterclass 1
11:30	Lunch (provided)	1:00	Trumpet ensemble
2:30	Break	3:00	Masterclasss 2
5:00	Dinner (on own)	7:00	Guest artist public performance

Things wrap up with a shorter day on Saturday (9 AM to 4 PM), which includes warm-ups, dress rehearsal, a fun lunch where attendees bid for prizes using "Bert Bucks," and a concluding student performance featuring the 30 to 45 high school participants.

Food

Unless your camp runs three hours or less per day, consider how and when campers will eat. There are several ways to organize meals:

- **Student provided.** This is the most common model. Be clear about this so no one starves.
- **Parent provided.** Parent volunteers supply meals or snacks each day, delegated in advance. This solution is nice since it's free, ensures that all eat, and gets families involved.
- **Camp provided.** You or a staff member purchases veggies, fruit, cheese, chips, drinks, sandwiches, desserts, and so forth. Avoid an excess of junk food or pay the price after mealtime.

- **Restaurant.** Eat at nearby cafeterias/restaurants, either individually or as a group. If students must pay, be clear about this expense in camp literature.
- **Catered.** This option is nice and convenient but often expensive. Account for this in tuition unless local food providers offer in-kind donations.

If providing food, inquire about allergies and dietary restrictions on the application. In just about all cases, supply vegetarian, peanut-free, and gluten-free options.

Music Is Delicious

In 2013, piano and guitar teacher Libby Wiebel (www.libbywiebel musicstudio.com) offered her inaugural Summer Songwriting for Girls camp. Open to middle and high school students, this Monday through Friday (9 AM to 4:30 PM) experience runs out of her home with Wiebel as the only faculty member, keeping overhead low. Priced at $500, the camp accommodates three to eight participants.

Each morning, they begin with "Song Talk," a discussion-based analysis of tunes by female songwriters. "Music Theory" examines scales, chord families, harmonic progressions, and rhythmic patterns. "Lit Talk" highlights literary devices such as character development and rhyming schemes. Two hours each day are devoted to "Individual Writing," where participants claim a different part of the house and compose independently. (On Friday, this period is used for recording songs and adding video.) Days end with "Group Critique," sharing works in progress, offering feedback, and tending to necessary business.

Surprisingly, one of the most effective aspects came on a whim. Each day, Wiebel provided ingredients and a recipe, challenging participants to cook lunch. At first, they thought she was crazy leaving them unsupervised. But this forced campers to bond and work together, transforming the dynamic. "I will absolutely continue this tradition. It was one of their favorite activities. Partly as a result, even the most shy student came out of her shell."

Venue

While it may be possible to host a small camp at your residence, most require larger venues. The best options are buildings that are vacant or underpopulated during your event. Be sure the facility fulfills at least your minimum needs. Is there an area for all campers to convene? Are there enough pianos, music stands, and rehearsal rooms? If you must rent or purchase additional equipment to make the space work, consider this in your cost analysis.

Space Matters

Part of the charm of Mountain Road Traditional Music Camp, founded by violinist, banjo player, and singer-songwriter Alex Caton (www. alexcaton.com), is its location. Each year, around 30 participants and their families head to West Virginia's Brazenhead Inn (www. brazenheadinn.com), built and owned by an amateur guitarist and singer with Irish roots.

On Friday night, things kick off with a "slow jam session," followed by dinner and a staff performance. Throughout Saturday, participants attend 3 classes chosen from a menu of 17, including Irish fiddling, Irish song, old-time banjo, dancing, and drumming. Saturday evening features another performance, followed by a dance. Festivities wrap up Sunday morning with "gospel sing."

Events are held in an outdoor pavilion, upstairs conference room, large tent, and 4,000-square-foot wraparound veranda known affectionately as the "picking porch." Though Caton has full run of the property, she is not charged a rental fee (beyond accommodations for herself and two guest faculty). The inn benefits financially from a guaranteed full house. Most participants rent 1 of the 20 rooms or camp on their grounds, in addition to purchasing cuisine and libations from the lodge restaurant and Irish pub.

Campers are encouraged to attend with their families. In fact, parents, spouses, and kids may enroll in individual classes (priced reasonably) and attend performances. They also enjoy exploring the beautiful, secluded surroundings that include a lake and scenic hiking trails. Families of five or six regularly make this a summer highlight.

"We have found a magical and inspiring space, perfect for delivering an authentic Irish music experience. The owner has a wonderful story and passion for the art we make."

Logistics

The American Camping Association (www.acacamps.org) is a fantastic resource, with helpful information on their website and employees happy to address questions. For music-specific issues, engage a noncompeting camp director as a mentor.

Timeline

While organizing a camp mustn't require a large, risky financial investment, it does necessitate upfront time and energy as you design the experience, oversee logistics, and recruit students. This is particularly true for the inaugural season, after which things become more efficient, having previously worked through major challenges. Start early, make a plan, and distribute work throughout the year. Here is a suggested timeline for camps beginning in early July.

Timeline	Activities
9–10 months prior (September–October)	Develop business plan and camp design. Secure venue and times needed. Research faculty. Research strategic alliances.
7–8 months prior (November–December)	Recruit faculty. Develop content for brochure and web. Engage strategic alliances. Write press release.
6 months prior (January)	Post camp content to website. Print brochures. Distribute brochures.
5 months prior (February)	Have strategic alliances plug camp. Send press release to local media contacts. Speak to local groups about camp.
4 months prior (March)	Recruit, recruit, recruit. Work closely with strategic alliances. Attract media coverage. Send out faculty contracts. Solidify curriculum. Set schedule.
3 months prior (April)	Big push for camp—use your network! Applications are due. Conduct scholarship auditions (if applicable). Hire counselor (if applicable).

(continued)

Timeline	Activities
6 weeks–2 months prior (May)	Mail out contracts. Deposit of 25% is required from students. Order and organize music to be performed. Organize food logistics. Compose preparation letter. Compile welcome kit. Recruit remaining students as necessary to fill out load.
1 month prior (June)	Payment in full is required. Receive signed contracts. Mail out preparation letter. Assign chamber groups based on ability and instrumentation. Get supplies. Last-minute students? Last day for cancellation and partial refund is 2 weeks before.
CAMP WEEK (early July)	Pass out welcome kit. Have a great time as a teacher and administrator! Pay employees on last day of camp.
1 week after (mid-July)	Send thank you letters to contributors describing camp highlights. Be sure all bills have been paid in full. Celebrate with a great meal, nice wine, and lots of chocolate.

Personnel

One challenge of running a camp is hiring the right number of faculty. With too few, things quickly become chaotic and diminish the camper experience. With too many, profits decrease, even causing a deficit. As a rule of thumb, there should be one instructor for every 5 to 10 kids (through high school) or 10 to 15 college/adult students.

Unfortunately, the number of attendees is rarely known when courting faculty six to nine months in advance. Unless you are confident about recruitment prospects, avoid getting yourself in a bind by remembering an important rule of business etiquette: *there are no take-backs*. When approaching teachers, be clear that positions are contingent upon attracting enough participants. Perhaps a spot is guaranteed as long as they personally acquire a certain number of students. This mutually beneficial arrangement helps you meet enrollment goals and provides them job security.

Obviously, you should aim to hire outstanding teachers who work well with your target audience. Beyond that, some questions to consider include the following:

1. Might their own students benefit from the camp?
2. Will they actively recruit for you?
3. Do they bring name recognition or "celebrity status"? (Since fame is perceived, clever marketing goes a long way toward creating the aura of stardom. Great players with a CD credit, interesting history, and compelling blurb may generate all the buzz you need.)
4. Do they offer something noteworthy or unusual that adds desirability to your event?
5. Are they local or "imported"? (Out-of-town faculty come with a host of expenses: airfare, rental car, housing, food, etc. Be sure the investment is affordable and worthwhile.)

When the total number of campers exceeds 18 or so, hire a counselor or assistant to oversee logistics, freeing faculty to focus exclusively on music and teaching. Look for a responsible high school or college student who loves music, is responsible, and has good people skills. If you can't afford this expense, consider an unpaid internship. Another possibility is asking parents to help in exchange for a partial tuition waver.

Bocal Majority

Jennifer Auerbach founded Bocal Majority Bassoon Camp (www. bocalmajority.com) in 2005, engaging 20 participants and five faculty members. Since then, it mushroomed. Four years later, a second component was added: Operation O.B.O.E. By 2014, there were 25 separate camps offered in eight states, each impacting 20 to 100 double-reed students. There are beginner, regular, and advanced programs, in addition to Band Director Boot Camp and a Camp Intern Program. "As with so many entrepreneurial ventures, I've taken a hole and plugged it."

The student-teacher ratio ranges between 5:1 and 7:1. Most faculty live locally, though Auerbach does import guest artists for advanced programs. Once a candidate has been identified, he or she is vetted. A phone interview explores collegiality and fit with the camp philosophy. In most cases, hires are contingent upon bringing at least five students. This policy guarantees that faculty recruit proactively and ensures a profitable business model.

In the early days, Auerbach was responsible for everything. Today she delegates certain tasks to her very part-time five-member "admin team." While it is not possible to attend every event, she is heavily involved in them all. Preparing for summer is a time-consuming endeavor year-round, though she still manages to juggle 45 bassoon students.

From a financial perspective, Auerbach earns as much as 50% of her annual income from this for-profit business. But that's not the driving force. "The foundation of what I do is primarily concerned with making a difference in the lives of campers, teachers, and interns. Creating a sustainable enterprise is a crucial—but secondary—goal." Spoken like a true SMT!

Recruitment

To achieve educational and financial goals, a critical mass of students must enroll. But because your camp is small and local, recruitment need not be excruciatingly difficult, particularly when just 15 to 30 participants are required. Remember, summer camps are extremely popular activities during a season when people are looking for meaningful experiences to fill the days.

No audience trusts you more than current students. If it's a good fit, 25% to 50% of this group may reasonably be expected to attend. From a studio of 30, this alone generates 7 to 15 campers. Some SMTs even integrate participation into a larger summer study package.

Whenever possible, hire local teachers likely to enlist their own students. In fact, why not engage any instructor—who you like—able to entice five clients?

Use "celebrity" faculty to your recruitment advantage. For example, arrange for them to perform for your target demographic months in advance. After being blown away, audience members may ecstatically anticipate rubbing elbows with your superstar. At the least, include video footage and powerful text on your website showcasing who they are and what they bring.

Put your key contacts to work. Find ways to encourage band/orchestra/choir directors, church music ministers, private teachers, and professional musicians to spread the word, maybe even offering some kind of incentive (financial or otherwise) for each lead they generate.

Chamber Recruitment

Flutist Jessica Sherer (www.jessicasherer.com) began planning what would become the Atlanta Chamber Music Festival (www.atlantachambermusicfestival.com) with two like-minded colleagues. Though this camp (three days, 9 AM to 6 PM) would highlight small ensemble performances, they hoped it would grow large enough to assemble a chamber orchestra.

Fifteen invited faculty members (one on each orchestral instrument plus a second on violin) were asked to recruit, though no specifics were cited on contracts the first year. Marketing consisted of a website, posters, flyers, Facebook page, Twitter feed, and personalized emails to at least 150 area band/orchestra directors and independent music teachers. Thirty-eight students ultimately enrolled, a number they found acceptable for the prototype.

A few marketing additions helped in year two: articles describing the camp appeared in the *Georgia Music Educators Association Journal* and *Target Audience Magazine*; camp faculty who attracted a certain number of students were given a bonus; and many first-year participants returned and brought a friend. Though faculty size remained the same, enrollment swelled to 57.

As the Atlanta Chamber Music Festival looks toward their third season, they hope to nearly double enrollment, bringing in enough participants to staff two chamber orchestras.

Communication

Develop the following communication items for your SMT summer camp:

1. **Website.** Devote a section of your studio website to the camp, or better yet, create an independent URL. Include an overview, what makes the camp enticing, target audience (age, instruments, and background),

faculty, dates, location, price, and application procedures. Testimonials and video from past camps are extremely effective. A page addressing frequently asked questions is also helpful.

2. **Physical marketing materials.** Though we live in a digital era, consider the merits of printed posters, brochures, and postcards.

3. **Application.** Create a simple one-page online application for prospective campers, accessible through your website.

4. **Student contract.** Clearly outline policies/expectations, including when and how payment(s) should be made.

5. **Faculty contract.** Outline conditions of employment and recruitment expectations.

6. **Welcome/logistics letter.** A few weeks before camp begins, send an email welcoming students and providing details. Include venue address, directions, parking instructions, drop-off and pick-up times, contact information, and what to bring (instrument, music, music stand, a pencil, etc.). If students are expected to learn music ahead of time, mail the parts along with specific instructions on performance expectations.

7. **Welcome kit.** Prepare a welcome kit for participants with appropriate items, which may include a nametag, schedule, notebook, manuscript paper, pencil, camp brochure, faculty bios, and/or fun musical puzzles.

Monetization

Tuition

Directing even a small camp requires significant time and energy. From a financial perspective, create a model where you earn enough after expenses to make this effort worthwhile.

For a five-day camp spanning five to eight hours per day, tuition typically runs from $300 to $600, or $60 to $120 per day per student. Some require as much as $1,000 per week, but something has to be extraordinary for people to invest that kind of capital. A shorter, three-hour experience might charge as little as $225 for the week. Though the lower ticket price generates less income, it also leaves afternoons and nights open to pursue additional work. Another option is running one camp from 9 AM to 12 PM and a parallel venture from 2 to 5 PM.

Many camps require a nonrefundable $25 to $35 registration/application/administrative fee, due with the application. To encourage early enrollment (and peace of mind for the coordinator), some programs waive this expense as an incentive for individuals enrolling by a certain date. Others charge a $50 penalty for those signing up at the last minute.

Scholarships and Discounts

You may have students who want to attend but can't afford full tuition. What options exist beyond closing the door?

One possibility is encouraging them to obtain financial support from relatives, neighbors, and teachers. Perhaps they can offer a minirecital in exchange for donations. Older participants might set up a crowdfunding account.

Another possibility is approaching donors—supporters of education and the arts—about underwriting student scholarships. "For just $500, you can send a student to camp, and the award is named after you!" Both full and partial scholarships are possible. Be sure that impacted students send thank you notes to their sponsors. Donations are tax deductible only if you are running the camp as a nonprofit or partnering with one.

A final option is simply lowering your rate and calling it a "scholarship." Obviously, this affects the bottom line, so make calculations accordingly. Why not offer partial scholarships to anyone who asks? Maybe the official camp tuition is $500, but a $100 award is granted to all accepted participants! This practice feels generous, and if just $400 per student is needed, why not? Everyone likes to feel they got a good deal.

To encourage greater participation, consider offering discounts to siblings, campers who attend multiple weeks (if several sessions are offered), or first-time attendees.

Deposits and Cancellations

To ensure that enrollees are committed, collect 25% to 50% of tuition a month or two before the event, with the remainder due at least two to four weeks before camp begins. Avoid collecting imbursement during the event itself. This can get complicated and ugly. If someone hasn't yet paid, should they attend day one? What if a check bounces?

Students will back out from time to time. Withdrawals at the last minute throw an unfortunate wrench in your financial model as commitments have already been made. Protect yourself with a clear policy. Perhaps registration fees are nonrefundable, cancellations until one month before the camp receive 50% back, and terminations after that are granted no refund.

Expenses

Camp expenses include the following:

1. **Venue rental.** This is the biggest variable in the expense column, so research thoroughly and choose wisely. Some teachers strike gold and are charged only a nominal fee (free to $200 for the week). Many venues require hefty rates of $150 to $500+ per day for multiple rooms. If so, try to negotiate extras such as a performance space for your final event.
2. **Personnel.** This is the biggest expense. For a week of day camp, faculty members typically receive $500 to $1,250 each ($100 to $250 per day), depending on number of hours worked and background. Rates for counselors or administrative assistants range from minimum wage to $12 per hour. You may not need a counselor present all day every day, or an intern or volunteer may be willing to perform this work for free.
3. **Promotion.** Shop around for good prices on website design/hosting, posters, brochures, business cards, letterhead, printing, and postage.
4. **Supplies.** These include sheet music; rented equipment (keyboards, microphones, sound system); other items such as pencils, folders, and extension cords; and "graduation" gifts (such as certificates or mementos). Take out the guesswork and carefully price everything ahead of time. Perhaps some items can be donated in kind.
5. **Food.** This includes snacks, meals, and drinks not provided by students.
6. **Insurance.** Be sure you are protected in case of emergency.
7. **Transportation/housing for out-of-town faculty.** If faculty is imported, expenses obviously go up. But some teachers are willing, even delighted, to do home-stays.

Camp Financial Jam

The inaugural year of Hilton Head Jazz Camp (www.hhjazzcamp.com), founded by trumpeter and pianist James Berry, involved just 10 local students. By its third season, this six-day experience attracted 52 participants, including a healthy portion of overnighters. Helping build momentum was the partnership with a local nonprofit devoted to jazz education.

Applicants were required to pay a $29 registration fee plus $279 in tuition. Discounts of $50 were extended to siblings, camp alumni, and all-state band members. In addition, around $4,000 in partial and full scholarships was awarded, thanks to money raised by the partner nonprofit. Attendees had the option of purchasing lunches or an overnight hotel plan for a supplemental fee, generating a small amount of additional revenue.

As is typical, the biggest expense was personnel. A total of 10 faculty ensured a low student-to-teacher ratio. In addition, Berry hired a staff member to address logistical issues, and one instructor doubled as a resident assistant.

The camp venue, a local school, charged 10% of tuition (but not scholarships). Another big expense was insurance, requiring $1,000. Though the standard waiver agreement for camps held at schools provides basic coverage, Berry felt it necessary to secure additional liability, particularly with overnighters.

One teacher volunteered access to his extensive music library, eliminating this expense, but a speaker system for each teaching room brought supplies to $500. The $1,000 marketing budget paid for posters, direct mailings to band teachers, Facebook boosts, and a few print ads.

Hilton Head Jazz Camp has turned a profit each year, with room to grow. Berry plans on capping participation at 75. Beyond the personal revenue it generates, this event is extraordinarily fulfilling, both socially and educationally.

The Savvy Music Teacher Income Blueprint

Following our blueprint, the SMT offers a one-week day camp during the summer. Tuition is $400 plus a $25 administration fee, with between 15 and 30 campers. Expenses are as follows:

- $500 venue rental
- $750 for each faculty member. One additional teacher is employed to support 15 students (two total with you); three are hired when there are 30 students (four total).
- $80 per student for food, music, and supplies
- $500 for marketing

$500 venue + $750 faculty + $1,200 supplies + $500 marketing = $2,950 expenses (15 students)

$500 venue + $2,250 faculty + $2,400 supplies + $500 marketing = $5,650 expenses (30 students)

In this model, the expense per student is $189 to $197.

$2,950 expenses ÷ 15 students = $196.67
$5,650 ÷ 30 students = $188.34

Number of Students	Tuition + Admin	Gross Income	(COGS)	Net Annual Income
15	$425	$6,375	($2,950)	$3,425
30	$425	$12,750	($5,650)	$7,100

From camps (stream 3), the SMT earns between $3,425 and $7,100 per year.

6 EVENTS: STREAM 4

The value of public performance is obvious, and most serious music teachers schedule at least one studio recital per year. But Savvy Music Teachers (SMTs) are known for making events core to their brand—whether attached to lessons, classes, or camps—exploring a variety of innovative and unconventional formats. While organizing these activities takes time, energy, and imagination, dividends can be great. Well-conceived events build community, increase confidence, motivate participants, and stress that music is a gift worth sharing. As a result, studios hosting extraordinary happenings see their demand, student commitment, and retention increase.

Innovative Event Design
Frameworks for Innovation

Most readers are familiar with the traditional studio recital format: a marathon of students performs one or more works in succession for an audience of family members. This structure clearly offers many benefits. But how might you go even further, designing unique, memorable, exceptional SMT occasions? Which modernizations would increase impact and differentiation? Events present an opportunity to mix learning objectives, studio biases, and ecstatic innovation.

One innovative strategy is called *feature tweaking*. Begin by identifying typical characteristics, and then imagine alternatives. The chart that follows demonstrates this process. The point is not to combine all these things or blindly adopt suggestions that happen to be listed, but rather to begin imagining just how many creative solutions exist.

Feature	Traditional Model	A Possible Tweak
Atmosphere	Serious	Fun
Repertoire	By master composers or method books	Original compositions (or more interesting: music by fellow students)
Ensemble	Soloists, perhaps with accompanist	Chamber music
Preparation	Pieces must be polished	Sight-reading event
Venue usage	All performers play from "stage" area	A "surround sound" experience
Speaking	Features the teacher	Features the students
Audience	Family members	Retirement home members
Transitions	Applause	Short video interviews with students
Prerecital	Audience enters and finds a seat	Music-related film in background
Postrecital	Reception and mingling	Host a "talk back," where audience members ask questions of performers

Another innovative strategy is *objective amplification*. Begin by identifying desirable objectives fostered by traditional recitals, and then imagine meaningful activities that intensify each value.

Objective: Student Involvement in a Live Performance
Traditional event role

- Students perform music in front of an audience.

SMT objective amplification

- Students write program notes.
- Students provide verbal introductions to music they perform.

- Students provide verbal introduction to music played by peers.
- Students vote on an upcoming event's theme.
- Students design the "set," seating arrangement, program order, reception, and so forth.

Objective: Flexibility in the Moment

Traditional event role

- Students must be flexible when adapting to a new venue and performance conditions.
- Students are challenged to be flexible if a memory slip occurs.

SMT objective amplification

- Students perform at sight-reading recitals.
- Recitals include improvisational components.
- Program order is drawn from a hat.
- Audience members suggest parameters (e.g., loud, slow, staccato, high) applied to pieces.

Objective: Community Building

Traditional event role

- Audience members sit together to observe event.
- Mingling occurs before and after, possibly at a reception.

SMT objective amplification

- Recitals include audience sing-alongs, clapping in time, or call-and-response.
- Games involving the audience are played.
- Participants dress in costume related to theme.
- Audience discussion groups are formed, addressing some kind of issue or challenge.
- Award is given to section of audience that cheers the loudest (first to enjoy reception food?).

Objective: Family Involvement

Traditional event role

- Family members attend the recital and listen adoringly to their loved one perform.

SMT objective amplification

- Family members accompany/perform collaboratively with their loved one.
- Family members introduce performers (e.g., hobbies, interesting anecdotes) or music.
- Recipes of dishes prepared by families for the reception are compiled into a cookbook and distributed to attendees (along with a photo and bio of each family?).
- Family members who "win" a raffle are required to share a talent (students earn tickets by practicing a certain amount, various achievements, etc.).
- Parent-of-the-year award is given.
- Families publically share strategies for maintaining a musical household.
- These frameworks for innovation are relevant to far more than event design. During a hunt for fresh solutions, such techniques can be applied to lessons, classes, camps, or any other aspect of your artistic/career/life model.

Fifty Formats

Once an SMT ventures into the world of innovative event design, a near-infinite amount of possibilities emerge. While traditional recitals are absolutely valid and beneficial experiences, 50 additional large-scale event ideas include:

50 Event Concepts	
1. Audience votes	8. Electro-acoustic shows
2. "Battle of the bands"	9. Field trips
3. Busking (street performances)	10. Flash mobs
4. Coffeehouse sessions	11. Full-length solo recitals
5. Competitions	12. Fundraisers
6. Concerts in the round	13. Game show formats
7. Costumed events	14. Guest artist events

(continued)

50 Event Concepts	
15. Holiday events	33. Parent/child duo night
16. Honors recital (most advanced/improved students)	34. Pizza and performance
17. House concerts	35. Roaming recitals (moving locations)
18. Installations (the audience roams)	36. Sight-reading recitals
19. Interdisciplinary events	37. Silent movie accompaniments
20. "Invite your stuffed animals/ dolls"	38. Single composer/style events
21. Jam sessions	39. Skits
22. Joint recitals (with other studios)	40. Streaming performances (audience can view online only)
23. Lecture recitals	41. Student music video viewings
24. Master classes	42. Studio parties with music
25. Minirecitals embedded within lessons	43. Talent shows
26. Multimedia elements	44. Tea parties
27. Musical scavenger hunt	45. Teleconferencing events (performers from two-plus locations)
28. "Name that tune/style"	46. Teaching events (students teach audience to perform)
29. Narrated shows	47. Themed recitals
30. Open-mic nights	48. Through-composed (no pauses, overlapping performances)
31. Original composition night	49. Unusual venue events
32. Outreach/community engagement	50. World-record-breaking events

The following sections elaborate on a few of these formats.

Themed Recitals

Rather than having students perform the random assortment of music they happen to be practicing, recitals can be built around a unifying theme. The premise can influence more than just literature, extending to stage decoration, costumes, multimedia elements, verbal introductions, program booklet design, and reception food. In addition to increasing the "fun factor," this approach presents an opportunity to engage students in the creative planning phases. Some SMTs even invite theme nominations from participants.

Possible Recital Themes		
• A musical style • Animal • Book (read by all members of studio) • Collaboration, creativity, or other skill • Cuisine (with a reception to match) • Current events • Dance music	• Emotions • Ensemble music • Fairytale/story (read between pieces) • Friendship • Halloween • Mother's/ Father's Day • Music and visual art• Nature • Patriotism	• Science • Single composer • Single period of music • Thanksgiving • The power of music/art • Trip around the globe • Winter holidays

Staying Busy

Pianist Jennifer Foxx (www.foxxpianostudio.com) faced a dilemma common to music teachers. Though students did well during the year, one third to one quarter discontinued study after each summer. As an experiment, she began scheduling major events every other month. This made a huge difference in curbing attrition and increasing student commitment.

The early March Keyboard Festival features students in duet with MIDI accompaniments played on Disklavier. Students perform in customized T-shirts with a studio logo and musical message, and these handsome items (which double as great marketing!) are theirs to keep.

The Halloween Festival is a costumed concert alternating musical performances with games involving audience participation.

The Spring Recital is fairly traditional, though parents can buy an "ad" representing their child in the beautifully designed color program ($50 full page, $25 half page, $15 quarter page), transforming a throwaway booklet into a lifelong keepsake.

Because there are few good performance venues locally, most events are held in Foxx's home. Since it accommodates just 30 people, recital days are often marathons of three to four events, each carrying a small price tag to cover costs and the instructor's time.

Foxx's students also participate in events organized by the local Music Teacher's Association. For Music at the Mall, several studios combine to perform Christmas tunes. Piano Ensemble features numerous keyboardists playing 13 grand pianos, led by a conductor.

Joint Recitals

Joint recitals, combining students of two or more teachers, are most common between small studios wishing to create full-length events. However, because of the unique benefits offered, even SMTs with full rosters opt to cohost this format from time to time.

1. Joint recitals with noncompeting studios (e.g., violin and cello, jazz and classical, beginner and advanced) expand the palette of sound, resulting in a more varied event.
2. Participants are exposed to alternate approaches.
3. Things get interesting when music studios combine forces with another art form, such as dance, drama, or visual art.
4. Joint recitals can serve as a marketing tool, attracting siblings, friends, or even participants interested in exploring a secondary area.

Honors recitals, which showcase the top or most-improved players, present a unique opportunity for collaboration among teachers. To be included, studio members must pass a special audition. Because of this event's distinction, some students work diligently to ensure participation.

The More, the Merrier

Following a move across Canada, violinist Joel Bootsma (www. reddoorstrings.com) began building a studio from scratch. Worried that a group recital with his handful of beginners might feel underwhelming, he got an idea. Why not team up with a sister Suzuki program?

The joint event he organized, held in a public library, generated some buzz. Suddenly this was a collaborative happening, and a local paper ran with the story. Bootsma's students, younger than their counterparts, were inspired by playing alongside more advanced players. The traveling guests were delighted to take a field trip and act as mentors. Following the performance, the library organized a scavenger hunt, challenging both studios to work together to discover treasures hidden throughout the building. "I look forward to returning the favor next time, reuniting my students with their new friends."

Guest Artists

An inspirational way to transform a student recital is by incorporating a guest artist. Whether this involves a fellow music teacher, symphony orchestra musician, local freelancer, college music student, or personal friend, several roles are possible for this "celebrity":

- Cameo appearance
- First half student performances, second half guest artist
- Guest numbers sprinkled throughout
- In addition to solo works, guest is featured alongside students

Concerts, not Recitals

"Some people associate student *recitals* with boredom and monotony," reflects pianist and singer Dana Rice (www.thefameschoolblog.com). "But I don't want anyone leaving politely commenting, 'Well, that was nice.' Instead, a *concert* experience should WOW the audience."

Rice's events, which typically integrate a guest artist specializing in something other than piano, have featured a drummer, singer-songwriter, dancer, saxophonist, and spoken word artist. "This gives students ideas about using their musical gifts in the larger world." In addition to interspersing solo numbers, guests collaborate with studio members.

One to two weeks before the show, Rice organizes a 90-minute group class with the guest, providing a forum for questions, dialogue, rehearsal, and feedback.

Events are notable in other ways. Audience engagement is integral: viewing videos of kids, clapping in time, and chanting to the music. Students are encouraged to perform jointly, accompanying one another or working as a "band." They showcase secondary skills such as singing, percussion, secondary instruments, or original compositions. Parents also participate. For example, one father spoke about the importance of music education.

Concerts, open to the public, are marketed to local school music teachers. Participants receive physical postcards and digital invitations to share with family and friends. Volunteers from the community help expand the appeal.

Students pay an annual $100 concert fee. This investment supports Rice's time, venue rentals, decorations, marketing, programs, and a photo session with a professional photographer.

Public Showcases

Studio performances can be arranged at bookstores, malls, libraries, airports, parks, and other public places. These venues are often delighted to host events, since they bring in customers and reflect well on the presenter. Public showcases not only benefit students but also bring a delightful surprise to unsuspecting passersby. They may even serve as recruitment.

Do It Like the Pros

In addition to running home teaching and recording businesses, guitarist Greg Henkin (www.gregsguitarlessons.com) is the board president of a youth center called The Oasis. Rather than scheduling traditional studio recitals, he regularly arranges for high school and college students to perform 30- to 45-minute sets at this venue, either as soloists or with a band.

Henkin uses the opportunity to teach about the music industry and what it takes to book a gig. In addition to musical preparation, lessons preceding the show address professional etiquette, business issues, and "the type of career stuff I wish someone had taught me."

The Oasis is run like a professional club. A $5 donation, charged to the 50 to 200 audience members who arrive each weekend night, is split among featured acts. Though Henkin does not get paid directly for these events, studio enrollment has exploded (currently 75 students!), and he commands lesson rates higher than the competition.

Outreach Events

Many SMTs schedule meaningful performances for those most in need. Underserved audiences are incredibly appreciative, which makes a huge impact on participants as well.

Potential Outreach Event Forums		
• Homeless shelters • Hospitals • Inner-city communities	• Libraries • Nursing homes • Orphanages	• Prisons • Schools • Retirement communities

Giving Back

In addition to traditional studio recitals, trombonist Rebecca Teiwes (www. joyfulsoundschool.com) organizes several outreach events at nursing homes around the Valentine's Day and December holidays. Performances involve 25 to 30 of her students playing short solos and duos, two minutes or less in duration. Performers also introduce the music, announce their age, and model their outfits (due to frequent requests).

It is difficult to discern who derives the most enjoyment from this experience. Residents, who often suffer from serious diseases like Alzheimer's, love interacting with young people. They often rave that the engagement "made their season." Students find it exhilarating to play for such an appreciative crowd. In fact, Teiwes's alumni often return to participate when on break from college. And parents are delighted to see their kids generously share musical gifts.

Outreach events motivate students and have attracted clients who were impressed by the gesture. "But I do it to give back, bringing joy and hope to folks who can use some."

Fundraisers

Teach students the value of contributing to meaningful causes. Fundraisers can collect money for any worthwhile endeavor: protecting local parks, supporting disaster victims, cancer research, a new instrument for your studio, and so forth. Be sure to clearly articulate the value of your cause to students and audience members.

The Piano Cottage Rocks!

The Piano Cottage (www.thepianocottagegr.com) was born when Jody and Wright McCargar bought a home in western Michigan with an 800-square-foot backyard structure previously owned by a stained glass artist. While the space itself is charming and perfect for lessons, it is not the only reason their studio quickly expanded. In addition to traditional training, students regularly transcribe, compose, integrate technology, and take field trips to recording studios or orchestra rehearsals.

And then there is the popular July event The Piano Cottage Rocks. Interested kids audition with rock or jazz piano arrangements, but only the lucky ones are chosen to "headline." These performers work intensely for six weeks preparing the show: arranging, orchestrating, staging, rehearsing. Students who weren't selected may also participate, playing secondary instruments, singing in a choir, managing the stage, marketing, and fulfilling additional roles.

Featured performers get makeup and hair done by local volunteers (pointy spikes and flaming neon stripes are particularly popular) and perform on a fully lighted stage complete with smoke machines. A professional rhythm section joins the excitement.

Two shows on consecutive evenings sell out a 500-seat theater. Tickets are $10 each, though $200 buys a VIP package complete with family pass, T-shirts, and VIP lounge access where attendees mix and match custom frostings on cupcakes (a student idea). The inaugural event netted an astounding $10,000; the next year generated $11,500! Proceeds go entirely to the Crescendo Foundation, McCargar's nonprofit that awards music scholarships to interested kids without the means to afford private instruction.

Competitions

Whether the environment is serious or fun, competitions can be great motivators for students to focus, practice effectively, and step up their game. Many teachers regularly encourage participation in competitions hosted by local, regional, or even national organizations. SMTs can also arrange their own contests, offering awards including musical items, gift cards, free class enrollment, opportunities (e.g., solo recital, make a recording), or just a silly title.

Lessons from the Trenches

One of my favorite events each year is Piano Idol, an in-house competition for all my students. Like *American Idol*, competitors vary in age, ability, and style. The student audience votes to determine the winner. Kids work hard for this event and love hearing their peers.

The festive competition occurs over a week (in lieu of lessons), with 10 to 12 students involved each evening. There is one grand-prize winner and smaller but fun awards, such as King of Pop or Dynamics Diva. Piano Idols are invited to perform in a separate Honors Recital.

Field Trips

Field trips to professional performances are a win for all involved. Attendees experience amazing art, the organization increases audience and impact, and SMTs strengthen student commitment. Any engaging, high-quality, and-age appropriate event can be effective. Don't feel confined to the instrument(s) you teach. In fact, rotating through a variety of experiences over time provides a broader perspective on the musical world.

Great Concert Experiences		
• Chamber groups • Dance with music • Early music • Educational events	• Jazz combos • Musicals • New music ensembles • Operas	• Orchestras • Multimedia events • Solo recitals • World music groups

SMTs often make field trips a point of studio pride and community building, inviting parents, grandparents, siblings, neighbors, and friends. This allows students to experience great music in the company of those who mean the most to them. Events that are "required" or "strongly recommended," scheduled from the beginning of the year, and enthusiastically plugged may attract as much as 200% to 300% the size of your studio. After a few seasons, expect the group size to increase for this anticipated tradition.

Ticket-selling competitions are fun ways to generate excitement and buzz. Many presenters offer groups discounts, which can be passed on to students or kept for your time.

Music on the Town

Each year, New York City–based pianist Asuka Fu (www.pianostudio545.com) organizes at least one field trip for students and their families. Attendees wore costumes to one Halloween orchestra concert. A chamber recital featuring a performer dressed and addressing the audience as Beethoven provided an engaging, historical perspective.

> While this activity does not produce direct income, her tuition model includes an extra $10 per hour to subsidize events and cover supplies such as sheet music and a metronome.

Considerations

Frequency

Scheduling the right amount of studio events is key, with the ideal number depending on who and what you teach. At a minimum, full-time SMTs host one per term, though it is not uncommon to arrange something every four to six weeks.

A steady flow of events allows students to share repertoire as it becomes ready, rather than stagnating for months. It provides regular opportunities for improving stage presence and overcoming performance anxiety. It also goes a long way toward making studio members feel like part of a vibrant community, rather than mere individuals in a lessons program.

In researching this chapter, it was interesting to discover a correlation between frequency and innovation of events. Educators with semiregular offerings tended to imagine more creative experiences than those limited to just one per year.

Monthly Recitals

Flutist/pianist Kristin Paxinos and guitarist Ben Westfall (www.dcmusicstudio.com) teach around 110 students combined. With a shared belief that performing is an essential part of the music learning experience, they host a minimum of one recital per month. Since beginning this tradition three years ago, they have held no less than 52 events; December 2013 alone featured 7! Performances—typically on Sunday afternoons—are held in the storefront they rent, which has a stage, a piano, and seating capacity for 60.

Students interested in participating must pass a preperformance hearing to demonstrate adequate preparation. While they are strongly encouraged to perform at least once every three months, many opt for more regular involvement. At least a dozen sign up monthly. One 11-year-old girl, who plays both piano and guitar, has been showcased in more than 30 shows!

Thanks to these frequent opportunities, the entire studio stays motivated, "practicing their tails off." Some members get competitive, aiming to rack up high performance credits, which are tallied in a frame by the front door.

Performers are charged $15 per event, added to their monthly tuition payment. Since shows are limited to 12 players, recitals generate up to $180.

Logistics

SMTs offering multiple events typically alternate venues. Homes, libraries, businesses, music stores, school auditoriums, religious institutions, and street fairs all present potential. Consider how the characteristics and quirks of each venue might be integrated into the experience.

Venue Considerations		
• Acoustics	• Electrical access	• Piano quality
• Audience (built in)	• Handicap accessibility	• Price
• Audience capacity	• Lighting	• Reception area
• Bathroom accessibility	• Performance area	• Seating

Most studio events last 30 to 90 minutes, depending on the age and number of participants. Shorter is better, particularly when kids are involved. Everyone is busy, and as nice as your production may be, there can be too much of a good thing. Two adjacent briefer events are preferable to an unbearably long one.

Many teachers have been shocked to find their show lasting significantly longer than anticipated. When projecting duration, don't forget about intermission (better yet, leave it out) and time between pieces (applause, resetting the stage, performers entering and exiting, tuning).

Beyond overall event duration, consider lengths of individual pieces. For beginners, even a 30-second cameo can be meaningful. Advanced students may certainly present lengthy, multiple movement works, but count on pieces over 10 to 15 minutes losing attention of younger attendees. In our attention deficit hyperactivity disorder–plagued society, extended works even elude some adults.

Think carefully about literature and sequencing, creating a program with continuity, variety, and logical form. Will it start with beginners and systematically progress to more advanced students? Open with an advanced player to immediately engage the audience? Group performances by instrument (trumpets first, then horns, then trombones)? Mix things up?

Recitals must not be limited to solo repertoire. In fact, it's often more interesting when duos, chamber groups, or even full studio ensembles are interspersed.

Before each show, think through logistical considerations:

- Where will musicians be positioned?
- Where will the audience sit/stand?
- What are the seating arrangements for performers?
- Is natural lighting sufficient, or do you need additional sources?
- If electricity is required (amplifiers, microphones, etc.), are there accessible outlets?
- Does the host have music stands, or must you supply them?
- Will the piano be tuned? Who is responsible for that expense?
- What food issues should be considered (placement, refrigeration, heating)?
- Where will guests park?

Pre-Event Rituals

The educational impact of an SMT event begins weeks before the actual delivery date. Pre-event lessons, classes, rehearsals, and blogs are great forums for addressing relevant issues like memorization, stage presence, bowing, microphone technique, memory slips, audience etiquette, active listening, and enjoying the moment. Create studio rituals that ignite your community.

Public performances can inspire self-esteem, dedication, and a passion for sharing art. Unfortunately, many students derive the opposite, developing extreme stage fright and insecurity. Attitudes and priorities stressed by teachers have a profound effect on whether this activity builds or destroys confidence. SMTs are careful to send the right message.

Timeline

Planned events should be solidified before each term or academic year begins. Clearly articulate dates, times, and locations on your newsletter and website, requesting that families save the dates and minimize conflicts. No matter how clear you are, there always seem to be a few who drop the ball, so incorporate periodic reminders.

Timeline	Activities
4–6 months prior	Set date. Secure venue. Add details (time, location, directions) to website and newsletter. Announce event to students.
1½–3 months prior	Secure lighting/sound/recording operator (if applicable). Hire accompanist (if applicable). Assign concert pieces. Remind students of performance date.
2–4 weeks prior	Send out press release to local media. Review performance strategies and etiquette. Send concert reminder email. Set order and type program. Plan reception (if applicable). Confirm with venue, accompanist, and others involved.
1–2 weeks prior	Do run-throughs with students in lessons. Employ pre-event rituals. Confirm that everyone knows the where and when. Find students or parents to: • Help set up • Pass out programs • Take photographs • Run video camera • Oversee reception • Clean up afterward Make last-minute program changes. Copy program (usually two to four times the number of performers involved). Purchase food, drinks, utensils, and paper products for reception.
Before the show	Set up (chairs, piano, stands, mics, sound, reception, etc.). Prepare video and audio equipment. Give program with notes to lighting/audio/video operator(s). Have performers arrive early and warm up. Do a sound check.

(continued)

Timeline	Activities
Event	Welcome guests. Keep things moving smoothly. Stay cool and positive. Enjoy!!!
After the show	Attend reception. Chat with performers and guests. Clean up.
1 week after	Make sure all bills are paid. Send thank you notes to anyone who helped. Upload recital photos and video to website. Reflect on experience with students.

Monetization

Though few SMTs generate substantial income from this stream, meaningful events add clear value to a comprehensive music education. Consider them part of your larger strategy.

Income Models

There are several ways to generate income through events.

Tuition Package

Rather than assessing separate fees, many SMTs build a certain amount into their tuition package to finance time and expenses related to events. Where this appears on your income blueprint is not important. Most teachers simply record it as part of their "lessons" stream.

Recital Fees

Other SMTs charge students a recital fee, either annually or per event. To determine an appropriate amount, consider the number of events per term/ year, complexity, direct expenditures, and preparation time. Fees typically range from $10 to $40 per performance or $25 to $100 per year. Some recital fees buy access to audio or video recordings as well.

Ticket Sales and Other Income Models

For traditional recitals, the wisdom of charging admission is questionable. Parents will feel nickeled and dimed if required to pay to hear their own child perform. Ticket sales or donations are acceptable, however, for themed or unusual concerts. Keep the amount low, perhaps $5 to $10. After all, tickets should not rival a Broadway show. Slightly higher prices are permissible when featuring guest artists.

Fundraisers are the exception, particularly if the cause is compelling, as many community members proudly support meaningful causes. Either charge a set ticket price or ask the audience to donate as they please. The generous level of giving may surprise you! Keep in mind that gifts are tax deductible only when given to nonprofits.

Another possibility is securing paying gigs for the studio, perhaps $50 to $150 in exchange for entertainment at a local store. While this compensation is small, every little bit helps.

Products can be sold at studio events: recordings of you and friends, video/audio of the event itself, studio merchandise, gift certificates for lessons, raffle tickets for donated goods, tickets to concerts around town.

A final option involves selling ads in your program.

Indirect Income

Interesting studio events generate indirect income, differentiating offerings while serving as a powerful recruitment tool for lessons, classes, and camps. They can also justify higher rates. Students often request additional meetings when preparing to perform. Demand is also created when involved chamber groups need coaching.

It's a Lifestyle

"Our studio is not just about flute lessons. It's a lifestyle!" This is a common claim by students of Bonnie Blanchard (www.musicforlifebooks.com), who find themselves involved with different events every six weeks or so: competitions, master classes, retirement home concerts. At the Annual Mother's Day Gala, studio members perform in ensembles, introduce one another, dress in costume, perform skits, and give moms a handwritten card. In lieu of a spring recital, they travel to a recording studio, make a DVD, and post videos to YouTube.

The summer retreat is a highlight. Each August, over 20 students plus chaperones travel to a resort in the mountains 2½ hours away. Staying in eight rented condos, they experience an intense three-day agenda of fluting, master classes with college professors, musical games, swimming, and community building.

These experiences are undoubtedly meaningful, but how do they impact Blanchard's financial model? For the retreat, participants pay around $475, which covers expenses and compensates their beloved teacher the equivalent of an hour lesson (24 students × $75 lesson fee = $1,800 for the event).

Blanchard does not charge a recital fee, but there are indirect economic benefits. For example, flute ensembles rehearse an average of five times to prepare for the Mother's Day Gala, with a flat fee of $15 per student per hour (meaning duets bring just $30, but a 10-person group generates $150). Demand for these meetings is high, since the show is just weeks away.

The constant stream of happenings keeps students committed. Almost all take summer lessons to prepare for the retreat. In fact, several sign up for two weekly meetings, and one apprentice recently paid $600 to live with Blanchard for a week in exchange for daily lessons, personalized projects, and shadowing. "Most teachers see a decrease in summer income. Mine actually goes up."

Expenses

Most studio events carry related expenses. Consider them cost of goods sold (COGS), since they exist only in tandem with the event. Deduct this amount when calculating income.

Possible Event Expenses	
• Accompanist(s)	• Program design/printing
• Audio system rental	• Reception drinks
• Decorations	• Reception food
• Guest artist fee	• Reception supplies
• Piano rental	• Student awards (trophies, certificates)
• Piano tuning	• Venue rental

There are usually ways to curb expenses. Parents may be willing to contribute, volunteering their home, serving as an accompanist, or catering. Churches, music stores, and other venues often donate space as part of a barter agreement or in exchange for ads in your program booklet. Some businesses gladly provide in-kind donations for the tax write-off, particularly when an employee has a child involved with your studio.

The Savvy Music Teacher Income Blueprint

Following our blueprint, the SMT arranges three to five varied and meaningful events annually (one to two each in fall, spring, and summer). A recital fee of $50 to $100 helps make this possible (either built in to tuition or charged separately). Related expenses run $500 to $1,250 per year, not including donated and bartered items.

# of Students	Recital Fee	Gross Income	(COGS)	Net Annual Income
30	$50	$1,500	($500)	**$1,000**
30	$80	$3,000	($1,250)	**$1,750**

From events (stream 4), the SMT earns between $1,000 and $1,750 per year.

TECHNOLOGY: STREAM 5

In an era where many industries have been crippled by technological breakthroughs, some skeptics have predicted doomsday for independent music teachers. Perhaps instructional videos would deem individualized lessons obsolete, virtual instruments would annihilate acoustic ones, or gifted robots would become a favored alternative to human pedagogues. Luckily, this sci-fi version of the future has not come to pass.

While the personalized, hands-on work of a gifted music teacher cannot be duplicated or replaced by gadgetry, the opposite is true as well. Certain electronic tools offer powerful features that mere mortals simply cannot emulate. Savvy Music Teachers (SMTs) recognize that the best learning environments incorporate both.

Using Technology

Purpose

The number of available technology-based resources is staggering and growing by the day, including a mountain of lesson, practice, event, and project tools that simply did not exist just decades (or even years) ago. How many of these assets must SMTs incorporate to remain hip, current, and relevant?

I have argued that the primary mission of SMTs should not be celebrating pedagogical traditions, composers of the past, authentic performance practice, or innovative solutions. The same can be said of technology. While these orientations can absolutely help define your studio and educational identity, *the primary purpose of teaching music is to serve students, families, and communities.* Everything else is secondary. Decide what you want to build before venturing into the toolbox.

Does media make your studio hipper or distract from grander learning objectives? Who is more "modern," the online teacher whose core methodology hasn't evolved in years or the one who energizes contemporary students through creative exploration but thinks a "tablet" is a just a pill? Are interactive theory games a great way to further musical commitment or unhealthy addictions that cause students to lose interest in acoustic, real-world music making? There is no one size fits all. Different students—and different studios—benefit from a diversity of approaches.

Though there is no prescribed percentage of lesson time SMTs devote to technology, it probably requires more than zero. In a world where gadgets infiltrate almost every aspect of existence, it is difficult to imagine a relevant education that completely ignores these resources. Just as an accountant relying on only abacus would seem oddly out of touch (even if doing great work), music education failing to embrace any technology misses a tremendous opportunity.

Beginning with an essential question and clearly articulated learning objectives, ask how technology can better help achieve your aims. Approaching things in this order, rather than the reverse, greatly increases the odds of achieving your greater purpose.

Gear

A fully functional SMT studio has Internet access, capacity for audio/video recording, a laptop or tablet with a variety of useful programs/apps, and perhaps an electronic keyboard. Effective setups needn't be cost prohibitive. You likely own many of these tools already, and gear gets better and less expensive with each passing year. For well under $1,000, a single tablet stocked with apps can fulfill many valuable functions.

Technology-related costs include a combination of one-time expenses (equipment, software, repairs), recurring charges (subscriptions, web hosting), and maintenance fees. Each year, consider investing in new/upgraded equipment and functionality, imagining innovative ways technology can strengthen the musical engagement of students.

SMT Technology		
Computing Devices	**Audio**	**Platforms**
• Laptop/tablet with web cam • Smartphone • Smart board	• Headphones • Mixer • Sound recorder—high quality • Speakers—high quality • Stereo microphone(s)	• Apps • Internet access • Software • Studio management software • Studio website

SMT Technology		
Instruments	**Video**	**Accessories**
• Amplification	• HD video camera	• Cables
• Clavinova	(multiple cameras,	• Carrying cases
• Effects pedals	a bonus)	• Power strip
• Electronic	• Projection/monitor	• Storage devices
instruments	• Tripod	• Wireless router
• MIDI keyboard		

Lesson Tools

Teaching Technology

Over time, technology transforms instruments. Consider an abbreviated history of the keyboard:

harpsichord → grand piano → electronic keyboard → iPad piano app

Each option provides unique benefits. Harpsichords are authentic to Baroque music; grand pianos offer the widest expressive palette; electronic keyboards produce near-infinite timbres; and the iPad solution is portable and so unique that concert pianist Lang-Lang performed an encore of *Flight of the Bumblebee* with the Magic Piano app.

Beyond instrument choice, many aspects of music offer a comparable array of products:

NOTATION:
manuscript paper → lines on whiteboard → notation software/app
RHYTHM TOOLS:
analog metronome → metronome app → recorded rhythms → drum machine
INTONATION/TUNING
ear alone → tuning fork/pitch pipe → electronic tuner → intonation apps

Which part of each spectrum should play a role in your teaching? Or is it important to incorporate them all? This is a personal decision, but one worth serious consideration.

Technology is a lesson topic in itself. Some SMTs offer instruction in areas such as recording, digital editing, sequencing, computer notation, electronic instruments, effects processing, and drum machine programming. Others integrate these aspects alongside more traditional disciplines, differentiating their studio while expanding learning outcomes.

Audio/Video Recording

When concerned with the complexities of making music, it is difficult to simultaneously concentrate on nuance or even large-scale considerations. Even skilled multitaskers experience brain overload and a loss of objectivity. Observing an audio or MIDI recording of what was just played, however, allows students to listen critically from a third-person perspective. For better or worse, recordings don't lie.

To facilitate, many SMTs permanently house a high-quality recording device (along with playback capabilities) in their teaching space. Taped passages can be critiqued by teacher and student immediately following a run-through or taken home for more detailed, measure-by-measure analysis. Slowing down the audio presents a brutally honest depiction, highlighting every uneven rhythm, intonation glitch, or tone inconsistency.

Video recording allows the examination of additional issues, such as stage presence and health-related performance habits, in ways with which no mirror can compete. Viewing the same footage repeatedly, perhaps with slow motion or freeze frame, allows musicians to pinpoint problems related to unhealthy posture, irregular breathing, unnatural tension, or awkward movement. Some SMTs maintain multiple cameras projecting live feeds, allowing students to observe several angles/views in real time.

Beyond "capture and critique," audio/video recordings can play many additional roles in the music learning experience. For example, students might:

1. Send a midweek recording via email to demonstrate progress between lessons
2. Transcribe music rather than starting from notation
3. Play along with recorded accompaniments, progressions, or grooves
4. Record improvisations for later compositional development
5. Compare interpretations of the same piece by master performers
6. Critique recorded performances of amateur musicians

7. Study teacher-generated recordings of assigned music as a reference
8. Bring recordings they *love* to lessons, articulating what makes that music great
9. Place lesson recordings in cloud storage, chronicling progress over time
10. Expand horizons by exploring new music each week

On the Record

Every minute of every voice lesson taught by Rachel Velarde (www.velardevoice.com) is captured on video. "This is the most hated tool I use, but also one of the most beneficial. I may make the same point 50 times, but only when a student sees the problem in real time does it register." During practice sessions, students can review footage, self-evaluate, and be reminded of major points.

With foreign language songs, Velarde commonly recites text directly into the camera so her disciples can study diction, how the mouth moves, and linguistic flow. Taping is also helpful when accompanying students on piano, making it possible for her to objectively review the footage afterward without distraction.

Velarde's Zoom HD Camera is perched permanently atop a tripod in her teaching space. Rather than wasting time transferring footage to a flash drive or website, students bring their own SD memory card and retrieve it after each lesson.

Digital Notes

Mentioning—or even stressing—something in a lesson is no guarantee it will be prioritized during practice. For greater assurance and accountability, a written record goes a long way. SMTs working with a laptop or tablet can type directly into websites like Music Teacher's Helper or word processing documents placed in a storage cloud such as Dropbox. Audio and video recordings may be uploaded to these locations as well.

Digital notes give students instant and unlimited access to feedback while providing a clear record of expectations. It also allows them to review assignments and progress over years. Say goodbye to forgotten talking points and notebooks mysteriously devoured by canines.

Lessons from the Trenches

Gone are the days of written assignment sheets or audio files lingering in parent email inboxes. I use an app called Evernote (www.evernote.com), essentially a digital assignment binder with everything at your fingertips. Document formatting options are comparable to Microsoft Word, and video/audio clips can be easily embedded.

Students with iPads bring them to lessons. A "Piano Lessons" file folder within Evernote allows us to add a new page for each meeting, providing a "paper trail" to track progress and activities, with the most recent date on top.

Video Exchange

In 2009, ArtistWorks (www.artistworks.com) introduced a radically new approach to online lessons with huge implications for the future of teaching all topics. Its superstar faculty includes Miles Davis's drummer Billy Cobham, Philadelphia Orchestra's principal clarinetist Ricardo Morales, mandolin legend Mike Marshall, and rock guitarist Paul Gilbert.

Enrolling in "lessons" with a given instructor costs $90 for three months, $150 for six months, or $240 for a year. Students gain access to "hundreds" of prerecorded instructional videos shot in HD, including slow-motion replays, multiple camera angles, sheet music, practice charts, and the ability to easily loop video segments when practicing along. Presentations are broken down by ability level or concept; students gain access to the full collection.

Though ArtistWorks lessons have high-quality content and production value, instructional videos are nothing new. What makes this service revolutionary is the *video exchange* option. Subscribers are able to upload videos of themselves playing, shot with a webcam or smartphone. Within days or weeks, the instructor provides a response video, addressing the student by name and offering personalized feedback. These student and teacher videos are linked together and placed in a central library viewable by their entire "school" so that every paying member in this exclusive community can benefit from each interaction.

This model differs radically from weekly one-on-one meetings. Though not appropriate for everyone, consider the benefits this format offers both students and teachers.

Student Benefits	Teacher Benefits
Study with your ideal teacher.	Manage more students than possible with one-on-one meetings.
There is unlimited access to a large library of instructional videos.	While there is a significant time commitment on the front end to create content, less work is required once a critical mass has been created.
View the same lesson repeatedly, as often as desired.	There is no need to teach the same lesson a zillion times.
Learn from interactions between other students and the teacher.	Individual sessions have a larger impact, since they are viewable by all students for all times.
This option costs less than private lessons.	Earning potential is more than with weekly lessons (if enough participants enroll).
Work at your convenience.	Work at your convenience.
There is a shared advantage with all online forums: no commuting, geography irrelevant, and so on.	There is a shared advantage with all online forums: no commuting and geography irrelevant.

ArtistWorks has grown into a large company representing some of the biggest names in music. While they are tightlipped about the exact business model, their most popular teachers reportedly generate six figures from this presence alone.

Though building an identical model is unlikely, technologically inclined SMTs have an opportunity to emulate this approach. The long-term potential impact and income payoff is huge.

Lesson Subscriptions

Adam Nitti Music Education (www.adamnittimusiceducation.com) features an ever-growing library of instructional videos for electric bass shot in HD. Rather than a random assortment of lessons, it features a logical curriculum-based approach with categories such as "technique," "ear training," "theory," "improvisation," "style," and "reading." With

150+ lessons for beginners through professionals, most videos are 9 to 18 minutes in duration.

Standard membership begins at $25 per month, though there are discounts when subscribing to quarterly or yearly plans. This buys access to the full lesson library and "bonus content" (live performances, interviews, studio footage). It also includes a "virtual advisor," helping students determine the best lesson choices based on playing level. Premium memberships, starting at $50 per month, also include entry to live webcast master classes and a "feedback forum" for submitting questions or work samples that receive personalized feedback.

Creating initial content before the launch required hundreds of hours, and Nitti continues to populate competencies with new lessons. In a typical month, two long days are spent recording videos, two more editing and tagging, and another two planning and giving master classes. As the library grows, his time commitment will diminish but not disappear, since subscribers expect a steady stream of new resources.

Creating a sophisticated website like this is a long-term investment. Getting started required a $10,000 investment and full year of working closely with a developer. Within six months, there were some 80 subscribers, about a third of whom selected the premium membership.

Though Nitti sees this model increasing in popularity, he concedes it is not for everyone. "Part of what people are looking for is a direct connection to the artist or instructor. The challenge is finding ways to offer personalized interactions with students online. I also have an active playing career, which attracts many people to the site. In a world of infinite choices, there has to be a motivating attraction—a renowned reputation, engaging teaching style, entertaining sense of humor, or other unique element."

Practice Tools

A Digital Partner

While technology can add value to lessons, it is transformative when integrated into regular practice. Many tools help students stay focused, learn more, and enjoy the process.

Imagine, for example, a program allowing learners to practice with orchestrated accompaniments, adjust the tempo, record run-throughs, assess performance, and compare takes. These are just a few of the features provided by SmartMusic (www.smartmusic.com). In addition to providing the world's largest solo accompaniment library, it offers fingering charts, ear training drills, improvisation exercises, an interface to submit assignments, and a grade book that allows teachers to view progress and monitor how much time students practice. Yearly subscriptions run $140 for teachers ($11.67 per month) and $40 for students ($3.33 per month).

Smart Practice

Violinist Lisa Creason (www.creasonstudios.com) has her students interface with a number of technological tools when practicing. SmartMusic is particularly effective for the little ones. Accompaniments from Suzuki books are available, and unlike the corresponding CD, this program allows musicians to easily adjust the tempo or isolate short passages. It can also mark incorrect notes or rhythms in red as they play. "SmartMusic is very picky, which is very good."

SmartMusic comes in handy for older students as well, particularly those in public schools where music teachers use the program as an assessment tool. Creason also loves how easily her own compositions, when notated in Finale, can be imported into its library.

For advanced students working to master shifting or other challenging techniques, she offers "Practice with Lisa" recordings, which allow studio members to imitate or practice along with their teacher at home. Students also work with a number of apps, including Violin Multi-Tuner, which plays drones for scale practice.

Practice Apps

A variety of apps are designed to make practice sessions more efficient and effective. Tablets loaded with relevant programs are great assets to any SMT teaching or warm-up space. Students who purchase these can reap the rewards at home. While new products are developed regularly, here is a sampling of programs, demonstrating a range of educational benefits.

Practice Apps		
Name	*Price*	*Description*
Music Journal Pro	$6.99	Set practice goals, time practice sessions (per activity and overall), track progress, work with a metronome.
Recorder Plus + HD	$2.99	Recording and reviewing practice sessions are extremely valuable for musicians of all ages and abilities. This app features decent quality sound recording, nondestructive editing, track organizing by category, text and photo annotation, and the ability to easily transfer files to other programs.
Tempo—Frozen Ape	$1.99	Sophisticated metronome that allows you to choose various meters, mute or accent beats, add subdivisions, create intricate click tracks, and make set lists.
Cleartune	$3.99	Chromatic tuner with settings for various instruments, transpositions, and temperaments.
Amazing Slow Downer	$14.99	Slow down audio by up to 25% without altering pitch or clarity. Helpful when transcribing or practicing along. Includes adjustable looping, transposition, and pan controls.
Avid Scorch	$1.99	View and play back scores created with the notation program Sibelius, change key and tempo, move between standard notation and guitar tab, view just the staves you want to see.
Voice Coach	$4.99	Warm-up, warm-down, and other exercises for singers. Let's you set range and tempo. Other helpful apps for singers: **Voice Tutor** ($4.99); **VoiceJam** ($6.99); **Italian/ French/German Diction for Singers** ($.99 each).

(continued)

Practice Apps		
Name	*Price*	*Description*
Fingering charts (app category)	Variable	**Fingering Strings** (beautiful app for bowed strings, $5.99); **Fingering for iPad** (beautiful app for wind instruments, trill options, $9.99); **FingeringCharts Pro** (for 21 wind instruments, $2.99); **Violin/Fiddle Fingering Chart** ($1.99); **ChordBankPro** (guitar chords, $3.99).
Scales/Arpeggios (app category)	Variable	**Scales Book** (method for woodwinds and brass, $7.99); **Piano Companion** ($2.99); **Scale Wizard** (for guitar, $.99); **Scales & Modes** (for piano, guitar, violin, bass guitar, $1.99); **Trumpeteer** ($.99); **Flute Scales** ($1.99); **Practice My Saxophone Scales** ($1.99).

Lessons from the Trenches

I am an iPad addict, and the educational benefits of this amazing device have transformed my teaching and studio! My top 10 SMT apps are:

1. **ForScore.** Read PDFs of music scores directly on your tablet.
2. **Educreations.** Music instruction, which allows educators to record their voice and draw while explaining concepts.
3. **Evernote.** Record keeping and organization.
4. **Flash Note Derby.** Note naming for beginners.
5. **GoodEar.** A series of specialized music theory apps on (a) intervals, (b) scales, (c) "pro," (d) chords, and (e) melodies.
6. **Tenuto.** Thirteen customizable exercises and five calculators addressing written and aural theory.
7. **Zite.** Customizable magazine for personal and professional development.
8. **MusicNotes.** Every piece of music purchased from their website magically appears here.
9. **Yamaha's NoteStar.** Provides backing track to pop songs.
10. **Spotify.** Paid subscription allows advertisement-free streaming of just about any recording imaginable.

Musicianship Tools

Developing solid musicianship requires more than playing or singing well. Software, websites, and apps help students develop additional aptitudes by providing games, flashcards, charts, repetitive drilling, and information centers. These tools save lesson time and broaden engagement. Some are free, others charge a one-time fee, and still others require subscriptions. The strongest programs are generally geared toward beginning or intermediate musicians.

Technology Musicianship Categories		
• Analysis	• Intervals	• Notation
• Chord symbols	• Keys/key signatures	• Note reading
• Chords	• Meter	• Rhythmic concepts
• Counterpoint	• Music history	• Scales
• Ear training	• Music literature	• Sight reading
• Fundamentals	• Music styles	• Solfege
• Instrument properties	• Music terminology	• Theory

Music Learning Community (www.musiclearningcommunity.com) provides 450 colorful, interactive games to its 75,000 subscribing studios, schools, and families. Geared toward beginning and intermediate musicians, some involve MIDI keyboards, while others require only a laptop or tablet. Activities, which can be organized by subscribing teachers, address musical literacy, ear training, and keyboard skills. A subscription of $20 per month or $219 per year buys full library access for up to 50 students. The price is halved for studios with fewer than 10 students.

A number of websites and apps address music theory and ear training. The free MusicTheory.net presents lessons and exercises around note reading, rhythm and meter, scales and key signatures, intervals, chords, and progressions. Also complimentary is Good-Ear.com, focused on aural identification of intervals, chords, scales, and cadences.

Teoría (www.teoria.com) investigates both theory and ear training. Though complimentary access is available, the annual $20 fee allows members to save scores and track progress. Teachers who join can create groups for their studio, monitor exercises completed, and view scores. Discounted rates are available for larger groups.

To date, no single comprehensive music history website or app exists for kids. Perhaps that is too big a topic, but there are many good resources, including the following:

- **Young Person's Guide to the Orchestra** (www.listeningadventures.carnegiehall.org/ypgto, free). Take a safari to learn about orchestral instruments, using Benjamin Britten's composition as a guide.
- **NY Philharmonic Kidzone** (www.nyphilkids.org/games, free). This website includes a number of activities where visitors learn about instruments and musicians, create original music, build an instrument, and more.
- **Classics for Kids** (www.classicsforkids.com, free). This website, app, and podcast include composer bios, quizzes, recordings, and games.

The Practice Loop

Bass, guitar, and cello teacher Brittany Frompovich (www.ladybassmusic.net) regularly incorporates "loopers" (looping pedals or apps) into lessons and encourages students to integrate them at home as part of their "deliberate practice" routine.

At the most basic level, loopers are powerful, user-friendly recording devices. Frompovich has students capture run-throughs, listen back, and mark problematic aspects in the score. "This immediate feedback produces incredible results, helping students advance quickly while developing their inner ear." They can also compare multiple takes, develop rhythmic accuracy with the built-in metronome, adjust the tempo, or practice with stored recordings of themselves or the teacher.

Loopers are also great tools for stimulating creativity, teaching improvisation, and applying theory concepts. Some students record a bass line and improvise over the harmonies. Others produce multilayered compositions with interlocking rhythms, thick harmonies, or sophisticated counterpoints. "Loopers have quickly become a staple of the practice studio. It not only helps students of all genres improve but also makes their practice more purpose driven."

Instructional Videos

While instructional videos have not usurped the need for independent music teachers, they do facilitate valuable supplemental learning. SMTs often incorporate videos that:

- Allow students to access vital information—perhaps an upcoming event or composer of the month—avoiding the time dump of repeating the same message
- Expose students to various topics (e.g., scales, rhythm, form) when they reach a certain level, allowing them to view the footage as many times as desired
- Demonstrate a technique (e.g., how to move your wrist), to be consulted while practicing
- Provide a reference practice recording

Many SMTs utilize preexisting material, embedding videos on their website or providing links. Others prefer original content. Creating your own instructional videos not only helps studio members but also contributes to the canon of available resources. In addition, they demonstrate teaching abilities, serving as marketing while building credibility.

Many instructional music videos are available for free through sites like YouTube and Vimeo. Others require a purchase. For example, On the Music Path is a free iPad app through which users can purchase high-definition video lessons (45 to 85 minutes in duration) for $2 to $20.

Lessons from the Trenches

After eight years of introducing five-finger major/minor patterns the same way, I decided there had to be a better way to maximize lesson time and save my sanity. The solution appeared when a student showed me how her school uses a program called Edmodo (www.edmodo.com) to create a "flipped classroom" environment, where students are introduced to new content online and then utilize class time for practicing with the teacher. This app/program, free and web based, changed my entire approach to theory training.

All theory lessons from preparatory through level 4 are class driven, created for groups of 20 students rather than individuals. The core content is explained through videos I created using ScreenFlow (www. telestream.net/screenflow), Classroom Maestro (www.zenph.com/cm3), and Educreations (www.educreations.com). Now in lessons, all I have to do is check assignments and address questions. This requires two minutes per lesson each week, versus eight the old way, and students progress exponentially faster. (Video example: www.vimeo.com/73641588)

Event Tools

Event Recording

Unlike a painting, which can adorn a wall for centuries on end, live music is an art form that moves through time. Each recital has a distinct beginning, middle, and end. Missing it means forgoing an experience never to be duplicated.

The moment can, however, be captured in an audio or video recording. This souvenir is not only exciting in the weeks and months that follow but also a wonderful flash from the past years down the road. (I still get choked up watching concert videos from my youth.)

A sophisticated mic system or multiple camera rig is certainly possible, but recordings mustn't be fancy to be effective. Even a high-quality recording app or static image from a single camera may sufficiently secure meaningful memories. Recordings can be burned to physical CDs/DVDs, uploaded to YouTube public/private channels, or made available through your website with a valid password.

In addition to preserving memories, recital videos are instructive. They allow you and the student to evaluate stage presence, facial expressions, bows, spoken announcements, and the performance itself. Video is helpful leading up to concerts as well. In the minds of most students (and pros!), run-throughs for a live camera are a terrific way to simulate the energy, focus, butterflies, and sweaty palms of performance.

Lessons from the Trenches

Inspired by a presentation challenging independent teachers to consider performance opportunities outside the traditional recital format, I realized that any positive musical experience is better than one students dread. Rather than hosting a holiday recital that year, I offered mini 30-minute recording sessions for $30. Students brought flash drives and walked away with professional-quality recordings of recital pieces and holiday music to give to family and friends. They could design their own CD cover or email digital copies.

I earned an extra $1,500 (less the piano tuning) for about 25 hours of additional work over three days. The best part? Students were ecstatic!

Live Streaming

Until recently, audiences interested in witnessing a live studio recital had to:

1. Travel to the performance venue—out of the question for nonlocal friends/relatives
2. Fit in the performance venue—often problematic for big studios using houses or other small sites

Both of these challenges can be rectified when events are streamed online. In fact, some SMTs now schedule streaming-only shows, where performers are the only folks to set foot in the hall.

Viewing Lessons from Home

Pianist Andres Hartmann (www.ppiano.com) keeps a webcam in his studio to film and stream lessons. This way, parents can view the action from the comfort of home or other locations via a password-protected site.

Digital Scores

When hosting events, SMTs finally have an alternative to the messy stack of books and awkward-looking page turner. The app forScore allows PDF documents and scans to be loaded onto a tablet. To turn the page, simply tap the screen or use a Bluetooth foot pedal (such as AirTurn BT-105, with two pedals for moving forward or backward). This program allows users to make markings on the score, rearrange pages, account for repeats, view one or two pages at a time, set up loops, create set lists, add bookmarks, and more.

Event Design

Technology transforms events. Electro-acoustic compositions, lighting, slides, silent movies, or a live projected video feed goes a long way to impact the atmosphere. When students help design these aspects, it also taps into creative potential.

Plugged-in Shows

With the tagline "fusing music technology with private lessons," pianist Stephen Hughes (www.musicalaccents.net) incorporates most approaches from this chapter and more: lesson recording; instructional videos created with the interactive whiteboard app Doceri; customized YouTube channels for each student; lesson notes in DropBox; and a huge range of apps including the SmartMusic-like interface Home Concert Xtreme. Hughes even incentivizes progress with iReward, which tracks points over the year and enters students in a drawing to win $100.

Not surprisingly, technology also plays a prominent role in studio recitals. During transitions, videos featuring students (describing historical significance or what they love about the music) are projected. These vignettes, typically 30 seconds, are filmed during lessons. When playing begins, a beautiful slide designed by his wife is shown, including the title, performer's name, and a related image. Videos and slides are organized through PowerPoint.

Hughes recently began streaming events, viewable by family and friends unable to attend. Past performance videos are available to students via YouTube and the studio website.

You may assume that Hughes has advanced degrees in computer science, but this is not the case. "I learned these tools myself. Incorporating a little at a time, the benefits were so great that technology ultimately became central to my teaching philosophy."

Project Tools
Studio Recordings

Though anyone today can make a decent audio recording on a laptop, tablet, or smartphone, a studio-quality product generated with professional microphones and sophisticated software is still superior. Imagine the thrill that occurs when advanced, intermediate, or even beginning students experience a "professional recording session." Whether the goal is a well-documented run-through or digitally edited masterpiece, this activity motivates and inspires. The final product provides permanent evidence of talent and hard work, treasured for years to come.

With equipment and expertise, one possibility is recording in your own teaching space, either during normally scheduled lessons or additional meetings.

An alternative is hiring an engineer and traveling to an external location with excellent acoustics such as a church, concert hall, or professional recording studio. Working in a new environment provides a shot in the arm. Since there are usually costs associated, make sure you understand the full economic ramifications.

Treat the recording experience as an exciting, educational journey. Before the big day, break down the process, answer questions, and involve students in devising a recording strategy (three complete passes, music broken into chunks, and so on). During the session, explain microphone selection/placement, explore equipment and software, and welcome feedback. Afterward, challenge participants to make edit choices. In some cases, technologically savvy individuals may possess the skills to edit recordings on their own.

Do It Like the Pros

Each year, Natalie Weber (www.musicmattersblog.com) organizes a yearlong practice incentive system for her students based around a particular concept or problem such as sight reading. When students successfully pass a hurdle, they are rewarded with "diligence dollars" (fun-looking currency designed by Weber).

At the end of one year, the top dozen earners won a trip to a major recording studio. Their three-hour field trip began with a tour of the facilities, examining fancy microphones, isolation chambers, and the impressive control room. Each participant then recorded a favorite piece on the beautiful nine-foot Steinway. Needless to say, students loved the experience and emerged with a souvenir for life.

For a community-building activity, why not "release" a studio "album" on your own studio "label"? No, you don't need to mass-produce and shrink-wrap 2,000 units. Instead, go low tech. Burn copies from your computer and have students decorate personalized adhesive labels. In addition to creating a sense of pride and kinship, this provides an item that can be sold or gifted—what a meaningful stocking stuffer! While downloads are not as much fun as physical products, they offer a lower-cost alternative and can drive traffic to your website.

Music Videos

Having students produce or star in their own music video presents an electrifying challenge. It gets them to consider aesthetic response, create a narrative, and make personal choices. Using photos, downloaded graphics, original artwork, captions, live shots, previously existing footage, self-generated video, and voiceovers, students can imagine their own concept, set minidocumentaries, or simply have fun. This can be every bit as creative and inspiring as composing music. Better yet, most students have all the tools and knowledge they need.

Uploading videos to sites like YouTube for the world to see can:

- Motivate students to practice in order to represent themselves well
- Instill pride and enthusiasm, since videos make them a little "famous"
- Serve as powerful marketing for the studio

Empowering through Technology

For British pianist Reuben Vincent (www.reubenvincent.co.uk), technology is more than a pedagogical supplement. It presents an opportunity to empower, engage, and inspire creativity.

Periodically, students as young as age 5 take "snapshots" of their musical activity. Recordings are made when pieces reach performance level, and a studio CD is "released" each year, giving participants an exciting keepsake to share with relatives or friends. Students submit cover art entries, with voting or a jury determining the winner.

Though learners work hard on standard literature, they are also encouraged to become composers. A Class Music Book—a computer notation compilation of studio compositions—rests on an end table for all to peruse. When the electronic collection circulates, students pick pieces by peers to learn and critique.

Video plays a particularly significant role. Students regularly create "film scores" or add visual dimensions to their own performance recordings. At its simplest, projects showcase a run-through shot by single camera. But others explore further, incorporating photographs, PowerPoint slides, opening/closing titles, or preexisting footage. For the grade one piece "Walking Fingers," a young student created a stop animation production of LEGO figures. Another, who had just recorded "Creepy Crawly," assembled a sequence of photos showing an inflatable spider sneaking up on an unsuspecting person napping. The final note is accompanied by a blood-curdling scream.

More than a fun activity for performers of all ages, video creation can aid musicality. "Sometimes there are students who have trouble connecting with musical content. They play with their heads, but not their hearts. When producing videos, however, they imagine a story. Giving direction and deepening connection, the transformation can be truly marvelous."

A friendly video competition ascends to the next level. This challenges students to produce creative statements, and anything music related is fair game: reflections on the learning experience, practice diaries, experimental music making, original compositions, creative montages on top of recorded performance. Or take the opposite approach, inviting everyone to set original video to the same recording. Embed these on your studio site, and have visitors or judges vote on favorites. This practice is so unusual and interesting that it may even be newsworthy to local media.

Monetization

There are four primary ways SMTs generate revenue through technology. The first is **direct income**, comparable to other aspects of our blueprint: money exchanged for a particular product or service. Perhaps recital DVDs cost $30 apiece.

A second option is generating **passive income**. Though work is required on the front end to create valuable products or content, sales and distribution are automated, allowing you to earn income even when sleeping. Examples include the following:

- Subscriptions to your content-rich website
- One-time memberships to your content-rich website
- Access to instructional videos
- Digital downloads of your recorded music, print music, ebooks, or recital/concert videos
- Downloads of apps you create
- Advertising revenue from vendors on your website or public videos

A third solution is charging students a fixed, mandatory **technology fee**, typically $50 to $100 annually. This covers all media-related expenses, buying students access to an assortment of valuable tools: web-based resources, lesson video/audio recording, recital DVDs. If you require a technology fee, give people their money's worth.

A final option, and SMT favorite, is requiring a **technology lab** as part of the tuition package. No, this does not require a state-of-the-art facility with 10 fancy keyboards, computers galore, and a disco ball. Instead, it is feasible with minimal equipment and preparation. Technology labs do not require additional teaching time, yet they can raise annual income by thousands while enhancing student learning. Now that I have your attention, see how it works in the following vignette.

Technology Labs

It sounds like a riddle: Each hour, two students arrive at the studio of Leila Viss (www.88pianokeys.me) for 60-minute sessions, yet they do not take group lessons. There is only one teacher and one room. How is this possible?

The answer is that learners encounter two distinct experiences: a piano lesson and a "technology lab." While one is at the keyboard, the other sits at a table just feet away, working on music-related computer software or apps. A half hour later, they switch positions. Most of the teacher's attention is focused on the piano, but she can easily shift between the two stations as necessary. How's that for educational multitasking?

Viss, author of the book *The iPad Piano Studio* (www.ipadpianostudio.com), is constantly in search of interesting music apps that engage and challenge studio members. In fact, she has two tablets loaded with options and is currently shopping for a third. At the beginning of each hour-long meeting, she unveils the surprise task(s) to be completed during the lab. Focus might be on intervals, ear training, theory, sight reading, music history, or something else. "Today," she explains, "it is so easy to find just the right assignment for students."

When possible, Viss schedules lessons/labs with siblings or performers of comparable ages and abilities. In addition to technology work, they can play the occasional duet, coach one another, or learn by listening in on their partner's lesson. But counterintuitive pairings that have resulted from scheduling complications can also be effective. She recalls a sweet friendship that blossomed between an eighth-grade boy and a first-grade girl.

The benefits of labs are numerous. Students develop musicianship and technological skills while playing fun, educational video games in a supervised setting. Parents love having the full hour, just enough time to run errands. The teacher earns more per hour and watches students grow at a quicker pace. From a financial perspective, Viss recommends charging your typical lesson fee plus an extra one third to one half for the lab.

The Savvy Music Teacher Income Blueprint

Scenario A

SMT trombonist Mitt Dampfer regularly integrates video into curriculum. An HD camera resides upon a tripod in the corner of his studio. Portions of lessons are recorded and then examined during meetings or uploaded to private YouTube channels for student review. Once a month, he films and posts helpful instructional content for students. Mitt also takes video footage of recitals, made downloadable to families with a password.

His main expenses were the camera and related accessories, costing $1,500. Though the equipment was purchased outright last year, he *amortizes* the amount over three years in his SMT blueprint. In other words, since this technology is expected to last at least 36 months, one third of the expense ($500) is deducted from his economic calculations each year. Mitt's 30 students pay a $50 annual technology fee (totaling $1,500).

Scenario B

SMT Abe Forforty, an oboist with impeccable intonation, believes in the power of educational technology. His 30 students pay a $100 technology fee (generating $3,000) and gain access to all the fantastic resources available through SmartMusic and Music Learning Community. The subscription to SmartMusic costs him $1,340 per year ($140 for the instructor plus $40 per student), and Music Learning Community requires $240, bringing expenses to $1,580.

Scenario C

SMT P. Anne O'Bench, an Irish keyboardist, added a required technology lab this year. Instead of paying $25 for 30 minutes, her 40 students each now spend $35 for a 60-minute lesson/lab. With two students in attendance at a time, her hourly income leapt from $50 to $70, an astounding 40% increase. P. Anne's lab is offered only when school is in session, 30 times per year. Therefore, the $20 hourly rate increase allows her annual income to grow by *$12,000*. To be clear, her workload has not increased, only revenue. What a game changer!

$20/hour lab fee × 20 hours per week × 30 lessons per school year = $12,000

There are some expenses necessary to make this arrangement work. In the first year, P. Anne spent lavishly, devoting $1,500.

P. Anne's Lab-Related Expenses	
Fancy tablet (e.g., iPad)	$600
MIDI keyboard	$500
Lots of cool apps	$400
TOTAL	$1,500

All of these items should last well beyond one year. Though $400 is a lot to spend on apps (since most are free or less than $20), P. Anne bought 40 fancy ones averaging $10 apiece.

Scenario	Gross Income	(COGS)	Net Annual Income
A	$1,500	($500)	$1,000
B	$3,000	($1,580)	$1,420
C	$12,000	($1,500)	$10,500

From technology (stream 5), the SMT earns between $1,000 and $10,500 per year.

8 PRODUCTS: STREAM 6

Music is not just a service industry. Each year, Americans spend millions of dollars on music-related products including instruments, accessories, sheet music, instructional materials, paraphernalia, recordings, and technology. As a Savvy Music Teacher (SMT), you are already an expert on many of these things: testing instruments, assigning repertoire, prescribing learning tools, recommending accessories, directing students to great retailers. There are savvy ways to turn these aptitudes into income. Many options increase impact and name recognition as well.

While nobody pursues all options in this chapter, choose a few that resonate with your interests. Monetization is incorporated throughout, rather than discussed separately at the end.

Sales

Dealership

If you have what it takes to peddle sizeable volume of a musical brand or product (instruments, accessories, and so forth), you could become a dealer. This is not an option to take lightly, as it means operating a second business, often with significant upfront investment.

Every manufacturer maintains a yearly sales minimum that must be met by dealers. After all, they want to partner with merchants who expand their market share and reach new consumers. Depending on the company, that could range from $2,500 to $15,000+. Some businesses require dealerships to operate from brick-and-mortar storefronts, while others are fine with a home office and Internet sales.

Manufacturers offer retailers a discount of anywhere between 5% and 50% off the list price, depending on a number of variables. Forty percent is average; expect smaller margins for high-end instruments. Since music retailers typically sell products for less than list price, however, earned income is typically around 20% to 25%. For example, let's say a trombone lists for $1,000. As the dealer, you receive a 40% discount, or a $600 purchase price. If the brass eventually sells for $800, you gross $200 (20% of list price).

Problem Solving

As is so often the case, it started with a problem. Canadian harpist Alison Vardy (www.alisonvardy.com) had students in need of instruments, but few local stores carried quality products. Despite her lack of business experience, research suggested that starting a dealership wasn't that hard, and she dove in.

Over time, her venture West Coast Harps (www.westcoastharps. com) grew. In its best year, she moved $140,000 with a 25% profit margin ($140,000 sales × 25% profit margin = $35,000). While hardly a full-time living, this niche enterprise provides a healthy supplement.

Today, Vardy sells harps, hammered dulcimers, and bowed psalteries. The five suppliers she represents are small, typically one- to two-person operations. Most have no minimum sales requirements, though one only signs with vendors maintaining a permanent physical display space (which she has at home). At any given time, there are some 30 instruments in inventory.

Vardy also rents her own harps, often in combination with instruction. For $160 per month, renters gain access to one of seven Celtic harps plus two lessons. For $80, retirees can enroll in her harpsicle (26-string lap harp) class at a senior center, which meets for four weekly 90-minute sessions. Use of an instrument during class periods is included, but bringing one home between sessions costs an extra $50 per term.

Buying and Selling

A more manageable strategy for SMTs hoping to sell the occasional instrument or accessory is finding great deals through pawnshops, instrument technicians, or Internet sites like eBay. These products can then be resold for a profit, perhaps with repair/refurbishing.

A related strategy is purchasing in-demand supplies in bulk (e.g., strings, reeds) and then vending items individually. This saves students the hassle of driving to a store or waiting for an Internet order, and clients are guaranteed a product sanctioned by you, the teacher. Shop around for the best price so you can resell at a fair amount while generating a profit.

Music-Related Accessories		
• Amplifiers	• Instrument stands	• Mutes
• Bows	• Mallets	• Recordable CDs
• Cables	• Manuscript paper	• Reeds
• Cases	• Metronomes	• Rosin
• Chairs/stools/thrones	• Microphones	• Software
• Chinrests	• Mixing boards	• Straps
• Digital recorders	• Mouthpieces	• Strings
• Effects pedals	• Music magazines	• Tote bags
• Effects processors	• Music stands	• Tuners

Lessons from the Trenches

Years ago, when looking to buy a grand piano for my studio, I came across an amazing Yamaha upright. The owners needed to sell it quickly because of an unexpected out-of-state move.

I looked up the piano model number and did some research on www. bluebookofpianos.com. Much to my surprise, similar instruments sold on eBay for $2,500 and retailed at dealers for $5,500. I snatched it for $650 and sold it to a student for $1,500 plus moving expenses. Though my price could have been higher, I wanted to pass along a great deal. Six years later, her family still loves the instrument.

Manufacturing

Homemade, with Care

For years, bassoonist Katherine Holland (www.hollandbassoon.com) made reeds for her students. But when band directors and other regional teachers began making inquiries, she started a side business.

Holland Custom Reeds currently offers three product lines: hand-crafted reed blanks ($10), student reeds ($20), and professional reeds ($30). In an average month, 6 to 10 customers purchase two to four units apiece. She spends three or four hours weekly manufacturing 10 to 12 products. Her stockpile has grown so that when orders arrive at busy times, the inventory exists.

In the near future, Holland hopes to grow the business into a subscription model, providing a reliable and steady income stream. An elite group of subscribers paying a fixed price automatically receive a given amount of reeds per month. Dropping the plan makes you ineligible to place orders and allows someone else to enroll.

Saxophonist Stephen Pollock (www.stephen-pollock.com) recalls the ugly, flimsy cardboard music folders they used to hand out in college band. Seeking a better solution, he made his own beautiful, durable leather version. Like Holland, he started selling them commercially after musicians expressed an interest in obtaining their own.

Each folder requires six hours of labor. However, most work can be done while watching TV or listening to music. With more than 1,000 folders in circulation, Pollock typically gets 30 to 60 orders per year. The folders are a great gift item, and Pollock's busiest times are around graduations and the holidays. "This income stream has definitely made a difference." He currently charges $150 apiece. Earnings have paid for trips, car payments, and living expenses. Future plans include more customizability, with different sizes, colors, and engraving options.

Another possibility is building instruments or accessories yourself. In this case, the investment is materials and—just as important—time. If you enjoy making these things anyway, why not incorporate them into your business model? For some SMTs, manufacturing is a welcome hobby that provides limited income. Others create an empire that grows exponentially over time.

KinderFluting

Over 25 years of teaching, KinderFlute founder Kathy Blocki (www. blockiflute.com) consistently observed young flute players (and older ones) directing their air stream in the wrong angle. To help, Blocki created Pneumo Pro, a headjoint-shaped device that fits into the body of a flute to assist with tone production. Spinning wheels show exactly where air is aimed.

Working with an engineer, she developed a series of prototypes. Version 1.0 was made of wood, with 48 independent pieces assembled by hand. It was a fairly expensive product, listing at $59, and just 25 units sold in the first year.

Blocki continued investing time and money into new prototypes. Designing a plastic version required $5,000, and $50,000 was the price tag for a mold. She then paid to manufacture 5,000 units. Financed entirely with personal savings, such a large and risky investment made her understandably nervous. But she believed in its potential and acted with prudence. The business is now profitable, with more than 25,000 units sold over 3½ years at $30 apiece.

Blocki is working on a second product called the Flute Tutor. This $25 frame, which rests on the right shoulder to keep a flute straight, forces players to adjust their embouchure rather than rolling the instrument. She also sells seven self-published flute method books and an instructional DVD, in addition to serving as a dealer for Di Zhao and Nuvo flutes.

Merchandising

Merchandising is fun, builds pride in your studio, and helps with marketing. Purchase a quantity of customized items at a discounted price, incorporating a design with your studio logo and meaningful text or images. Perhaps students submit original artwork, with the best one(s) etched into your treasure. Around the holidays or throughout the year, sell these items (sometimes called *merch*) at a profit. People will want them because they're amusing, beautiful, useful, and personal, while celebrating an organization they support. Introducing a contrasting product each season is better than bombarding clients with endless supplies of coffee mugs.

Customizable Items		
• Baseball caps	• Money clips	• Studio yearbooks
• Calendars	• Mouse pads	• Sweatshirts
• Coasters	• Photo albums	• T-shirts
• Coffee mugs	• Placemats	• Teddy bears
• Cutting boards	• Puzzles	• Tote bags
• Gloves	• Scarves	• Travel mugs
• Hats	• Socks	• Wine glasses

A number of companies offer low prices for decent-quality, attractively designed paraphernalia sold in quantity. Shop around for a desirable design and manufacturing price. The trick is ordering the right amount. Large quantities trigger less cost per unit, but a great price on 300 trinkets that go unsold isn't helpful to your bottom line. A better policy is taking prepayments from families (think Girl Scout cookies), ensuring that most or all of the supply is claimed.

How much can you expect to sell? With 30 private students and a little proactivity, moving 50 units may be possible without breaking a sweat. For example:

- 20 bought by existing lesson students/families for themselves
- 10 bought by existing students as gifts for relatives, neighbors, and so forth
- 5 purchased by alumni students
- 15 sold to family members, friends, neighbors, fans, and students in your classes

If hoping to peddle more—say, 120 to 150 (4 to 5 per student)—host a studio-wide selling competition, awarding a prize to the top mover.

Consider a hypothetical five-year cycle, selling 50 to 150 units per year. The chart to follow shows your costs, selling price, and profit.

Year	Product	Unit Cost	# of Units	Investment	Retail Price	Gross Profit	Net Profit
1	T-shirt	($5)	50–150	($250–$750)	$18	$900–$2,700	$650–$1,950
2	Coffee mug	($3)	50–150	($150–$450)	$10	$500–$1,500	$350–$1,050
3	Tote bag	($15)	50–150	($750–$2,250)	$30	$1,500–$4,500	$750–$2,250
4	Baseball caps	($7)	50–150	($350–$1,050)	$19	$950–$2,850	$600–$1,800
5	4 wine glasses	($11)	50–150	($550–$1,650)	$25	$1,250–$3,750	$700–$2,100
						AVERAGE	$610–$1,830

Recordings represent an obvious category of merchandise for musicians. While the details of bringing a recording to market fall outside the scope of this book, financial considerations are comparable to issues discussed in the following section on publishing.

Teaching, Playing, and a Whole Lot More

Though Scottish fiddler Ed Pearlman (www.edpearlman.net) earns the majority of his living teaching and playing, he also sells a variety of items through his website and elsewhere:

- **Performance CDs.** Featuring collaborations with his son and others recordings are available through his website, CD Baby, and iTunes and sold at shows.
- **Instructional CDs.** These feature Scottish tunes broken down for learning phrase by phrase.
- **T-shirts.** The customized design displays text every teacher has heard repeatedly: "I played it better at home!"
- **Finger finder.** A patented slide ruler helps violinists grasp finger patterns in every key. It is distributed by Shar Music.
- **Tune groups.** For $15, people can access one of five collections of melodies for three months, including sheet music and mp3s, with phrases broken down for quick mastery. To date, he has had 70 unique subscribers, many who have paid for multiple tune groups.
- **Fiction book.** His self-published title is called *Franck's Wild Ride*.
- **Scotland tour.** Pearlman also organizes group trips to Scotland, where participants hike during the day and experience private concerts by prominent musicians at night.

By themselves, none of these items generates significant income. But in combination, they add up, contributing about 20% of Pearlman's annual earnings. In addition, these things bring joy, attention, and unexpected opportunities.

Instructional Materials

As a creative SMT, you have undoubtedly discovered "better ways of doing things." Perhaps you've invented technical exercises, musical games, or original compositions. Whether these instructional materials are hip, unique, superior, or all of the above, why not introduce them to a larger market, expanding impact and income?

Types of Instructional Materials		
• Arrangements • Books on pedagogy • Children's books about music • Collections • Composition workbooks • Computer-assisted instruction (CAI) • Ensemble pieces • Flash cards • Games • General MIDI disks • How-to books • Improv guides • Instructional DVDs	• Instrumental transcriptions • Lesson plans • Method books • Motivational tools • Music apps • Music dictionaries • Music trivia • Online games • Orchestral excepts • Original compositions • Parent guides • Popular music transcriptions • Practice guides • Practice logs • Public domain music editions	• Recorded/MIDI accompaniments • Recordings (CDs/downloads) • Seasonal music • Software • Style guides (gospel, jazz, folk, etc.) • Subscription-based websites • Teaching guides • Theory books • Video music lessons • Website templates for music teachers • Workbooks

Engaged Educator, Passive Income

After moving across country when her husband started graduate school, Joy Morin (www.colorinmypiano.com) was challenged to imagine a viable career model. Though most income would come through a newly built private studio, her interest in diversifying led to an assortment of educational products available commercially through her website.

To date, she has designed eighteen $10 lapbooks representing great composers. Each package includes lessons plans, a biography book, and beautifully designed items that students can cut, fold, glue, and color. The $8 Ice Cream Interval Game helps young musicians quickly identify the distance between notes. Comprehensive curricula for summer camps—one focused on composition and another on world music—are available for $40 each. She also sells five sets of rhythm cards for $5 to $6 and a rhythm flipbook for $20.

These items, marketed to teachers, are not distributed physically. Instead, customers gain access to a downloadable PDF and a license to reproduce as many times as they want (for their students only). Buyers can print onto card stock, laminate, or use other treatments.

Since all items are all electronic, there are no associated production or shipping costs. Because they are distributed only through her site, she retains 100% of profits. Within 15 months, 700 units sold, and these numbers are projected to snowball.

Morin emphasizes a basic premise of passive income: "For lessons, you have to put in time for every paycheck. But products like these continue to sell even after the hard work is done. I love teaching, but having money magically appear in the bank is a great perk."

There are three publishing options available, each with unique strengths and weaknesses. Before selecting a model, do your homework.

Traditional Publisher	
Pros	Publishers invest in design, production, distribution, and basic marketing while providing limited guidance along the way. They fulfill orders and have existing relationships with book distributors and vendors. You may negotiate a cash advance.
Cons	You earn much less per sale and sacrifice creative control. Things take longer (at least a year getting products to market). Securing representation is cutthroat and not attainable for many aspiring teacher-authors. Unless your book is expected to move thousands of copies, don't count on this option.
Self-Publishing	
Pros	You earn the most per unit sold and maintain full control and ownership. Things go faster, and it forces you to be proactive and entrepreneurial. Products can be sold at a reasonable rate and still generate profit.
Cons	It requires significant upfront investment for design, printing, and shipping—expenses that may not be recouped if your product fails to sell. To make this option worthwhile, at least 500 units should be produced at a time. You are responsible for distribution, marketing, and financial risk.

(continued)

Print-On-Demand (POD)	
Pros	This is similar to self-publishing, except you purchase a handful of units at a time, rather than large quantities. It prevents you from getting stuck with a large supply of unsold products. Many POD companies fulfill orders as well and offer design templates.
Cons	POD costs significantly more per unit than the previous option, driving list prices up and profit margins down. It is only recommended when small sales are anticipated.

Releasing instructional materials takes time, energy, and financial investment. Make sure the commitment is worthwhile. Be forewarned: this path is rarely lucrative. Though there are exceptions, traditionally published authors who see income beyond the cash advance are the exception rather than the rule. Self-publishers frequently lose money.

That said, the benefits of creating instructional materials—that people care about—expand beyond direct income (or loss) through product sales. They can enhance impact, credibility, celebrity, and web presence. Authors often see a spike in speaking engagements, media coverage, gigs, students, hourly wages, and more. People want to be associated with *you*.

Though a comprehensive study of publishing falls outside the scope of this book, briefly consider some major issues:

- **Outsourcing.** There are many types of professionals eager to help bring your instructional materials to life, from ghostwriters and designers to marketers and publicists. They all cost money. Because that capital comes from your piggy bank, carefully determine which investments are most beneficial, and what you can do on your own. Will you pay with time or money?

- **Production.** The larger the quantity, the less expense there is per unit. It might cost $17 to photocopy a single book, $800 to digitally print 100 copies ($8 each), or $1,500 for offset printing of 500 ($3 each). The trick is producing just enough so that the list price is reasonable without burdening you with unsellable inventory or an earning deficit.

- **Price.** As with any product, getting the price right is crucial. Set it too high and sales are lost. Mark it too low and you'll never break even. Keep in mind that income generated must first pay off the initial investment before profits are generated.

- **Marketing.** Marketing is always the author's responsibility, even when working with traditional publishers. The average self-published or POD book sells fewer than 100 units. However, SMTs perform better than average! Produce an outstanding product and promote it heavily.

When self-publishing, limit distribution to your website and "back of the room" sales unless realistically expecting to move more than 500 to 1,000 units per year. This way, 100% of transactions go to you, minus expenses (cost of goods sold [COGS]). The prospects of getting into Barnes & Noble (almost impossible) and Amazon (quite feasible) may sound great. Here's the problem: most wholesalers and distributors require a 40% to 55%+ discount off list price. You may also be responsible for shipping and fulfillment, and most products are bought on consignment. (In other words, items that don't sell can be returned, and you are stuck paying for shipping and refund.) To generate profit through external vendors, experts suggest a list price at least six times the production cost. When ordering 2,500 books at $2 each, this model can work. But if it costs $4 to $10 to manufacture each product, do you really expect consumers to pay $24 to $60?

Downloadable products (e-books, audio/video/MIDI files, computer games) change everything. In this case, without the expenses of physical production and shipping, external distribution through visible sources may make sense.

Self-Published, Pronto

When living abroad in Sweden, Jennifer Eklund (www.pianopronto. com) had several piano students. Because Swedish music stores carried little suitable music and downloading wasn't yet possible, she bought music notation software and started creating her own arrangements. Within six years, these evolved into a method series called *Piano Pronto*.

Since most established publishing houses already represented piano methods, Eklund decided to self-publish. This turned out to be a great choice. Within years, she had an eight-volume method book series, supplemental titles, and hundreds of sheet music items on the market.

With physical sheet music stores disappearing, Eklund seeks to re-create or surpass that customer experience online. Many items can be purchased in multiple formats at various price points through the Piano Pronto website: hard copies, single-user e-books, and editions with lifelong "unlimited reproductions licensing" for teachers to share with their studios. Every book and sheet music title includes full-length audio samples and page-by-page previews, allowing consumers to make informed purchases.

Physical products are also available through Amazon, since many consumers are accustomed to shopping there. However, everything is carried on consignment, and the company charges 55% of list price plus shipping. (Following our interview, Eklund discontinued Amazon sales because of their high commission and her strong direct-to-consumer sales figures.)

Electronic copies of individual works are sold through Sheet Music Plus (www.sheetmusicplus.com), which also takes a 55% commission. Creating an account and uploading files through this site is easy, and it comes with an additional benefit: they own expensive digital rights software that allows consumers to print only once.

While the exact amount earned from product sales fluctuates month to month, it is significant. Today, Eklund consistently generates as much or more income through retail ventures as she does from lessons.

Sales Tax

If selling products in states where you have a presence, you are legally required to charge and report sales tax. This typically runs between 1% and 10% of the purchase price, depending on the area and type of product. Out-of-state sales (e.g., over the Internet) may not require this levy. For more information, check with your state's Department of Revenue.

Lessons from the Trenches

To conveniently serve my studio, I make bulk music purchases every few months and distribute as necessary. An annual enrollment fee (currently $145) covers all music, administrative fees, recital costs, assignment binders, and additional services. Because students are not charged directly for items, I am not liable for sales tax, making life much simpler!

Instrument Rentals

SMTs who have acquired a number of instruments over the years or are looking for a new investment strategy should consider renting to students and community members. Once an instrument has been paid off, 100% of the rental fee is yours to keep (minus upkeep).

Instrumental students choose whether to purchase or rent. Primary advantages of buying are that money goes toward an asset that can be kept long term or sold later. This option also allows consumers to handpick the specific instrument. Benefits of renting include the following:

- **Expense.** It avoids a large, upfront expenditure.
- **Loss of interest.** It allows students to test an instrument without large financial consequences if they decide to stop playing.
- **Upgrade.** It permits students to upgrade without the hassle of selling an old instrument first. Young string players easily move into different-sized models as they grow.
- **Insurance.** Many rentals include insurance (for an extra fee). When problems arise, the owner—you in this case—repairs the damage instead of the renter.

A minimum rental period for instruments is typically required (e.g., one year). Rates vary drastically depending on the dealer, purchase price, quality, whether it's used or new, and demand in a given region. The approximate charges listed as follows provide guidelines for student-quality instruments.

Instrument	Rental Fee
Flutes, clarinets, trumpets, trombones, violin, viola	$10–$30/month
Amplifiers	$15–$25/month
Guitars	$20–$40/month
Alto sax, oboe, piccolo, cello, drum set	$30–$50/month
Bass clarinet, bassoon, horn, baritone, tuba, bass	$50–$70/month
Cheap console pianos	$35+/month
Synthesizers/digital pianos	$45+/month
Baby grand pianos	$100+/month

Rentals are often priced to pay for themselves within a year or two. Suppose a $300 student violin rents for $15 per month. After 20 months, the initial investment has been recouped, and each subsequent payment turns a profit. Be sure to have renters sign a contract detailing the agreement, making it clear what happens if the instrument is damaged.

Drumming Up Rentals

Not atypical for percussionists, Greg Giannascoli (www.greggiannascoli. com) owns a large assortment of instruments. In college, he discovered a business opportunity in renting this inventory. Since then, his collection has grown to include multiple timpani sets, cymbals, ethnic percussion, drum sets, toys/sound effects, and a wide range of mallet percussion instruments.

Giannascoli rents to two types of customers. The first is students (frequently his own) looking for practice instruments. Families often prefer renting by the month over making a robust investment in, say, a full-size marimba. At a given time, there are typically 10 such rentals. Since they are used for practicing, this equipment needn't be top of the line. "Worn" instruments also remove pressure from renters to maintain immaculate condition.

The second market involves leasing high-end gear to theaters, orchestras, chamber series, and other organizations for specific events. With shorter rental periods of days or weeks, the price tag is higher than when borrowing for the long haul.

Giannascoli is always on the lookout for good deals, regularly scouring sources like eBay and Craigslist for underpriced, used gear. As a rule of thumb, he seeks equipment that can pay for itself in under a year, though high-quality purchases may require longer.

Partnerships

Local Music Stores

Whether or not you have a financial agreement, do all you can to support good local music stores. These businesses are invaluable. In addition to selling merchandise, many offer a performance space, instrument repair, guest artist series, workshops, music scholarships, and solid advice. Unfortunately, brick-and-mortar merchants have been hit hard as consumers increasingly purchase highly discounted items through the Internet from vendors without comparable overhead or services. Alas, many longtime fixtures have closed their doors.

If you plan to send students to a particular location for major purchases such as instruments, some vendors pay commissions. Typically that ranges from 2% to 5% for regularly priced products or 1% to 3% on sales items.

Others offer a fixed amount in exchange for business, such as $50 on $1,000 to $2,000 purchases, $100 on $2,000 to $3,000, and so forth. The challenge for dealers is that markups on instruments tend to be low (thanks to price comparison shopping online), so there is not much profit margin left over to share.

Most dealers prefer giving vouchers or in-kind donations to loyal music teachers: free recital hall usage, free event piano rental, free tuning, and so forth. If you require these services anyway, their value is equivalent to cash (except that you aren't required to pay income taxes on it, as is the case with earned income).

To explore this possibility, get to know local dealerships and come to an agreement. In truth, building relationships with vendors who offer extraordinary services, convenience, and customer service is a savvy move even if no recompense is offered. The best solution here may be sacrificing income to support a great local company.

Affinity/Affiliate Programs

Affinity programs exist to promote and reward customer loyalty. Frequent flyer initiatives are probably the most-known variety, awarding faithful customers with perks like seat upgrades, free tickets, access to special lounges, early boarding, and free checked luggage.

Prima Music (www.primamusic.com), self-described as "the first online store designed especially for music teachers," is an example of a music-related affinity program. In addition to a large collection of print music, Prima Music sells teacher aids, music gifts, instruments, and accessories. After joining the program (free), you receive discounts based on your level of membership. The more you spend over a lifetime, the higher your status.

It doesn't take long for SMTs to move up the membership ladder. Students pay list price (which they do anyway, since most music has a fixed price regardless of vendor), but you place the order and keep the difference. The same discount is applied to all items.

Membership Level	Discount	Requirement
Silver	10%	Register with Prima Music
Gold	15%	Spend over $300 lifetime
Platinum	20%	Spend over $700 lifetime
Diamond	25%	Spend over $1,200 lifetime

Similarly, *affiliate programs* allow SMTs to build virtual "stores" on studio websites or add links to merchant sites. When someone makes a purchase, an embedded identification number gives you credit for a given amount per sale. Check with online vendors about their structure and policies. Setting up links is not difficult; good companies walk you through the process. Students place orders at their convenience, and you don't get stuck with unclaimed music. A few examples include:

- **Sheet Music Plus** (www.sheetmusicplus.com). This site starts with an 8% commission.
- **All Piano Sheet Music** (www.allpianosheetmusic.com). This company pays $4 per sale. If referring new people to the affiliate program, they also give 20% of that individual's commission.
- **Virtual Sheet Music** (www.virtualsheetmusic.com). "The leading source of Classical Sheet Music Downloads" pays affiliate partners an impressive 30% of sales.

Affiliate relationships can expand beyond sheet music to include recordings, books about music, and accessories. Other companies with affiliate programs include iTunes and Amazon. For a more thorough list of possibilities, visit the music page from AssociatePrograms.com (www.associateprograms.com/directory/entertainment/music).

Certifiably Affiliated

One lonely Christmas Eve, drummer Mike Veny was working on his music teaching business website (www.musiclessonbusiness.com). Aiming to add quality content, he placed an affiliate link to his favorite electronic drum kit without any expectation it would lead to revenue. Imagine his surprise when, six months later, a check arrived for $600.

Excited about the prospect of generating more passive income, he got serious about affiliate marketing. His 10 websites (yes, 10!) now link to 20 companies, many with multiple products. Each month, some of these businesses send him payments ranging from $10 to $1,000. Transforming this into the largest portion of his income is a medium-term goal.

Sometimes Veny places affiliate links in product reviews on one of his sites. Other times, they simply appear as ads. Either way, he only shares quality products, since building trust is paramount. Represented items include:

- **Instruments and accessories.** These include drums, cymbals, sticks, and drum heads. He is currently working to launch a new instrument price comparison site.
- **Instructional materials.** These include percussion-related instructional DVDs.
- **Websites.** One of these is Music Teacher's Helper.
- **Books.** Veny reads a book a week and places Amazon links for his favorites. One day, he hopes to start a website focused exclusively on great reads.
- **Marketing products.** Infusionsoft, which Veny fondly describes as "email marketing on steroids," is a product he uses personally. Though his links have generated just two sales, the product runs $350 per month and pays a healthy return.

From a financial perspective, how much income can a sheet music affinity/affiliate program provide? That depends on the percentage earned and total dollars spent. Consider what budding musicians typically spend on print music.

Younger students work primarily from graded method series. For example, *Piano Adventure,* by Faber Publications, has levels Primer, 1, 2A, 2B, 3A, 3B, 4, and 5. There is also an accelerated series for older students and another for adult beginners. Each level contains books, CDs, and MIDI accompaniments. Here is a full list of Level 1 products:

Product	Price
Lesson Book	$6.95
Theory Book	$6.50
Performance Book	$6.50
Technique and Artistry Book	$6.50
Sightreading Book	$6.95
Gold Star Performance with CD	$7.95
Popular Repertoire Book	$6.95
Christmas Book	$4.95
Lesson Book CD	$10.95

(*continued*)

Product	Price
Popular Repertoire CD	$10.95
Popular Repertoire MIDI	$10.95
Background Accompaniments MIDI	$24.95
TOTAL	$111.05

Few teachers require students to buy an entire collection like this, instead picking and choosing depending on student needs and personal instruction style. On average, students work through one to two levels each year, often supplemented with additional materials.

Advanced students require fewer books, but purchases are more expensive. And unlike beginners, who tackle every piece in a collection, advanced players skip around. Here is a random sampling of prices for print music (edition names not provided).

Music	Price	Music	Price
Beethoven Piano Sonatas, Book 1	$24.95	Orchestral Excerpt Books, Various	$15-45
Chopin Etudes	$11.95	Ives: 3 Songs	$9.95
Barber, Complete Piano Music	$16.95	The Beatles: White Album (guitar)	$19.95
Prokofiev, Violin Sonata Op. 56	$20.95	A Chorus Line	$14.95
Bach, Cello Suites	$12.95	The Real Book	$29.95
Flute Project: New Pieces for Solo Flute	$25.95	Jamey Abersold Play-A-Longs	$10-20

Active students often spend $50 to $100+ per year on music. For a studio of 30, this means $1,500 to $3,000 is paid. By earning 15% through affinity/affiliate programs, you get $225 to $450.

Other affiliate programs exist as well. Music Teacher's Helper, described in chapter 11, offers a 20% recurring monthly commission when you refer a customer. If the subscriber enters a promotional code identifying you when signing up, monthly passive income is generated throughout the life of his or her account. (Incidentally, if you learn about them through this book, please consider entering the SMT promotional code 84EBC9.)

The email marketing company Constant Contact (used by many musicians) currently pays $2 for each "qualified lead" signing up for a 60-day free trial, and $50 for paying customers.

Outside the virtual world, affiliate-like opportunities exist as well. Some piano tuners and instrument technicians provide referral fees in gratitude for new customers. In fact, you may want to offer this benefit when people point new students in your direction. Referrals, as we will see, are a powerful and cost-effective marketing tactic.

The Affiliate Retailer

"Years ago, students would come to me with a hole burning in their pocket. They wanted an instrument, accessory, or music and would happily have purchased it through me. But I didn't sell these things and sent them elsewhere."

This seemed like a squandered opportunity to violist Jarrod Haning (www.thesixfigureartist.com), and after researching various possibilities, he stumbled onto the affiliate retail model. Today, he deals directly with one of the largest online music manufacturers. He can order any of their products wholesale (typically receiving a 50% discount off of list price) and sells them at the normal retail price.

This sounds a lot like a traditional dealership, but there is one major difference: *no inventory or upfront investment*. Haning has no expenses until a client buys something, at which point he collects payment, places the order, and pockets the difference. For new instruments, he contacts the company and requests three models to test on consignment. If something sells, Haning pays the wholesale amount. If not, they are returned, the only expense being shipping.

To establish this relationship, Haning had to obtain a retail license, requiring a little paperwork and a nominal fee. He collects and pays sales taxes each month and is required to report how much was made that period (ranging anywhere from nothing to thousands of dollars). "I can't believe I didn't start doing this years earlier!"

The Savvy Music Teacher Income Blueprint

Scenario A

One hundred percent of SMT May Jorskale's product income comes from discounts and referral fees.

1. **Affinity program.** May's 30 students spend an average of $65 per year on sheet music, or $1,950 total. She is involved in an affinity program, effectively earning a 10% discount, or **$195**.
2. **Affiliate programs.** May has an affiliate relationship with several websites. This year, two musician friends named her when signing up for a Constant Contact account, generating **$100**. Five others maintain Music Teacher's Helper websites at $348 each annually ($2,088 total), for which she gets credit. That program pays 20%, generating an additional **$418**.
3. **Equipment sales.** This year, three of her piano students bought new keyboards: a grand, an upright, and a sampler. The combined price tag was $9,567. In thanks for her loyal support, the shop offered her a 3% commission, or **$427**.

Scenario B

SMT Mel O'Dee is the handy type. As a hobby, he builds, sells, and rents instruments.

1. **Equipment sales.** Each year, Mel sells three new instruments, with a profit margin of $300 each, or **$900** per year.
2. **Equipment rentals.** Mel also rents a collection of instruments he made years ago to students and other locals. Currently impacting eight people at an average of $20 a month ($240 a year), this generates **$1,920** annually.
3. **Instructional materials.** Three years ago, he self-published an e-book guide about instrument building. Just 18 copies sold this year, netting $10 per book, or **$180**.

Scenario C

SMT Barry Sacks is a natural salesman.

1. **Equipment sales.** Barry is always on the lookout for great eBay deals. Each year, he buys and sells an average of five instruments to students and locals.

After doing any necessary repair work himself, he averages a $400 profit per instrument, or **$2,000** total.

2. **Merch.** Each year, 100 *limited edition* customized items are manufactured and sold. Barry does a big push not only to private students but also to members of his classes and camp. This year, the product is a T-shirt with a profit margin of $11 apiece, or **$1,100**.

3. **Instructional materials.** Barry has two instructional method books that do pretty well, available through his website. He sells around 500 units per year, averaging a $3 profit for each, or **$1,500** total. In addition, 13 compositions playable by beginning to intermediate-level musicians sell modestly, generating another **$400**.

Merch	Scenario A	Scenario B	Scenario C
Equipment sales	$287	$900	$2,000
Paraphernalia	—	—	$1,100
Instructional materials	—	$180	$1,900
Equipment rentals	—	$1,920	—
Affinity program	$195	—	—
Affiliate programs	$518	—	—
NET ANNUAL INCOME	**$1,000**	**$3,000**	**$5,000**

From products (stream 6), the SMT earns between $1,000 and $5,000 per year.

9 ADDITIONAL: STREAM 7

Beyond the impact/income streams investigated in the previous six chapters, many additional pursuits contribute to the well-being of Savvy Music Teachers (SMTs). This is one of the great things about becoming a professional musician—opportunities are everywhere.

The best options offer fresh challenges, personal growth, expanded networks, and inspiration. Certain engagements also fuel recruitment and influence teaching philosophy. Gigs during tough-to-fill teaching periods also solve a scheduling puzzle.

Please note that fees for most activities are highly variable depending on location, experience, employer budget, and other factors. The figures in this chapter are just guidelines.

Teaching Options
Directing a Music Academy

This book centers on SMTs who run solo enterprises. However, as big thinkers, their preoccupation with inventive ways to increase impact and income often leads to a different conclusion. Transforming studios into academies is the most common way music teachers exceed the $100,000 earning benchmark while providing a path to positively influencing hundreds of students on a weekly basis.

Not to be taken lightly, running a music academy involves startup investment (buying pianos and supplies, fixing up teaching space) and continued expenses (facility rental, maintenance, utilities, insurance, staff). It requires vision, leadership, people skills, ongoing marketing, disciplined financial management, meticulous accounting, and extreme organization. But for those willing to take the risk and responsibility, the educational and financial payoff can be enormous.

Music academies recruit students, organize scheduling, provide teaching space, collect payment, hire teachers, make payroll, and administer logistics. The best programs also coordinate a variety of intriguing initiatives, with all seven SMT streams playing an active role:

1. **Lessons.** While some academies hire any willing, qualified music teacher on instruments they need, SMT programs favor passionate instructors with compatible educational philosophies. Most programs claim 20% to 50% of tuition, passing on the rest to instructors. Some charge a fixed rate for all comparable lesson packages, while others vary this according to teacher experience, specialty, and demand.

2. **Classes.** Academies typically pay class teachers a set fee ($30 to $65/hour) and then claim the remainder of tuition, making this a particularly lucrative option. The larger the program, the easier it is to fill exciting courses with existing clients. Some programs also organize workshops, master classes, and competitions.

3. **Camps.** Most SMT academies host intriguing camps and summer programs. Economics are similar to those described in chapter 5, though recruiting is often easier with a larger pool of clients. When existing facilities are used, a supplemental expense is avoided.

4. **Events.** It is easier to populate a series of innovative, meaningful events when serving a larger community. Interstudio options expose participants to musical variety.

5. **Technology.** Many SMT academies offer technology classes, house media workstations, or integrate technology throughout their curriculum.

6. **Products.** A larger established client base makes it easier to maximize sales from a shop peddling accessories, sheet music, merchandise, or even instruments.

7. **Additional.** SMT academies have many opportunities for integrating additional streams: renting out performance space, presenting ticketed events, and so forth.

While some SMTs invite employees to work from a room in their home, running an academy typically requires renting/purchasing external facilities, whether choosing a commercial space or a converted residential property.

Considerations for Music Academy Facilities	
• Acoustical properties	• Potential to expand/add on
• Bathrooms (men and women)	• Practice rooms
• Character/charm	• Proximity to client base
• Handicap accessibility	• Rehearsal space(s)
• Local business regulations	• Rent/mortgage amount
• Maintenance issues	• Sales area
• Neighborhood safety	• Storefront
• Office space	• Teaching spaces (quantity and size)
• Parking	• Utility costs
• Performance space	• Waiting area

Staff performance reflects directly on your business. Employees who routinely arrive tardy or fail to connect with families can quickly damage reputation and credibility. Therefore, it is essential to vet employees and develop clear written policies outlining expectations.

Some programs merely represent a random collection of independent contractors, connected by little more than the desire to teach music and work through an umbrella organization. But SMTs are known for building academies around differentiated essential questions, learning objectives, activities, brands, philosophies, and pedagogical approaches.

Lessons from the Trenches

I founded Centre for Musical Minds (www.centreformusicalminds.org), an academy specializing in multiple styles of piano instruction, my third year after graduating from college. My motivation was less financial and more about creating a spectacular environment where I could work with great colleagues to develop an innovative and meaningful curriculum.

Hoping to run a "destination location," I rented a 1,200-square-foot efficiency. The space has a nice kitchen, a library, a bathroom, a waiting area, and four teaching spaces each equipped with a piano, desk, and shelves. The lack of a performance hall turned out to be a blessing, forcing us to arrange performances around town that engage the community.

I interview every student who walks through our doors and have been known to turn folks away. Because creating a positive sense of community is so important to me, it is essential we involve the right people.

My nine teachers are paid well, based on a two-tier system depending on degrees and experience. Many are graduates from a local university with a strong pedagogy program. Though careful never to micromanage, I do provide a good deal of training on the front end, particularly when it comes to incorporating popular music and relating to "average" students.

During the first several years, my take-home salary was actually less than as an independent teacher, thanks to startup expenses including first and last month's rent ($2300 each), as well as making payments toward a $25,000 business loan and $20,000 instrument loan. (I'm happy to report that both were eliminated within five years.) Beyond teachers, I also hire an accountant and graphic designer and am responsible for taxes, utilities, and other overhead. Twenty percent of what the program earns is placed in a business account for future investment.

Though my salary—whatever is left—is not directly tied to the number of students on my roster, I truly love teaching and always take a large load.

Running a music academy requires tremendous work, but the educational, social, communal, and ultimately financial benefits are significant. This was a great decision for me.

Teaching in a Music Academy

For financial reasons, this book advocates teaching independently. Working for someone else's music store, academy, or other community school results in a diminished hourly rate, typically 20% to 50% less than what clients pay. It also erases income potential from supplemental streams like products, events, and technology, since the employer reaps these rewards. Many programs also require teachers to sign a "noncompete" agreement, meaning that they are legally forbidden to recruit students to their own independent business.

That said, many academies offer appealing employee benefits, particularly when teachers are in college, moving to a new area, or scheduling hard-to-fill slots. They are largely responsible for marketing, recruiting, communicating with parents, collecting payment, arranging logistics, and providing a teaching space, allowing you to focus exclusively on music and teaching. Some employers provide perks such as teacher training and mentorship. Furthermore, the best programs offer dynamic environments that are gratifying socially and expand beyond the realm of possibility for an isolated, independent instructor.

There is no one size fits all. Some programs clearly offer employees a bum deal, while others are quite compelling. As with anything, carefully weigh the pros and cons before signing on. Consider financial, educational, artistic, and communal implications.

Do It for the Community

In addition to teaching independently, Todd Van Kekerix spends two days per week giving lessons and classes at the New School for Music Study (www.nsmspiano.org), a nonprofit community music program specializing in keyboard music. This requires at least an hour drive in each direction, and the pay is less than his private rate. Yet he has chosen to work there for seven years. Why?

Like many community programs, NSMS recruits students, collects payment, and arranges scheduling. They tune pianos regularly, have an extensive print music library, and house a performance space. Though only full-time teachers are eligible for benefit packages, Van Kekerix can contribute to a 401k retirement fund, receiving a company match.

"But the highlight of working here is the collegiality among teachers. I love the sense of community, that everyone is devoted and on the same page."

The faculty gathers formally to discuss pedagogical issues every other week, and fascinating accidental conversations transpire when strolling the hallways or eating in the kitchen. "There are legendary educators in this building, making interactions truly inspiring."

Four times per year, NSMS organizes faculty recitals. One show was even scheduled at Carnegie Hall. Each term, the academy hires a master pedagogue to conduct professional development workshops, observe teachers, and provide feedback. Preceding student performances, instructors routinely arrange impromptu "performance exchanges."

Years ago, Van Kekerix taught lessons through a music store that did not provide most of these benefits. But NSMS is different. Though he could easily fill his own studio with local students alone, earning more and commuting less, the perks of this particular position make the trade-offs worthwhile.

Classroom Music

Occasional SMTs are classroom teachers by day and independent instructors by night. While this makes for a busy schedule, the two activities are nice complements. Typically, teaching in public school requires certification and a content-area college degree. Private schools may or may not require this pedigree. Full-time positions pay $35,000 to $80,000 annually, depending on the district, teacher education, and years in the system. As with most "jobs," guaranteed employment means dependable paychecks and scheduling.

When public/private school music educators take sick or vacation days, the schools are always delighted to have a real music teacher step in, rather than wasting entire periods with an unqualified substitute. Classroom music teachers put in special requests for substitutes with musical backgrounds. Substitutes are allowed to specify what (e.g., music only), when (e.g., Tuesdays and Fridays), and where (e.g., three local high schools) they are willing to teach. The more flexible you are, the more likely it is that you'll get hired. At least a bachelor's degree, but no teaching credential, is required. Compensation is $65 to $110 per day.

Double Duty

Following 19 years as a junior/senior high band director and 5 years in the corporate world, trumpeter Larry Shudra (www.larryshudra. wordpress.com) now balances two major education-based jobs. As an elementary general music teacher, he interfaces with each of his school's 760 students at least once a week. Kindergarten through third-grade classes integrate Orff, Kodaly, American folk songs, drum circles, and games that promote teamwork, respect, and critical listening. Forth and fifth graders also learn recorders and theory. Before the school day begins, he offers a number of half-hour "electives" such as recorders, choir, and keyboard percussion.

Shudra also runs a private studio, impacting (1) 6th- to 12th-grade brass players and (2) younger students learning guitar. None of these clients overlap with his "day job," avoiding a conflict of interest. Lessons are scheduled from 4:30 to 9 PM Tuesdays through Thursdays. Weekends are left wide open, thanks to a great feature of elementary music: no football games.

Shudra's elementary school experience has undoubtedly influenced lesson dynamics. Beyond the virtue of patience, it has convinced him to place more emphasis on singing, phrasing, music requested by students, and always keeping it fun.

Balancing these two careers does more than generate significant income. "Teaching in so many contexts keeps me fresh and current with a variety of methodologies. I love both sides!"

Assistant Teaching/Coaching

Healthy music programs at junior and senior high schools often hire assistants to run ensemble sectionals, help with the marching band/show choir, rehearse the school musical, or operate in additional capacities. Youth symphonies and regional honors ensembles also employ coaches. While these positions are not known for paying lavishly, perhaps $1,000 to $5,000 annually, they can supplement income while placing you in a vibrant environment.

Lessons from a Coach

Percussionist Dan Hostetler holds the title of assistant band director at an area high school. Responsibilities include rehearsing marching band percussion, directing the percussion ensemble, and arranging music for both groups.

Hostetler's schedule varies greatly by the season. Intense band and drum line camps are scheduled each summer. In the fall, with marching band in full swing, his leadership is required four to five days per week plus competitions and shows. Things slow down during spring, when most duties can be accomplished one afternoon per week.

Part of his salary comes through the school district, offering the equivalent of a coach's stipend. The remainder is paid by a robust band booster organization. The school also permits him to offer lessons in their facilities, free of charge. Between 80% and 90% of the percussion section take advantage of this opportunity, providing an additional layer of income and impact.

Adjunct College Instruction

Universities, colleges, and community colleges hire adjunct faculty to teach classes on a variety of topics including theory, ear training, class piano, Alexander technique, pedagogy, Eurhythmics, music appreciation, applied lessons, and special topics. In fact, the number of adjuncts has skyrocketed as schools curb their budget by hiring fewer tenure-eligible faculty members. Payment, typically $1,500 to $4,000 for a two- or three-credit class, is far from spectacular when considering preparation and commute time. But involvement in higher education may make the opportunity worthwhile.

Part-time positions rarely involve high-profile searches. If interested, get to know people with clout. Send a resume and letter of interest to the chair, director, or dean, even if no post currently exists. When opportunities arise, as they often do, committees start with what's on file.

> ### Adjunct in Higher Education
>
> In addition to gigging and running a private studio, saxophonist Michael Keepe (www.mikekeepe.com) works as an adjunct college instructor. Three mornings per week, he teaches at a university where responsibilities include saxophone lessons (eight students), weekly studio classes, and a three-credit methods course for music education majors. Originally offered quarter-time employment, he successfully negotiated a half-time position. In addition to a higher salary, this arrangement enables access to health insurance for his family of five.
>
> Keepe also travels to a community college two afternoons per week, leading a two-course music industry sequence. Compensation for these three-credit offerings is $2,500 each. In addition, half-hour applied lesson slots generate $450 per semester. During a given term, two to five students typically sign up for primarily hour-long meetings.
>
> A semester-to-semester adjunct contract does not guarantee stability. If a class fails to meet enrollment minimums or responsibilities shift among faculty, work can be cancelled with little warning. However, Keepe is grateful for the opportunities, revenue, and benefits his positions provide and aspires to become an indispensible member of these communities.

Teaching Artistry

Teaching artists are individuals who use their art to connect with schoolchildren. Unlike classroom music teachers, who engage a fixed group of learners throughout a term, teaching artists typically serve one-hour to two-week residencies in a given school or class. They may present to music ensembles but just as often interface elsewhere, linking music to reading, math, science, history, or other topics. The best examples of this practice, known as *arts integration*, further participants' comprehension of and passion for both music and the other subject.

Paid opportunities for teaching artists exist in every US state and many countries. Compensation is typically $50 to $150 per individual session, or $75 to $250 per day. To learn more about this burgeoning field, read the most comprehensive resource on the topic, Eric Booth's *The Music Teaching Artist's Bible.*

Music Is Magic

In addition to private teaching, singer/songwriter Greta Pedersen (www. greta.net) works as an elementary school teaching artist. Most residencies last one to two weeks, placing her in contact with three to five classes per day. Alternate scheduling, such as six consecutive Mondays, is also possible.

One of her programs, called "Music and Dance in a Multicultural World," celebrates the similarities and differences of people worldwide. Attendees learn a Mexican or Danish dance, world percussion, and a song that translates hello, goodbye, please, thank you, and the numbers 1, 2, and 3 into several languages (including those native to class members).

Songwriting residencies can connect to literally any topic. While Pedersen leads the compositional process, she depends on the class's "expertise" on, say, volcanoes, geometry, or reading strategies. After learning and reinforcing everything they know, she helps them craft a song. By week's end, classes record their new masterwork. In several instances, she has allowed groups to leave a long-term legacy by composing a new school anthem.

Pedersen also offers 40-minute assembly programs (typically two per day, divided into kindergarten through second grade and third through fifth grade). During "America's Story through Folk Songs," she accompanies historical tunes on mountain dulcimer and guitar, teaches sign language, and invites audience members to play spoons and washboard. "La Musica es Magica/Music Is Magic," balancing instruction in Spanish and English, features bilingual sing-alongs.

When Pedersen lived in California, most engagements were arranged independently, paid for by schools, districts, or parent teacher associations. Now in Oregon, she works with agencies including Young Audiences, the Right Brain Initiative, and Wordstock that typically pay a fixed hourly rate for residencies but allow her to set assembly pricing.

Like most teaching artists, Pedersen has a seemingly endless supply of inspiring stories: disengaged students moved to participate for the first time, new friendships resulting from collective art making, liberated learners empowered by nontraditional approaches.

Nonteaching Options

Performance

Performance is the most common stream SMTs combine with teaching, providing an artistic outlet, personal fulfillment, and often significant income. As an added benefit, students love hearing their teachers perform. A few options and typical wages are listed to follow. For more ideas, see my prior publication *The Savvy Musician.*

- **Accompanying.** $10 to $50 per rehearsal hour; $50 to $200 per performance
- **Solo/chamber concert, high profile.** $300 to $3,000 per show
- **Solo/chamber concert, lower profile.** $75 to $500 per show
- **Hired church musician.** $50 to $150 per service, may include rehearsal
- **Orchestra member (semiprofessional).** $40 to $100 per service
- **Orchestra sub (professional).** $50 to $150 per service
- **Pit musician.** $50 to $150 per service
- **Private parties** (weddings, graduation, Bar Mitzvahs, etc.). $100 to $500 per engagement
- **Recording artist.** $30 to $150 per hour; $100 to $2,000 per project
- **Restaurant background music.** $25 to $75 per hour
- **Soloist with educational group.** $100 to $1,000 for residency

Genre Hopping

The genre-hopping cellist Alex Kelly (www.alexkelly.com) balances a true portfolio career. "I feel like a chameleon." He performs with string quartets, jazz combos, rock bands, new music ensembles, symphony orchestras, Klezmer/Balkan groups, and bluegrass jams. Looping effects have opened up a world of possibility as a soloist (or duo partner when paired with violin, guitar, or DJ) including wedding gigs, church services, house concerts, large-venue events, dance recitals, and even shows with a circus troupe. Featured engagements in front of orchestras have ranged from the Vivaldi Double Cello Concerto to collaborations with Grateful Dead founding member Bob Weir. He also records and produces music on a weekly basis—several local studios seem to have him on speed dial.

As a composer and arranger, Kelly has written everything from film scores to video game soundtracks to a concerto featuring tabla guru Zakir

Hussain with the National Symphony Orchestra. His book *The Seven Points* teaches cello fingerboard mapping techniques.

This intense variety not only makes for a challenging and exhilarating career model but also impacts his teaching. Private students learn to be curious, well-rounded musicians, equipped to play written music, improvise, compose, record, and integrate electronics.

Composing/Arranging

SMTs with composition and arranging skills have an array of professional options: commissions, transcriptions, sacred music, film scores, jingles, video game soundtracks, ring tones, and more. There is a robust market for settings with educational merit. Because this work is so varied, it is difficult to approximate compensation.

Minor Internet Celebrity

Tubist Peter Opaskar (www.TubaPeter.com) began arranging for low brass out of necessity. With a lack of interesting repertoire available, he wrote *20 Duets for Low Brass* based on public domain composers such as Bach, Mozart, and Sousa. That collection has since been recorded and released on CD Baby and iTunes, as well as transcribed and published for several instrumental combinations. Since then, his arranging has expanded to low brass duos, trios, and quartets based on Baroque, classical, film, TV, and video game music.

One evening while eating buffalo wings, he experienced "what may well have been the only good idea of my life. Why not make ensemble videos overdubbing all parts myself?" Shockingly, at least to Opaskar, they caught fire. As of our interview, his 241 YouTube videos had acquired 2.3 million hits, with over 4,500 subscribers. The most popular, tallying some 300,000 views, is a tuba duet on the theme to *Family Guy*.

Most videos prominently display his web address, where PDF downloads may be purchased. This process is automated, meaning that once an arrangement becomes available, income is 100% passive.

The popularity of these videos brings credibility when seeking students or gigs. Though arrangements currently provide a small percentage of annual earnings, this minor Internet celebrity hopes that will soon change. "The more they generate, the happier I'll be, since I love arranging, performing, and producing videos." Something else he loves: walking into a new school and—by sheer coincidence—discovering one of his arrangements on a music stand.

Other Music Opportunities

Here are a few more music-related, income-generating possibilities:

Gig	Description	Earns
Arts consultant	An SMT with skills as a marketer, leader, problem solver, advocate, or community builder may find freelance consultant work with ensembles and arts organizations.	$40–$120 per hour
Competition judge	Evaluate performances or compositions for local/national contests.	$100–$500 per event
Copyist	Transcribe compositions or arrangements into computer notation software like Finale or Sibelius.	$10–$20 per hour
Guest conducting	Engagements range from church choirs to honor bands.	$50–$500 per service (unless famous)
Repair	Repair instruments for students and others in town.	$30–$100 per hour
Music journalist	Write music-related articles for magazines, newsletters, or online sources. Some professional organizations hire freelance writers to compose program notes.	$75–$300 per article (or free)
Piano tuner	Full-fledged piano technicians require extensive equipment and training, so basic tuning is a more realistic aspiration for SMTs.	$75–$150 per tuning
Radio host/ employee	Share great music with others, hosting your own local radio show or working behind the scenes.	Free–$50 per hour
Recording engineer	SMTs with home recording studios can record, edit, mix, and master. Students may become recording clients, and vice versa.	$20–$100 per hour

> ## Tuning In
>
> An effort to be frugal originally led keyboardist Paul Whitson (www. whitsonteachertuner.com) to learn about piano tuning. Why hire someone else? Discovering a sincere interest in this activity, he began apprenticing with a local technician. Currently, this work accounts for 10% to 20% of his annual income. Revenue generated is deposited into its own savings account and left untouched until the quieter summer months.
>
> Whitson's two businesses undoubtedly benefit one another. Many students entrust him to care for their instruments, and tuning has proven an effective recruitment strategy.

Nonmusic Work

Far too common are tales of starving artists forced to take on dreaded "day jobs" just to support their musical habit and make ends meet. Though they rationalize this gig for its temporary financial support until better times emerge, the opposite often occurs. Grueling, unfulfilling work has a way of sucking life energy, causing physical and mental exhaustion. When each workday finally comes to a close, employees are too drained to make good progress toward meaningful musical ambitions. Do not fall into this trap.

If following some semblance of the SMT blueprint, you won't be forced to wait tables, work from a cubicle, perform hard manual labor, or pursue other forms of indentured servitude (unless this is what you want). There are many better paths to earning a living.

However, the right kind of nonmusical employment can provide variety, teach transferable skills, and even inspire. Perhaps music around the clock is simply too much. No shame is bestowed upon music teachers who pursue non-music-related streams. The best positions fulfill at least three, and hopefully more, of the following characteristics:

1. You enjoy the work.
2. You are paid well.
3. You can work during nonpeak music hours, or at times of your choosing.
4. You learn a new skill that helps your music/teaching career.
5. You are challenged to grow personally.
6. You interact with great people.
7. You network with people who may benefit your larger goals in some way.

A sampling of my personal favorite part-time jobs that complement the schedule and lifestyle of an SMT follow. It's up to you to research salaries.

Great Supplemental Work for Musicians	
• Aerobics/yoga instructor • Anything that develops marketing skills • Arts administrator • Babysitter • Baker (particularly of cupcakes) • Bookstore clerk • Caterer • Consultant • Copywriter • Daycare worker • Food critic • Home-based business (allowing maximum flexibility) • Journalist	• Librarian • Museum/art gallery employee • Mystery shopper • Personal assistant (for local musician?) • Pet sitter/dog walker/animal groomer • Something related to your hobbies • Survey taker • Valet parking attendant for wealthy people at a five-star resort that provides you free gourmet meals and fancy perfume • Web designer (for musicians?)

Beyond Music

In addition to freelancing and teaching flute, Melissa Lindon (www.melissalindon.com) makes money through another passion: yoga. Her classes, workshops, and private sessions help participants "stretch, strengthen, relax, and find a balanced peaceful state of mind." While many meetings are open to a general audience, some are geared specifically toward musicians. Interestingly, a number of aspiring flutists have contacted her specifically because they thought this yoga background would add value to music lessons.

As a guitarist, teacher, composer, and lyricist, the professional life of Rik Jonna (www.avantzato.com) revolves around music. But there is another side to his career. Jonna is also a painter and sculptor whose work features modern interpretations of instruments. Creations are available through his website and a number of exhibits. "I believe that I am one of the happiest creatures in the world because I found what I am meant to do on this earth. My music and art define my life as a human being, not simply as an artist."

The Savvy Music Teacher Income Blueprint

Following our blueprint, the SMT labors an average of three to eight hours each week, earning $500 to $1,000 monthly through additional work. Many SMTs generate considerably more through this stream.

# of Months	Monthly Income	Net Annual Income
12	$500	$6,000
12	$1,000	$12,000

Let's further break down the numbers to understand exactly what they imply.

$6,000 ÷ 52 weeks = ~$116 per week
$12,000 ÷ 52 weeks = ~$231 per week

On average, somewhere between $116 and $231 must be earned weekly.

$116 ÷ 8 hours = $14.50 per hour
$231 ÷ 3 hours = $77 per hour

This model requires an hourly wage of $14.50 to $77 when divided over three to eight hours. At a minimum, hopefully you can identify work that pays more than $14.50. Perhaps $77 per hour seems high, but gigging musicians and presenters often command higher fees. Two or three private parties per month may be all it takes to generate the minimum income needed.

From additional work (stream 7), the SMT earns between $6,000 and $12,000 per year.

Space matters. Where you teach influences everything from opportunities to client base to quality of life. The physical studio itself presents a platform for innovation and branding. Savvy Music Teachers (SMTs) set up shop strategically, understanding that teaching sanctuaries are sacred.

Zip Code

A common adage describes the three most critical factors for a successful business: "location, location, location." Though the implications of that statement have diminished in an era where cyberspace deems geography largely irrelevant, music teaching is still primarily a local venture. Most students take lessons in real time and real place.

Successful music teaching happens everywhere. Sprawling cities, suburbs, small rural towns, and options in between offer potential. That said, not all locations hold equal promise. Each place presents unique circumstances, with most requiring at least some compromise.

The possibility of moving may be unthinkable at this point in life: you love your neighborhood, you're well connected, you live near family, your spouse has a great job, moving would disrupt the children. In this case, take full advantage of your current surroundings without giving relocation a second thought. Where you live is the best solution, because it is the *only* solution. If you are flexible, however, do thorough research and make informed decisions before choosing a zip code.

Career Potential

With the possible exceptions of advanced students, a dearth of instructors, or truly unique SMT approaches, most people are unwilling to make extended commutes for music lessons. In some cases, even 10- to 15-minute drives are deal breakers; walking distance is better. Therefore, choose a conveniently located neighborhood, easily accessible to a critical mass of your target audience.

Desirable SMT Locations	
Family friendly	Choose communities that are overflowing with kids.
Strong music education	Find school districts with robust music programs or areas with an established youth symphony/drum corp/amateur music scene.
Affluent clientele	Some SMTs cater specifically to wealthier individuals. If that describes you, identify an area desirable to these clients.
Niche market	If specializing in a particular niche, such as seniors, special needs learners, or a particular career field, select your location accordingly.

Moving where there is far more demand than teachers in your specialty is a great thing. Oversaturated markets, on the other hand, make recruitment difficult and drive down rates. For example, graduates are often tempted to stay put in small college towns with large music schools. Despite obvious benefits, it places them in direct competition with current music majors, alumni, faculty who teach on the side, and perhaps a precollege program.

Because SMTs balance portfolio careers, consider zip code implications on additional income streams and artistic outlets:

- Going rates for gigs
- Interdisciplinary avenues
- Music teaching network
- Musical colleagues/community
- Performing arts venues (quantity and quality)
- Level of philanthropy
- Professional ensembles
- Regional orchestras
- Additional teaching opportunities

Life in Suburbia

Jazz vocalist Julie Bishop taught for five years from a two-bedroom row house in downtown Philadelphia. Following the birth of her child, it quickly became apparent the family needed more space. They moved to a bigger house in the suburbs with a dedicated teaching room, about 10 minutes away. Unfortunately, this was an unreasonable commute for most members of her studio. So she found herself with a baby and in desperate need of income, essentially starting from scratch.

When meeting with one of the few students who continued, she asked a neighborhood girl to babysit. Afterward, the sitter explained she had a lead role in her high school's musical. Might she take voice lessons? From there, Bishop's reputation spread quickly. People involved with three high school programs (and their feeders) quickly learned about their new community member, filling her studio to capacity by year's end.

The surrounding area has a high percentage of dual-income households, with families accustomed to setting aside money for activities like lessons. In addition, there are more potential students within a small radius. "My mother always told me that once I got to the suburbs, finding students would be easy. I didn't believe her, but once again, Mom was right!"

Cost of Living

Cost of living varies widely from city to city, or even neighborhood to neighborhood, impacting prices on just about everything: housing, groceries, utilities, transportation, health care. This, in turn, influences how much you need to earn, the quality of home/studio you can afford, and a host of other life decisions. To emphasize the point, consider salaries required to afford a lifestyle comparable to $70,000 in Chicago, IL (according CNN Money's cost-of-living calculator: www.money.cnn.com/calculator/pf/cost-of-living).

There are compelling reasons for moving to expensive cities like Manhattan, to be sure. Many musicians are seduced by its incredible diversity, vibrant arts culture, and ecstatic energy. But this decision comes with a substantial price tag. Reaching financial independence becomes nearly impossible, and count on renting a tiny apartment rather than buying a house. Because everything is expensive, money is always tight no matter how well you do. In addition, teachers are often forced to charge relatively low rates despite the exorbitant cost of living, thanks to a market oversaturated with eager instructors who drive down the going rate.

Chicago, IL	Conway, AR	Tampa, FL	Atlanta, GA	Denver, CO
$70,000	$53,522	$56,024	$59,380	$64,080
reference	−23.5%	−20.0%	−15.2%	−8.5%
Baltimore, MD	San Diego, CA	San Jose, CA	Honolulu, HI	Manhattan, NY
$72,685	$79,703	$91,726	$102,406	$133,530
+3.7%	+13.9%	+31.0%	+46.3%	+90.8% (!)

Leaving the Big Apple

One frigid winter afternoon, violinist Diana Anderson (not her real name) announced a shocking decision. After 12 years, she and her husband would move from their 800-square-foot New York City apartment to Raleigh, NC. Her friends were stunned and prophesized "you'll be back." But 15 years later, she couldn't be happier. "For me, New York was a silly place to live. The quality of life was very difficult. Though I often worked 16-hour days, it was barely enough to eek out a living. With growing credit card debt and retirement a lost cause, moving saved my finances and family."

Anderson is now debt free other than her mortgage on a 3,000-square-foot, five-bedroom, closet-rich house. Her neighborhood (which includes sidewalks and "greenway" trails connecting various parts of the city), friendly community, and proximity to beaches and mountains are tremendous perks. It is a great place to raise kids, and her daughter attends a strong public school with plenty of access to sports, music, and more.

As an independent teacher, recruitment has been fairly easy. With four local youth orchestras and healthy school music programs, this community truly values arts education. Her $68 hourly rate may be less than what some New York teachers charge, but money goes a lot further in this affordable town. "And I love my students. In NYC, people rich enough to afford lessons often treated me as a servant. Here, I feel like a cherished family member."

Anderson does miss some things about the Big Apple: friends, restaurants, shoe shopping, the Museum of Modern Art. Ironically, she finally has enough disposable income to explore these very things when traveling back there each year with her family.

Lifestyle

Beyond career potential and cost of living, your zip code impacts many things on a daily basis. For example, proximity to family often trumps all else. Few incentives replace living by parents who share home-cooked meals, help with laundry, and babysit the grandkids in a pinch. How important are the following lifestyle considerations to you?

Lifestyle Considerations	
• Airport proximity	• Points of interest
• Amusement/theme parks	• Political leaning
• Arts culture (for you to enjoy)	• Proximity to your family
• Bike trails	• Public schools
• Community	• Restaurants
• Commute to important locations	• Safety/crime
• Dating scene	• Shopping
• Economic health of area (general)	• Sidewalks
• Family friendly	• Sport teams (pro or college)
• Kid-friendly activities	• Spouse opportunities
• Major city proximity	• Traffic
• Neighbors who share values	• University environment
• Parks and hiking trails	• Weather/climate
• Places of worship	

The ideal location is not necessarily an obvious one, and some locales known to few are hidden treasures. For example, *Money* magazine ranks the "Best Places to Live" each year, highlighting small American towns that thrive economically and are well suited for raising a family, with "plenty of green space, good schools, and a strong sense of community." Might rankings like this provide clues about fertile SMT ground?

	"Best Places to Live" *Money Magazine*'s List of America's Best Small Cities (September 2012)		
Rank	**City**	**Population**	**Avg. home price**
1	Carmel, IN	80,100	$303,340
2	McKinney, TX	136,100	$245,917
3	Eden Prairie, MN	61,200	$413,566
4	Newton, MA	84,700	$850,117
5	Redmond, WA	55,200	$518,982
6	Irvine, CA	213,600	$904,753
7	Reston, VA	60,300	$467,934
8	Columbia/Ellicott City, MD	100,700	$406,943
9	Overland Park, KS	175,300	$278,204
10	Chapel Hill, NC	59,000	$376,660

While few places have it all, there are many potential hotspots for music teaching businesses with sufficient artistic opportunities, reasonable cost of living, and a desirable lifestyle. The benefits of discovering this magical intersection are immense.

Lessons from the Trenches

In graduate school, I came to three realizations:

1. I want to change the world by becoming a full-time piano teacher.
2. I want to reach financial independence.
3. The best way to accomplish these things is through a home-based studio.

What lacked clarity were the details. Seeking a perfect location, I conducted literally months of intensive research. Two of the most helpful resources were the Census Bureau (www.census.gov) and local chambers of commerce.

Finally, I decided on Frisco, TX, a suburb of Dallas. This community appeared ripe with opportunity. With a young and growing population, the cost of living was average, public education was strong and valued, and the city had big plans. A nearby mall housed five anchor stores, indicating that locals had disposable income. Better yet, the music teaching market wasn't saturated. In fact, there was a shortage.

Moving to Frisco was one of the best decisions of my life. True, I offer unique, quality services that would likely generate interest anywhere. But joining this incredible community didn't hurt either. Through research and a little luck, my assumptions turned out to be right!

Home Studio

The benefits of teaching from home have been articulated previously. Beyond saving a large, recurring expense, it increases convenience while giving you maximum control.

This book is not a real estate guide. Only you are qualified to determine the relative importance of walk-in closets, Jacuzzi tubs, kitchens with islands, double ovens, attached garages, heated floors, wine cellars, swimming pools (liabilities for home businesses, incidentally), or walls without peeling lead paint. For SMTs planning to teach from home, however, the role and potential of six essential areas must be considered:

1. Street/neighborhood
2. Studio entrance
3. Teaching space
4. Waiting area
5. Studio restroom
6. Office space

Finding an affordable residence in your desired zip code that adequately addresses business and personal concerns is no easy task. Few options are flawless with even a hefty dose of imagination, forcing you to make difficult concessions. Which is more important, a nicer neighborhood or fancier house? A bigger master bedroom or superior teaching space?

If teaching from home is central to your career model, it may make sense to invest more upfront, purchasing or renting real estate that works well for both you and students. But debt is not something to take lightly. Carefully think through ramifications.

Street/Neighborhood

Before falling in love with any property, check with city hall to learn the rules and regulations for running a home-based business. Some communities have no red tape, while others require costly permits or prohibit this practice altogether. It would be a travesty to purchase your dream home/studio only to learn that doing business there is strictly forbidden.

Teaching studios should be in areas where families feel comfortable. Safety, or *perceived* safety, is crucial. Parents are wary of sending children into seedy, rundown, or crime-infested neighborhoods, even if your particular lot poses little threat.

Parking is also important. Favor areas with ample street/driveway options and no permit requirements. Annoyance, or even anger, occurs when the hunt for a space requires 45 minutes.

As music teachers, we help students produce glorious sound. The neighbors, however, may have a different perspective. Some communities regulate strictly enforced quiet hours. Even if they don't, music in apartments, duplexes, or "shotgun" (close together) houses can create tension and ill will. Evaluate sonic ramifications of residencies in close proximity to others. Consider soundproofing, particularly when teaching a loud instrument, and always use common courtesy. (Another solution: earplugs make great stocking stuffers for the neighbors!)

Teaching Space

At the physical heart of SMT businesses is a teaching space, serving three large-scale purposes:

1. **Function.** Large enough to accommodate needs while being acoustically fit
2. **Education.** Contains tools necessary to maximize learning
3. **Atmosphere.** Sets a tone for your studio brand and expectations

Whether your home studio is a transformed living room, family room, bedroom, basement, or garage, the best options are large enough to comfortably accommodate instruments, cases, a piano (if applicable), teaching tools, you, a student, and an extra observer or two. Experiment with various furniture placements that are comfortable and set the stage for effective learning.

The ideal space is comfortable, placing all necessary teaching supplies within close reach.

Possible Teaching Room Assets	
• Amplification (if required)	• Music stand(s)
• Artwork (walls)	• Pencils/pens
• Audio recorder/playback	• Piano/keyboard
• Books	• Primary instrument (for you)
• Chalkboards	• Recording equipment
• Clock	• Recordings (library)
• Computer	• Rugs
• Corkboards	• Seating (for observers)
• Dry erase board	• Seating (for student)
• Electrical outlets (easily accessible)	• Seating (for you)
• Fan (ceiling or floor)	• Sheet music
• Flash cards/teaching games	• Spare instrument
• Instrument repair tools	• Stickers and fun "prizes"
• Large-screen TV/monitor	• Supplies: strings, reeds, valve oil
• Lighting (as appropriate)	• Tablet
• Manuscript paper	• Teaching materials and handouts
• Metronome	• Tissue
• Microphone and stand (if required)	• Video camera and tripod
• Mirror	

SMTs understand that the decoration and layout of a teaching space are more than aesthetic. They set a mood and forecast expectations. Artwork, furniture style, the color of the walls, knickknacks, and density of "stuff" make psychological impressions. Whether hoping to create a serious, fun, inviting, creative, or scholarly environment, reflect your priorities through interior design.

What items should adorn your teaching space? Fine art? Photographs of students? Music theory/history posters? Inspirational quotes? Recital programs? Student artwork? Whiteboards and Post-it notes? Knickknacks that inspire conversation? Is the look static, or does it change over time? Walls and floors present opportunities for innovation. Don't let them go to waste.

Lesson Space

Soprano Andrea Veal (www.andreaveal.com) teaches out of a relatively small home in rural New Hampshire. Her 18 × 14-foot living room fulfills multiple functions. Black chairs divide the chamber, with about one third of the space devoted to lessons and the rest used as a waiting/

personal area. With a little rearranging, the whole room works well for master classes.

On the teaching side, permanent fixtures include a digital piano, mixing board, and nice set of speakers. Students bring SD cards to lessons, inserted into a digital audio recorder to capture the experience. When needed, she sets up a microphone, video camera, and/or additional devices like a Chromebook tablet.

On the other side are a sofa, coffee table, rug, and TV with DVD. A bookshelf provides easy access to music. Veal typically leaves a newspaper and singing journal on display for parents to peruse (sadly, the former gets more attention).

Veal decided not to decorate with musical posters or inspirational quotes. Instead, her space displays pottery by friends and souvenirs from her international travels. "When students enter my home, they experience an honest representation of who I am. This helps build trust and a personal connection, two things essential to effective voice teaching."

Temperature and Humidity Control

Temperature and humidity control are critical. Extreme conditions cause instruments to go out of tune or worse, and guests feel uncomfortable. Whether through central air/heating or another mechanism (ceiling fans, space heaters, fireplace, humidifier, dehumidifier), regulate climate conditions year round.

Acoustic Considerations

While spaces needn't be on par with Carnegie Hall, treat them acoustically to optimize sound. Dry environments are brutally honest, letting you hear exactly what is played—a teaching blessing and curse. Unfortunately, there is not much you can do to add resonance to a room. Overly loud or boomy spaces disguise mistakes and make clarity difficult. Curtains, area rugs, egg cartons, and other acoustic treatments absorb sound and deaden a room.

Soundproofing not only appeases neighbors but also blocks out noise. This is particularly helpful when recording or multiple activities compete (e.g., practice room by teaching space).

Distractions

Running a business out of your home requires discipline about cleanliness. Clutter, dirt, and disarray are unprofessional and off-putting. Similarly, keep distractions like pets, ringing phones, and screaming kids to a minimum, as they detract from the semblance of professionalism, the quality of instruction, and student concentration.

Studio Entrance, Waiting Area, and Restroom

As with any business, your "storefront"—the first and last area that clients experience—makes a strong statement about your studio's brand. Create a good impression, keeping things tidy and pruning the bushes.

Some dwellings have just one door, making the choice of entrance obvious. When more than one option exists, be clear how students should enter and exit your home. The ideal solution is exclusively designated for business (rather than shared with family) and close to the teaching room so students aren't forced to traipse through your abode. Depending on weather conditions, items like a floor mat, coat tree/hooks, shoe rack, and umbrella stand may be appropriate.

A waiting room for family, friends, and early arrivers can be a true SMT asset. Ideally, it should be adjacent to the teaching chamber, whether a family room, a living room, a bedroom, a sunroom, or simply a piece of furniture that divides the lesson space. Beyond providing comfortable seating, transform this area into an engaging, interactive haven.

Wait . . . Here's a Great Idea

For many parents and siblings, music lessons mean wasted time as their loved one receives instruction. Not so in the studio of guitarist Ronnie Currey (www.currey.musicteachershelper.com), who transformed a portion of his basement into a waiting oasis. A designated studio-only entrance leads visitors to a rather large room, approximately 15 × 20 feet. Features include:

- **Seating.** Two large couches form an L-shape, placed on plush carpeting.
- **Coffee table.** This is around 5 feet square.
- **Snacks.** Candy bars, cookies, and other goodies are available, along with drinks stored in a minifridge. Some clients look forward to their treat all week. Items are $1 each, on the honor system, creating a very minor income stream.
- **Reading materials.** Displaying magazines and newspapers turned out to be a hit. In fact, parents eventually suggested a "take one, leave one" policy. Bookshelves store publications on music and musicians.

- **Large-screen TV.** Watch cable or concert videos from the DVD collection.
- **Wi-Fi.** Guests are given the password.
- **Payment box.** Parents drop checks here, avoiding time wasted on money matters.
- **Business cards.** Currey's cards are left on an end table. Parents can also leave promotional materials to advertise their services.
- **Bulletin board.** This is used to feature announcements, photographs, graduation invitations, and so forth.
- **Computer.** This desktop cycles through a PowerPoint presentation with studio news, student photos, music trivia, and more.
- **Other amenities.** His collection includes board games, a garbage can, and a collection of Beatles memorabilia (Currey is a self-proclaimed Beatles "nut").
- **Also in the basement.** The teaching room and bathroom are also in the basement.

With such a nice space, parents and other guests look forward to *their* lesson experience.

Guests need easy access to a bathroom. Keep this area tidy and stocked with toilet paper, hand soap, tissue, hand towels, and cleaning products. Basic first aid supplies may also come in handy.

Business Office

A designated office space is ideal, though some teaching or waiting rooms perform double duty. At the least, find a place to park your computer or tablet.

Home Office Items	
• Accounting records	• CD/DVD jewel cases
• Achievement awards	• CDs/DVDs (recordable)
• Books	• Chair (comfortable)
• Bookshelf	• Computer
• Brochures	• Contracts (students,
• Business cards	employees, etc.)
• Business checks	• Copier
• Business receipts	• Desk

Home Office Items	
• Fax machine • File cabinet • Folders • Ink/toner replacements • Insurance policies • Internet access • Letterhead • Mileage records • Official documents (wills, life insurance, etc.) • Paper • Paper shredder • Pencils	• Pens (ballpoint, Sharpies, highlighters) • Postage/envelopes • Practice logs • Printer • Rechargers (cell phone, etc.) • *Savvy Music Teacher* (your copy) • Scissors • Stapler • Storage box (programs, etc.) • Student files • Tax records • Telephone

With so many wonderful resources digitized today, fewer physical items must be in an office than ever before. In addition to standard software (Internet browsers, email communication, photo storage, etc.), helpful SMT platforms are listed in the chart that follows. Because programs and apps are constantly updated, no versions are listed.

Helpful SMT Software		
Type	*Purpose*	*Examples*
Word processing	Create text-based documents.	Microsoft Word, Word Perfect, Apple Pages
Spreadsheets	Organize and track finances, student information, contacts, listening library, etc.	Microsoft Excel
Time management	Plan your schedule; be sure important projects don't slide between the cracks.	Replicon, Tenrox Timesheet
Note taking	Keep track of information, people you meet, web pages, and more.	Evernote
Finances	Record expenses and income.	Quicken, QuickBooks, Mint

(*continued*)

Helpful SMT Software		
Type	*Purpose*	*Examples*
Taxes	Calculate taxes on your own (though hiring an accountant usually saves more for complicated SMT careers).	TurboTax
Audio editing	Edit, mix, and master recordings.	Audacity, SoudForge, ProTools
Labels	Create labels for recital CDs and DVDs.	Avery CD/DVD Labels
Video communication	Conduct video lessons and virtual face-to-face business calls.	Skype, Oovoo, Google Hangout
Video editing	Edit teaching, recital, or promo videos.	iMovie, Final Cut Pro, Corel VideoStudio
Photo editing	Edit photos from master classes, recitals, and other engagements.	Adobe Photoshop, Corel PaintShop
Graphic editing	Design posters, newsletters, and other graphic documents.	Adobe Creative Suite, CorelDraw Graphics
Music notation	Notate compositions, arrangements, and worksheets.	Finale, Sibelius, Notion
MIDI/digital audio sequencing	Record, edit, and play back music either from MIDI instruments or audio sources.	Digital Performer, Cubase, Logic Pro
Music studio management	Send invoices, receive payment, schedule lessons, and more.	Music Teacher's Helper, Studio Helper, Privio

Lessons from the Trenches

My office helps organize three essential components: (1) digital financials, (2) paper financials, and (3) student records. One of the best investments I make is for a QuickBooks Online account, which provides instant access to my entire financial profile. In a few simple steps, I can set up a new budget with estimates based on last year or pull up any quarter, month, or year with pie charts and graphs to learn exactly where things stand.

My financial records are "audit ready"—organized and up to date with a paper trail. Tax preparation after the first of each year requires no more than three hours to tie up loose ends. Each week, I stay disciplined about recording purchases according to category. At the end of each month, my bank statements are reconciled with QuickBooks, where every penny is accounted for and categorized. I also have a physical accordion-type organizer for filing receipts (in case of an IRS audit) with corresponding headings.

It would be nice to say I did this from the start, but it took a few years to get savvy. Finally, I invested in three hours with a CPA. Nervous when meeting her, I was embarrassed by how sloppy my bookkeeping had been. She helped me set up QuickBooks and get organized. My financial approach has definitely improved as a result.

I am an admitted "piler." At one point, there were no less than 12 mounds of paperwork and music sprawling across my office. Finding anything became a bear. With diligence, I now permit the accumulation of just two piles. The first contains items requiring immediate attention, while the second is less urgent.

Following years of paper record keeping in lessons, I am finally 100% digital. Using a free Evernote account as both a webpage and an app, I am able to create shareable and unlimited "binders" for each student. This shift alone eliminated four piles from my office!

Separating Work and Personal Space

Though teaching from home offers numerous benefits, there is a downside. When business and living space overlap, where does one end and the other begin? If your bedroom doubles as an office and conditions get stressful, how can you turn things off for a sound night of sleep? Where do you go to simply enjoy life when signs of your job inhabit every corner?

The best solution is dividing your residence into separate work and living areas. Not only does this make clear delineations for you, but it also strengthens your case to the Internal Revenue Service when deducting a "home office." While few SMTs enjoy the luxury of enough square footage to do this definitively, designate at least a few sacred spaces where business activity is strictly prohibited.

If you struggle to separate "work" from "life," draw up a personal contract detailing rules and regulations. Where are you permitted to check email?

Which counters may professional documents never touch? As with time, space management requires discipline and strategy.

Backyard Music

Drummer Jeff Cowell (www.locuststreetstudio.com) taught out of his Toronto-area home for several years. When students arrived, his already small residence felt even tinier, inconveniencing family and causing stress. And then there was the noise issue. "Drums are loud! I like my neighbors and want to keep it that way." Rather than moving or renting a separate space, Cowell ultimately built a detached backyard structure.

The new Locust Street Studio is a sight to be seen. Its exterior copper panels surround several colorful doors. Five round windows framed by actual drum shells and covered with thick glass "are the best sounding windows I've ever played!" He has plans to grow grass and plants on the flat green roof.

The interior is just as intriguing. A large teaching space, around 18 × 20 feet, is actually a "room within a room" to help with soundproofing. The structure also contains a small waiting area, bathroom, and utility room with an electric panel and storage. Floors are heated, electric outlets are plentiful, and Wi-Fi flows freely.

This structure required a significant investment. While it won't pay for itself any time soon, it increases the home's value, avoids the need to rent teaching space, and serves as a seductive recruitment tool. It is also a wonderful place for bands to rehearse and for his own children to practice, while adding quality of life for the whole family.

Other Locations

Venues

When teaching from home is something you are unable or unwilling to do (no suitable space, large classes, summer camp, personal preference) a number of alternatives exist. The choice of venue influences brand and image. Represent your business well.

Other Teaching Venues	
Music stores	Economically, it is better to rent space rather than working as an employee, signing a "noncompete" agreement, and forfeiting autonomy.
Public/private schools	The occasional school allows music teachers to use their facilities for free, since better playing benefits the program directly. If not, favor fixed rental rates over a percentage. Some public schools offer free room usage during the summer to nonprofits. While you may not want the hassle of filing for 501(c)(3) status, consider partnering with an organization that shares a similar mission. They may be willing to file the paperwork in exchange for marketing or minor compensation.
Rental spaces for musicians	Some private enterprises rent rooms specifically to musicians in various time increments. Even if they primarily target bands, this space may work just as well for lessons and classes.
Arts centers	Some state arts commissions/agencies rent space to artists at reduced rates.
Churches/ synagogues	Many worship centers have rooms appropriate for music learning, often with pianos. Congregation members may be able to negotiate use for free, for extremely cheap, or in exchange for volunteering.
Office buildings	Some commercial structures offer flexible conditions, rentable by the hour, day, week, month, or year.
Businesses closed when you teach	Though unconventional, businesses closed when you teach (e.g., offices with morning hours only) may consider renting out a room.
Other buildings that rent rooms	Community centers, retirement homes, libraries, warehouses, small hotels, restaurants, and other establishments may rent rooms at reasonable rates. Many locations offer Wi-Fi access, a waiting area, and additional benefits.

(continued)

Other Teaching Venues	
Nonrented properties	When a landlord is unable to secure tenants for either residential or commercial properties, they are simply bleeding money. The proposition of leasing vacant space for limited hours may be compelling. Of course, when they do find an occupant, the opportunity evaporates.
A neighbor's home	Some households welcome a guest teacher in exchange for easy income. In fact, music lovers may volunteer their dwelling for free.

A potential benefit of renting is gaining access to students already connected to that location. For example, some schoolchildren are more inclined to enroll in music lessons at their school, capitalizing on a convenience. The same is true of seniors at a retirement home.

Many variables impact the price tag of a room rental: zip code, size, fanciness, equipment, business type, demand. Some hosts offer different rental packages, with options by the hour, block (e.g., Thursdays, 4 to 8 PM), day, week, or month. Discounts for multiple rooms may be available—helpful when running a summer camp or music academy.

Monthly leases are the most expensive but provide unlimited access and freedom to control the environment more or less as you please. In some regions, nice spacious rooms can be found for just a few hundred dollars. Identifying a hole in the wall for less than $1,000 to $2,000 in a major metropolis like New York City is unlikely.

Hourly rentals have the highest per-minute rate, but you pay only when space is in use. In this case, you are essentially stuck with equipment and decoration as is. Options appropriate for music lessons and classes generally cost $5 to $20 per hour.

The best rental rate, clearly, is gratis. Of course, free rentals are rarely ideal, and the wisdom of asking for favors beyond the already generous offer is precarious. If individuals or businesses let you use their space without charge, do not take this for granted. Bend over backward to avoid creating inconvenience or complication. Tokens of appreciation like holiday cards and fresh-baked brownies go a long way.

Businesses specializing in rentals are likely to have fixed rates and a clear contact person. Nonrental agencies, on the other hand, may require digging to identify who has authority to make those arrangements. In schools, this individual often has a title like business manager, facility manager, athletic director, or assistant principal of student activities. With religious organizations and community centers, there may be an activities director or building coordinator. For other businesses, start with the owner or manager. Even places that have never before considered renting may find the promise of artistic presence and passive income persuasive.

Many landlords check credit scores and do background checks (criminal records, child abuse, etc.). Some places require a special business permit, which may or may not be accompanied by a fee. Check whether the property owner's insurance policy covers renters.

Rental Space

Baritone saxophonist Wayne Leechford (www.wayneleechford. com) began teaching woodwinds through an academy in an upscale neighborhood. Unfortunately, they claimed a whopping 50% of the tuition he generated. Because this made it impossible to reach financial goals, he began renting a room through a music store as an independent contractor. When they closed unexpectedly, he founded Leechford Music Teaching Studios (www.leechfordmusic.com).

LMTS is located in what used to be a chiropractor's office, with five 9 × 11 rooms, a bathroom, and a reception/waiting area. Beyond providing his own teaching address, Leechford rents rooms to independent instructors by the hour ($12) or day (e.g., $110 per month for full access every Monday). Currently serving seven teachers, LMTS has the capacity to expand by three.

Leechford signed a three-year lease and left a security deposit. Insistent on creating a professional and warm environment, he used $3,500 of startup expenses to pay for carpeting, repainting, signage, and music stands. He and two other teachers store their personal pianos there.

Beyond covering rent, revenue from this investment currently contributes 5% to 10% of Leechford's annual income. He ultimately hopes to move in to a larger space of roughly twice that size that includes a rehearsal/performance space and small store. "To earn more than the average music teacher, you must look for additional income streams. This is what I chose."

House Calls

Home Schooling

After college, vocalist Melissa Blasek (www.melissablasek.net) began working through music schools that claimed up to 50% of her earnings while failing to generate many students. Without an adequate teaching space of her own, a better solution was necessary.

Voice, piano, and guitar students of Blasek now have three options:

1. **Weekly in-studio lessons.** She still teaches through one school, where half-hour weekly lessons run $100 per month. The program charges a commission, leaving $72.
2. **Biweekly in-home lessons.** For $120 per month, she travels to your home. Rather than 30 minutes every seven days, this buys a one-hour meeting every other week.
3. **Weekly in-home lessons.** These half hour slots are priced at $130 per month, available only on weekdays before 3 PM.

Blasek, who began making house calls in her own neighborhood, quickly expanded into 17 local towns. Within 10 months, she had a full schedule and waiting list. She clusters meetings geographically, and openings are filled by a combination of place in line and location. When traveling, she packs her guitar, half-sized keyboard (for voice lessons only, as budding pianists own an instrument), necessary books, and laptop.

The "current" rates listed previously are charged to new students. After signing on, that amount is guaranteed for as long as study continues. Blasek's policy requires full participation from September through June and at least one prorated lesson during both July and August. Students who don't want summer lessons may drop out, but re-enrolling means higher tuition and possibly joining the waitlist. This policy brings greater financial stability to summers.

"For me, in-home lessons are a great solution. The pay winds up being higher, and my only overhead is gas. More importantly, I grow closer with families when visiting their homes. Turnover diminishes, and problems with pets, siblings, or noise have been rare. People investing in this service go out of their way to ensure it is a positive experience."

Another option is becoming a traveling teacher, providing lessons directly in students' homes.

In-Home Lessons	
Pros	*Cons*
This is a good option when you have no appropriate space for a home studio.	You have no control over physical lesson environment.
It does not require the expense of renting a room.	It requires commuting, which costs time, money, and inconvenience.
You can charge extra for travel expenses and troubles.	Students may be less focused in their home.
Commuting provides a break in your day.	It may inconvenience the student's household.
It eliminates inconvenience associated with teaching from home (your family disrupted, constant cleaning, etc.).	You can accommodate fewer students, since time is eaten up commuting; travel fees are rarely equivalent to teaching rates.
You help clients create a musical home.	You must transport all supplies with you; there is no access to unanticipated resources.
Parents love this convenient solution.	This puts wear and tear on your vehicle and requires fuel expenses.
Liability insurance is not needed.	Technology access may be less than optimal.
Travel miles are tax deductible.	It is difficult to keep on schedule.

Lessons requiring a keyboard must take place where the piano is situated. Otherwise, find a room with few distractions like an office, living room, spare bedroom, or basement.

A traveling teacher's vehicle serves double duty as a storage locker. (The bike is out!)

Possible In-Home Lesson Items to Transport	
• Amplification • Audio playback system • Books on music • Instrument (yours) • Laptop/tablet • Method books • Metronome • Mileage log • Music stand • Paperwork (contracts, newsletters, etc.)	• Receipts for payments • Recordings • Sheet music collection • Supplies: strings, reeds, valve oil • Teaching games/tools (e.g., flashcards) • Theory books • Tools for instrument repair • Workbooks

If you provide house calls, get compensated fairly. Reimbursement for fuel is not enough. How much is your commute time worth? Some SMTs ask affluent families to pay as much or more for travel minutes as the lesson itself.

Music Lessons in the Office

TravelClef (www.travelclef.com), a "traveling music school" in Singapore founded by Benjamin Kwan and Edmund Chew, began by offering guitar and ukulele lessons in the homes of clients. Then one day, an unexpected inquiry opened up a new market with near-unlimited potential. The call came from an engineering firm, asking about scheduling a weekly music class for interested employees in their building.

The encounter was so successful that they started marketing lessons and classes to other businesses. To date, these "products" have impacted the staff of banks, telecommunications firms, community centers, a shipping company, and a hospital. Teaching space costs TravelClef nothing, as employers are excited to host such a meaningful activity for their personnel.

In most cases, interested workers pay to enroll, though some companies partially subsidize the experience. One 11-employee business fully funded participation for everyone on the payroll. After all, these experiences improve morale and build community, contributing to a positive workplace environment.

Corporate engagements are divided evenly between lessons and classes. In addition to guitar and ukulele, TravelClef now offers "piano" instruction on lightweight, battery-operated, roll-up instruments. At the request of clients, some sessions highlight themes like leadership, team building, motivation, or happiness, while others have a pure musical focus. "Our goal is not to develop virtuosos," explains Kwan. "Instead, we just have fun making music. We laugh and laugh and laugh." As a result, their students can't wait to get to work!

Making the Business Run

Business Structures

In the United States, self-employed individuals can operate under several business designations, each with unique tax and legal implications. Most SMTs who run a studio (as opposed to an academy) operate as *sole proprietors*, or nonincorporated businesses run by a single person. This is the easiest and cheapest kind of enterprise to operate—essentially just go about your work. Few regulations and little red tape are imposed on sole proprietorships, allowing the studio to be run as you see fit.

With this legal status, your business and personal financial life are intertwined to the core, at least in the eyes of the Internal Revenue Service. In the unlikely event your company gets sued (e.g., your piano falls on a student), personal assets may be seized, making it essential to carry commercial general liability insurance. Profits can be reinvested in the company (and are tax deductible) or given directly to you, the owner.

If your business grows to incorporate additional employees, other business structures should be considered. Consult an accountant to explore the myriad options available.

Savvy Music Teacher Inc.

Tubist Bernard Flythe (www.theflythegroup.com) balances a varied career. In addition to 24 private students, he gigs as a freelancer, runs sectionals at three schools, and serves as an adjunct professor. Following years of operating as a sole proprietor, he formed an *S Corporation* called The Flythe Group Inc. at the recommendation of an accountant.

The primary benefit of this legal status is that it allows additional tax deductions. Though his earnings (around $60,000 annually) have remained fairly consistent, three new write-offs totaling $21,600 enable Flythe to keep more of this money:

1. **Rent.** The full amount of his rent plus some utilities ($800/month × 12 months = $9,600/year), paid by the company, is tax deductible.
2. **Salary.** The business entity pays Flythe a monthly salary ($600/month × 12 months = $7,200/year). Though required to send himself a 1099, this relatively small but official income amount is taxed at a low rate. Keep in mind that many life expenses (e.g., rent) are paid by the company, rather than his salary.
3. **Dividends.** The company divides after-tax profits into *dividends*, paid to stockholders ($400/month × 12 months = $4,800/year). Since Flythe is the sole stockholder, all this money goes to him. However, dividends are taxed at an even lower rate than his salary.

Running a corporation requires a certain amount of extra legwork and expense. The initial $50 fee to incorporate was processed by his bank, and another $50 per year owed to the state of Georgia is comparable to paying for a driver's license. Paperwork is relatively uncomplicated.

Flythe is the president and CEO of The Flythe Group Inc. Its board has just one other member: his brother. "It is great having a sibling as a sounding board for career issues. Additionally, there is now a legal rationale for deducting travel expenses when I make the eight-hour round-trip drive to visit family."

Contracts

Many young teachers start their careers without student contracts. At some point, they get burned, and then discover why these documents are so crucial. Avoid the learning curve by incorporating binding documents from the beginning.

Effective contracts needn't be long or complicated. In fact, the best examples are just one page and use normal, comfortable, comprehensible language rather than confounding legalize. The point is not to scare students or trick them into something unexpected. Instead, clearly articulate studio policies and expectations.

A good contract protects both you and your students. It lets them know what is expected while outlining resources provided in return. Signed each year or when there is a policy/rate change, they should include the following:

1. **Your contact information.** Include your studio name, address, phone number, website, and email.
2. **Student's contact information.** Include the student name, address, phone number, email, and contact parent for children under 18.
3. **Rates.** Clearly state tuition and all other applicable charges.
4. **Payment policy.** When must bills be paid? Before the beginning of each semester? By the first day of each month?
5. **Payment methods.** What payment methods do you accept? Cash, check, or credit card? Can people pay via your website (highly recommended)? Is there an auto-charge option?
6. **Late payment charge.** What penalty is assessed when payments are not on time?
7. **Cancellation policy.** Clearly outline your policy. How far in advance must students notify you to reschedule? How many cancellations are permitted?
8. **Refunds.** Do you grant refunds for prepaid lessons (not recommended)? What happens if a student decides to halt study midterm?
9. **Signatures.** Both you and the student (or his or her legal guardian) should sign the contract.

In addition to contracts for students, craft legally binding documents for your employees and employers. Though most people are honest and true to their word, these agreements become invaluable when problems arise.

Payment Methods

SMTs accept three payment methods. Consider the benefits and deficits of each.

Form	Pros	Cons
Cash	• Ensures you get paid • No expense incurred • Can be spent immediately	• No way to reclaim if misplaced • Requires bank trip to deposit • Must be vigilant about recording for taxes • Few people use cash today

(continued)

Form	Pros	Cons
Check	• Clear record of payment • No expense incurred • If misplaced, can be cancelled and rewritten • Many banks have apps that let you deposit through your phone	• Checks can bounce, resulting in penalty • You may not be able to cash a check to your business name • May take several days to clear
Credit	• Convenience • Can be automated or paid for through website • Payment sites keep clear records • Payment guaranteed and immediate	• Requires vendors to pay a fee, often 2%–4% unless you do a lot of volume • Harder to take payment in person (though apps like Square make this easier)

Lessons from the Trenches

When starting to teach, my payment policy was a little "squishy." Frustrated after not being compensated a handful of times, I made a change. Instead of assessing late fees, my policy now states that lessons will be terminated if fees are 10 days late. It sounds extreme, but so far, nobody has tested the waters.

I have accepted credit cards since 2009. In addition to making things more convenient for clients, this option has caused late payments to drop to near zero. PayPal through my website and Square on my smartphone simplify and streamline the process. Because processing fees are tax deductible, the actual cost to me is minimal.

11

FILLING YOUR STUDIO

You have musical talent, teaching expertise, and a profound passion for your work. The challenge? Your studio has just 13 students but can accommodate 32.

For serious Savvy Music Teachers (SMTs), the value of a full studio cannot be overstated. Beyond the obvious implications on impact and income, it also allows you to pick and choose students, referring problematic ones elsewhere without inflicting detrimental economic consequences. That keeps you inspired, which in turn benefits the entire studio. A full load even helps with marketing, as satisfied clients enthusiastically refer others. Ironically, the hardest time to recruit is when you need students the most. When enrollment booms, this happens almost automatically!

No doubt, you're convinced. The problem is not a lack of ambition, but rather a roster marked with vacancies. The solution: marketing.

Marketing Strategy

Filling a music studio is simply not that hard, especially for accomplished, innovative SMTs with a likeable personality. In fact, it's easier than promoting most other kinds of businesses.

For starters, you don't need thousands of customers, just 20 to 40. Music studios appeal to specific niche markets, which is easier and more cost-effective than reaching the masses. And people taking lessons often stay loyal for 3, 5, or even 10+ years. True, all instructors experience turnover when students switch teachers, discontinue study, or advance to college. However, SMTs who integrate the kinds of initiatives described earlier develop a committed following. Once a studio reaches capacity, there are typically only a few openings each year.

Over time, the glowing reputation of great teachers alone generates plentiful leads. But when quickly growing your studio is important, employ an SMT marketing strategy.

What Rarely Works

I often encounter independent teachers with underpopulated studios. The lack of clientele is killing them financially, but what can they do? When asked about a marketing plan, some bashfully concede there isn't one. Truth be told, they have little interest in this activity. Isn't great teaching enough? (Hint: no.) But others make a valiant attempt, incorporating some combination of the following: (1) ads, (2) posters, (3) business cards, and (4) a basic website.

If this strategy describes you, and your waitlist is mushrooming, feel free to skip this chapter. You are doing just fine. But the aforementioned tactics, at least in isolation, are rarely enough to generate enough excitement to quickly fill a roster.

Advertisements are expensive (e.g., one Midwest suburb–specific children's magazine charges $700 monthly for a quarter-page ad and requires a one-year contract) and largely ineffective in a world oversaturated with competing messages. While many companies are delighted to take your money and run an ad, SMTs are generally wary of this tactic unless the opportunity is cheap or free and extremely targeted. There are more effective ways to market a studio.

Lessons from the Trenches

Though not a fan of print advertising, I have found a few effective online options.

On Facebook, the "boost" option is different from its advertising channels, which normally appear in the left-hand margin. Instead, a boosted post enters into news feeds of my chosen demographic. I typically use this tactic when sharing videos, investing $20 to $30 per post (though it is possible to devote as little as $5). Beyond reaching new clients, this strategy helps maintain buzz about studio activities.

Thumbtack.com has proven an effective recruitment tool. Prospective students request price quotes and additional information through my page at no cost to them. Responding to inquiries (direct advertising) costs two credits, or approximately $3. I have generated around three students for every $100 spent, making Thumbtack both affordable and effective.

Google AdWords (www.adwords.google.com) is also moderately helpful, primarily for increasing search engine optimization to attract new visitors to my website. This service allows users to create ads connected to keywords (e.g., "Dallas piano lessons"). When someone does a related search, my ad may appear. Clicking delivers them to my website, and I am charged a fee depending on the popularity of these keywords. No click, no pay—finally, targeted advertising that costs only when people pay attention!

Posters hung in strategic locations and business cards distributed generously can in fact lead to inquiries. Yet serious students today rarely find teachers this way. Even if a promotional item grabs attention, most clients seek referrals or conduct online research before inquiring about lessons, which brings us to the final point.

Websites are crucial, but simply having one isn't enough. Unfortunately, far too many music teacher sites fall somewhere on the effectiveness continuum between boring and disastrous. They certainly fail to excite visitors in ways that generate immediate, positive return.

So what's an SMT to do?

Success in marketing is not measured by the number of promotional items created or amount of time/dollars spent. All that matters are results: gaining clients. With that in mind, here are five SMT strategies that work. Follow them, and it won't take long to fill your studio and grow a waitlist.

Strategy #1: Unique Selling Proposition
What Students Seek

Someone new enters the market for private music instruction. After considering several options, which factors are most influential in determining the ultimate decision?

Some flip a coin. Others gravitate to the lowest price or closest destination. But for something as personal as music lessons, *most clients are drawn to accessible studios that connect personally and offer high perceived value.* This is true even when tuition is more.

Why Study with Me?

In 30 seconds or less, every SMT should be able to concisely answer "Why study with me?" What makes my instruction so special, so valuable, so *remarkable* that it clearly rises above the competition? (Or am I simply another competent/wonderful but generic music teacher?) Simply stated, what is my *unique selling proposition* (USP)?

Of course, not all rationales are equally effective. Consider the message of Sue Saphone.

Why Study with Sue Saphone?

1. Weekly lessons!!!
2. Yearly recitals!!!
3. Excellent teaching!!!
4. Over 23 years of experience!!!!
5. I studied at a top music school!!!!!
6. I won prestigious awards!!!!!!!!!

Comparable merits commonly appear on promotional materials by independent music teachers. Yet in a competitive marketplace, this sales pitch is unlikely to conjure much excitement:

1. **Weekly lessons.** Every music teacher offers weekly lessons. Why waste the ink?
2. **Yearly recitals.** Recitals are imperative, but again, just about every respectable studio does this. Those that don't are substandard, but nothing is remarkable here.
3. **Excellent teaching.** Let's hope so. However, self-praise is a hard sell. All people claim they're outstanding (have you ever seen promotions for "mostly adequate but 30% subpar" work?). How does Sue excel? The assertion is unsubstantiated.
4. **Over 23 years of experience.** The implication is apparently that because she's done it for a while, she *must* be good. That requires a leap of faith. Some veteran teachers should have retired decades ago. Hopefully that's not the case here, but why is this significant? Plus, what does "over 23 years" mean: 24 years? 23 years, 47 days, and 14 minutes?
5. **I studied at a top music school.** Many music teachers have degrees in music, often from good programs. This claim is hardly unique, particularly if Sue lives in a big city or college town with a decent music program.
6. **I won prestigious awards.** Way to go, Sue! But does winning a prize automatically qualify you as a good teacher? More troubling, these last three points are all about the teacher (me, me, me) while completely ignoring the student (you, you, you).

7. !!!!!!!!! Why all those exclamation marks??? People who overpunctuate often do so to disguise uninteresting words!!! :-(The same goes for CAPS LOCK, AS IT LOOKS LIKE YOU ARE SHOUTING AT THE READER.

Lessons from the (Other) Trenches

I (David Cutler, author of *The Savvy Music Teacher*) also went to top music schools (through my doctorate!!!) and have won buckets of awards!!!!!!! Yay me!!!!

Do you truly care? Perhaps it's interesting trivia, perhaps not. Maybe you're happy for me (thanks, Mom); feel free to create a Wikipedia entry. But is that why you decided to read this book? Probably not. More likely, you hoped it might help solve *your* problems. Perhaps you noticed the frequent use of "you" throughout.

Accolades provide credibility but should not be your primary message. SMTs are careful to demonstrate value to *students*, rather than merely singing their own praises.

Meaningful USPs are typically informed by an essential question, chief learning objectives, and unusual/innovative studio initiatives. Keeping this in mind, consider the following message:

Why Study with Dijer E. Doo?
1. Friendly, personalized learning environment
2. Monthly master classes
3. Yearly performance for an underserved community
4. All students improvise (no prior experience necessary!)
5. Technology integrated regularly
6. Students have won prestigious awards

Dijer certainly has a USP:

1. **Friendly, personalized learning environment.** This says something about studio attitude and philosophy. It's not substantiated here, but it at least suggests that the teacher is no tyrant and takes an interest in tailoring lessons to each learner.
2. **Monthly master classes.** Because these aren't commonplace, it makes a stronger impact than the "yearly recital" claim. This is a nice bonus for certain types of students.

3. **Yearly performance for an underserved community**. A socially conscious studio? Now that's interesting. These must be good people.
4. **All students improvise**. Though scary to some, this priority excites others seeking a holistic and creative education. The "no experience" clause quells fears of a novice.
5. **Technology integrated regularly**. Dijer sounds hip and current, not your grandmother's music teacher.
6. **Students have won prestigious awards**. This message is client centric. He must be good if students win prizes.

From these 34 words, it becomes clear that Dijer is no typical teacher. True, some students will be turned off by his distinctive positioning, instead seeking a more traditional approach. But others will be compelled by the unique biases of this program. Though he charges $7 per hour more than Sue, we are clearly not comparing apples with apples.

In a world where virtually anybody can study with anybody, thanks to the growing popularity of online lessons, USPs have never been more important. Carefully determine how to best explain the differentiated value of your studio (rather than just music lessons in general). Beyond marketing, getting this right can make you a better, more impactful teacher.

Why Study with Me?

Lily Shang's (www.lilyshang.com) website specifically addresses this question:

1. **International Experience**. Lily has studied and performed all over the world in places like Beijing, Tianjin, Hawaii, Toronto, New York, Stanford, Orlando, and Montreal.
2. **Timeless Methods**. Violin methods are an oral/aural tradition passed down from teacher to student. Lily has been lucky enough to study with many great violin teachers.
3. **Cross-Genre Secrets**. Lily has experimented with many forms of music. . . . She has jammed and recorded with indie-rock bands and improvises jazz, oldies, and electro. She can seamlessly incorporate non-classical music elements into lessons, whether it's a YouTube beat-boxer or dance tracks from DJ Tiesto.
4. **An Exciting Performer**. Lily is an active performer. She believes that in honing her performance experiences she'll have more wisdom to pass on to students.

5. **Ever the Student.** Lily still practices on her own so she understands what it's like to be a student.
6. **She's Good At It.** Lily is a great music teacher because she enjoys it and has fun every lesson. . . . Chances are you will as well.

Shang's site also lists a "menu of lesson options," including focus on theory, ear training, improvisation, chamber music, orchestral rep, recording, video production, and "jam nights."

Strategy #2: Direct Interaction

The most potent marketing tool in your arsenal is *you*. The greater your visibility, the more opportunity you have to connect with prospective students. Both one-time encounters and extended interactions may yield results. When working to fill a studio, *schedule at least one engagement per month* that places you and your target audience in direct contact.

Performance Opportunities

Playing for or alongside your target audience is a great way to energize, build trust, and generate leads. Many SMTs consider performance opportunities central to their marketing efforts.

Performance Opportunities Providing Direct Interaction	
• Birthday party performances • Camp performances • Carnivals, festivals, athletic events, career fairs, dance recitals, etc. • Classroom performances • Concerts and gigs • Day care center performances • Educational concerts • Featured soloist with student ensemble • Guest artist at talent shows	• Guest conducting • Open rehearsals • Preconcert show played by invited youth group for your event • School/amateur/church choir accompanying • School assemblies • Side-by-side concerts • Spontaneous playground performances • Teaching artist work

Don't let a performance go to waste. Let people know about your studio and USP, as well as how to get in touch. Pass out promotional materials and hang posters in areas where this audience typically convenes (e.g., music rooms in schools where you perform) so they are reminded of your work.

Meeting Your Customers

Following a cross-country move, hornist/brass teacher Sarah Younker (www.sarahyounker.com) needed to build her studio, and fast. Getting proactive, she sought opportunities that brought her in direct contact with young players.

One new student struggled with band music. Contacting her director, Younker requested to mentor this musician in context during a school rehearsal. During the session, interactions with the whole group led to a great time for all, and several classmates signed up for lessons. Following that positive experience, Younker voluntarily offered sectionals at other area schools. Conductors loved the generous offer, and her studio grew steadily.

Hoping to network and have an artistic outlet, Younker joined a semiprofessional wind symphony made up of military personnel, band directors, and other locals. One evening, a trumpet player remarked, "I love how you play! Do you teach?" Of course, she did. He happened to lead a local youth symphony and sent several students her way.

Another recruitment opportunity emerged when teaching after-school classes to first through third graders. Called "Young Musicians," these musical petting zoos met once a week for two months, exposing participants to a variety of instruments. When "graduates" showed musical promise, Younker approached parents, inquiring if their talented child might consider music lessons. For kids interested in brass, she was the obvious teacher of choice.

Nonperformance Opportunities

Performing isn't the only musical setting that facilitates close contact with potential students.

Nonperformance Opportunities Providing Direct Interaction	
• Adjudicating/coaching local music competitions • Coaching/leading sectionals: youth symphonies, church choirs, community ensembles, school music programs • Composing/arranging for ensembles	• Hosting your own competition • Preconcert talks • Speaking to student groups • Teaching classes • Working at summer camps • Workshops through music stores

Parental Engagement

Also consider ways to engage parents. Organizing gatherings with titles like "How Music Lessons Transform Your Family," "Getting Your Child Excited about Practicing," or "Why Music Lessons?" is a great platform for meeting moms and dads. Though these free talks—complete with cookies and tea—should not be disguised commercials, inspired parents may immediately schedule a trial lesson.

Or have your students do the marketing. Arrange minirecitals at local parent teacher association meetings. By transforming sessions into dynamic artistic encounters, attendees may consider whether their own children would benefit from music study (with you).

Strategy #3: Strategic Allies

Imagine the impact when a community leader, teacher, friend, or other influential voice declares, "You really should take lessons with _____!" Word of mouth is powerful marketing. Luckily, the unique features of SMT programs provide plenty of fodder for igniting this chatter.

Identifying Key Allies

Plenty of people can direct students your way: family, friends, colleagues, neighbors, current students/parents, former clients, other teachers, college faculty, church/temple staff—you name it. When looking to fill your studio, consider how each person you know might help.

In addition to your current network, brainstorm respected leaders connected to your target population(s), though not in direct competition with you. For cellists, possibilities include youth symphony conductors, school string educators, summer camp directors, music store managers, luthiers, and string teachers of different styles/levels. Vocalists might consider general music teachers, choral instructors, church music directors, musical theater casting agents, club owners that book bands, and karaoke bartenders. If targeting seniors, don't forget retirement community activity directors and concert presenters that cater to retirees.

The Direct Plea

Each year, trombonist Linda Yeo Leonard (www.yeodoug.com/ young_players.html) mails a single-page letter to 30 band directors in the greater Chicago region. Its four paragraphs address her teaching credentials and offer an observation: "Students who take private music lessons progress at a significantly swifter rate than those who do not. I take pride in assisting my many students to fully realize their potentials in band, jazz band, and orchestra classes as well as solo and ensemble competitions year after year." She then makes a direct plea for referrals. The letter is accompanied by a resume and 7 to 10 business cards.

The simple act of reaching out to these key allies year after year has paid dividends. Several cite her as their first-choice low brass instructor. Some include her studio information on band e-newsletters. Three public high school programs have even invited Leonard to teach from their facilities, free of charge. "This arrangement is convenient for students, I have a place to teach, and directors see their members improve rapidly. Everybody wins!"

Cultivating New Advocates

Transforming someone from stranger to advocate requires more than a clever email. A good first step is scheduling an in-person meeting, preferably over coffee or lunch (on your dime). This is the surest way to begin building meaningful relationships. With that goal, make first contact through a brief, personalized email:

1. **Break the ice.** If possible, find something that connects you with this person: a past encounter, mutual acquaintance, similar background. If nothing else, include a sincere comment about the person's work and why you are moved to make contact.
2. **Introduce yourself.** Provide one to two sentences describing who you are and what you do.
3. **Make the offer.** Invite the person to meet. Mentioning your studio is fine, but avoid asking for favors during an initial contact. Instead, show a sincere interest in people and they will become interested in you.

If no response arrives within a week, do not get discouraged. This may indicate busyness rather than disinterest. Follow up with a second email or phone call. Most people are accessible to those who demonstrate persistence. If no sign of life emerges after several attempts, cross that person off your list and move on.

The purpose of a first "date" should not be manipulating someone into helping you. Rather, begin a sincere, long-term, professional relationship. Create a friendly rapport, asking questions about the individual's projects, interests, and needs, balanced by sharing a little about yourself and your teaching. Before leaving, ask how you can help the person (e.g., coaching an ensemble for free) and leave the door open for further communication. It is permissible to share your quest for new students, but don't make that the conversational centerpiece.

Over the next several months, interact with each new connection several times through follow-up meetings, collaboration, social media, attending the person's concerts, or other means. As the association grows in mutually beneficial ways, referrals will come. Just as important, you make new friends and expand your network. Who knows where that will lead?

Motivating Your Network

Knowing the right people is only part of the challenge. For them to produce actual leads, your allies must advocate. Why exactly would anybody do that?

- **A fluke.** Someone might refer you unprompted. While it's great when that occurs, don't rest your strategy on accidental recommendations. If you need students, be proactive!
- **Extraordinary work.** If aspects of your teaching are innovative and wonderful (common for SMTs), those in the know may have no choice but to share the gossip.
- **Recent contact.** Human beings have short memories and tend to refer the person with whom they've been in most recent contact.
- **Reciprocal agreement.** For example, a piano teacher might agree to send all students to a particular tuner, and vice versa.
- **Incentives.** The referrer receives a free lesson, referral fee, or some other goodie that rewards their support (see marketing strategy #5).
- **Asking.** Sometimes all it takes is asking for referrals. Without the prompt, it may never cross the mind of even your closest friends.
- **They like you.** None of the previous rationales works unless people truly like you and the work you do. Be good to everyone.

Partnerships

A core marketing strategy for singer-songwriter and music therapist Rachel Rambach (www.rachelrambach.com) is forming strategic alliances with local businesses that have overlapping clientele and shared values.

One partnership is with a photographer specializing in newborns, kids, and families. Appealing to similar audiences, both professionals link their websites and mention one another periodically on social media. The photographer distributes Rambach's business card with every package sold, while the music teacher displays beautiful photo samples on a studio wall (including one of her own baby). Both parties have generated numerous leads from this arrangement. More important, they are now close friends.

Another affiliation grew out of a need. Though lessons and therapy sessions were comfortably conducted in Rambach's home, she lacked adequate space to accommodate early childhood classes. Searching for an appropriate venue, she stumbled upon a therapy clinic with a compatible philosophy and unused room during the day. In addition to reasonable rental rates, the clinic hangs posters and distributes informational postcards describing Rambach's offerings. This promotion has generated numerous clients for classes and lessons. Conversely, several music families have become clinic customers.

A third alliance is with a music store where Rambach used to teach. Rather than hiring a replacement, this business is quick to refer its former employee, proudly displaying her cards and brochures. In return, Rambach encourages studio members to buy method books, accessories, and instruments from this vendor, which grants them a 5% to 10% "preferred partner" discount. She also receives a finder's fee when students make large instrument purchases.

Great business, like great teaching, benefits everyone involved.

Strategy #4: Powerhouse Website

A business without a web footprint is one that doesn't exist, at least in the eyes of the public. If you are serious about promoting your teaching studio, a designated website is nonnegotiable. That said, the mere act of erecting a basic site—or even an elaborate one—doesn't guarantee success. Not all domains are created equally. In fact, many instructor websites fail to do their teaching justice. Sometimes it even hurts their cause. SMTs settle for nothing less than a *powerhouse website*.

10 SMT Powerhouse Website Tips

1. **Display vitals in plain sight**. Many websites neglect to mention essential details; others require viewers to dig for data. If you mandate a hunt, you risk losing students. Place essentials on the landing page or another intuitive spot.

Studio Essentials	
• Business/teacher name • Email address • Instruments/topics taught	• Location (if not a street address, at least city, state, and neighborhood) • Phone number

2. **Load your site with value**. A teaching website serves up to four audiences: (a) you the teacher, (b) prospective clients, (c) current students, and (d) other groups. Clearly identify the communities you hope to benefit, and provide meaningful content.
3. **Delete anything and everything that fails to add value**. Every page, link, and even word should serve a function. If not, take it out. Many sites include seemingly random information or verbosity that does little more than dilute the message.
4. **Show your commitment**. Should performer-teachers have a single umbrella website or multiple independent ones? While there is no "correct" answer, a robust performance URL with just one page devoted to teaching seems to indicate that education is merely a side business. If choosing the all-in-one model, connect the dots. Emphasize your devotion, highlighting how this multifaceted existence benefits students directly.
5. **Make it *student* centric**. Average teachers compile considerable content about themselves—teacher bio, teacher photos, teacher awards, teacher policies, teacher rates, teacher calendar, teacher expectations—with little to no mention of students. SMTs, on the other hand, highlight student issues, student news, student profiles, student photos, student tips, student exercises, student games, news for students, and events for students. In addition to providing valuable resources for current clients, this emphasis functions as potent marketing. Powerhouse sites make prospective clients believe, "Wow, I want to be a part of that community," rather than "Hmmm . . . sounds qualified. . . ."

6. **Create a brand.** It is not enough to say who you are and what you do. SMT websites tell a story and establish a dynamic. If you are a fun/engaging/demanding teacher, reflect that reality. Be consistent and interesting!

7. **Make your site musical.** SMT websites should include music, whether teacher recordings, student performances, or videos of superstar players.

8. **Both content and design count.** The words on your site are important, but so are visual components such as layout, clear menu, and graphic elements. Create an online home base that is beautiful and full of quality, mirroring your instruction.

9. **Avoid barriers.** People have a range of expectations when visiting websites. Some like text, others prefer videos, and still others are intrigued by photographs. SMT websites incorporate all these elements. On the flip side, eliminate anything that might discourage your audience from engagement, such as complex forms or hard-to-read CAPTCHAs (strange characters that visitors must duplicate to convince the site they are human).

10. **Keep it alive.** Powerhouse websites are not static. They are kept current and incorporate new materials to keep visitors coming back.

Building Your Website

A powerhouse website needn't cost a fortune, and there is no direct correlation between the amount spent and level of effectiveness. Many SMTs today design compelling sites on their own. If you feel underqualified or overwhelmed, consider asking a high school student, college media arts major, or professional for help.

How to design a website falls outside the scope of this book, but doing so is certainly easier than it used to be. You no longer have to understand HTML or install a separate program on your computer. To secure an address, go to a host such as GoDaddy.com and buy your .com and .org domain. Many are purchasable for under $10. Several companies offer templates that are fully customizable and easy to program. For example, WordPress.com has a wide range of free and flexible designs. Better yet, they work well with Google Analytics, which tracks traffic and breaks down your reach.

Well before construction begins, the first line of business is compiling content that will live on the site. This process consists of writing passages and collecting photos/videos/recordings. Also essential is designing a logical web map that shows site organization, including menu and submenu items. Creating this navigation model forces you to think through design, considering what to emphasize and prioritize.

Features

The next several pages describe features common to SMT websites. Rather than incorporating them all, choose elements most helpful to your brand and message. When developing material, consider the questions and perspectives of likely visitors.

Welcome Video

Typically appearing on your landing page, a welcome video presents an opportunity to tout your USP and philosophy alongside teaching demonstrations, student interviews, and performances.

A Welcome Video

The simple, low-tech welcome video for Chris Goslow (www.pianolessonsinsacramento.com) features about two minutes of speaking over a faint piano recording. His message addresses the benefits of piano lessons, studio priorities, and types of students he has impacted. A caption with web address and phone number appears twice.

In addition to a minute-long overview video, Brannon Littleton's (www.iteachkeys.com/our-teaching-approach.php) site features a 13-minute "Welcome Movie." Following captions with questions like "I've always wanted to sing but don't think I can. Do you work with people like me?" and "I have taken piano lessons before and was bored. What makes you different?" his approach is discussed.

Our very own Kristin Yost, featured in *Lessons from the Trenches*, invested in a professional videographer. In just 30 seconds, viewers encounter several of her students providing compelling testimonials (www.vimeo.com/24850363).

USP and Teaching Philosophy

Though your unique selling proposition and teaching philosophy intersect, they are not the same thing. USPs, often shown with succinct bullet points, explain what makes your studio special. A teaching philosophy expands upon this, explaining your essential question while pointing to specific *features* (e.g., students use method book X) and *benefits* (students develop this creative skill) of your approach.

Philosophically Speaking

The website of Chad Twedt (www.students.twedt.com) explains his teaching philosophy:

Musicianship: I strive to turn students into musicians, not just pianists. They undergo collegiate rhythmic and theory training after three years of lessons since there is no good reason to wait until college. It isn't enough to teach good musical values—students must also learn to experiment and be inventive in their music making.

Flexibility: I adapt teaching to each student. While all are taught core curriculum, they are also encouraged to find "dessert music," whether from Harry Potter, Coldplay, ballet transcriptions, or video games (all of which have been featured on studio recitals).

Gentle Honesty: There is always a nice way to speak honest criticism, and it is my goal to find those words so that students will not only like me, but seek and trust my professional opinion.

Serious Levity: I am a serious teacher who loves to joke around. When students complete pieces, I fasten stickers on their music with images ranging from broccoli to "Intel Inside!" because gold stars are boring. When they scoot across the bench playing scales, I write "no scooting butt" in their notebook after explaining that my furniture doesn't need polishing.

Slogans: I regularly tell students that there is no such thing as *too hard*. There is only *too fast* or *too much*. They also frequently hear that practice does not necessarily make perfect; *practice only makes permanent.*

Studio Policies and Logistics

Policies, expectations, tuition schedules, studio news, upcoming events, class homework, and dates you'll be out of town are common items on SMT sites. Generally speaking, it is also advisable to publish lesson rates. When charging more than the competition, be sure to present a compelling case that justifies your augmented value.

Lessons from the Trenches

I approach the business side of music teaching with a firm but kind hand. As my own boss, I am in charge of paying myself and seeing that all financial responsibilities are met. Therefore, it is essential to clearly communicate policies both verbally and in writing. My website includes the following documents (many of which are reproduced in Appendix D):

1. **Financial policy.** This indicates when tuition installments are due, and for how much.
2. **Attendance policy.** This includes makeup lesson information, what tuition covers, and possibly an outline of the calendar year.
3. **Expectations.** I lay out expectations and responsibilities for students, parents, and even the teacher. "If you put in this much effort, here is what you will get in return."
4. **Makeup lesson policy.** My no-makeup-lesson policy is strict but fair.
5. **Practice policy.** Each spring I issue a practice challenge, complete with a prize of approximately $100. Students who practice a set amount of time over a given number of weeks (depending on ability level) are entered into a drawing.

Teacher Bio and Photos

Don't make the mistake of so many musicians and have your bio read like an obituary. While it can certainly highlight qualifications, education, professional activities, awards, and other accomplishments, remember that the purpose is to engage, not simply brag. A bio is not just commentary on what you've done; it suggests who you are and what you believe. Therefore, let the teacher in you shine. Consider statements about teaching history, philosophy, and students. Personal anecdotes are worth consideration, and be sure to get the right tone (formal vs. friendly).

People like to put a face to a name. Include at least two recent personal photographs on your teaching website. Be sure the impressions broadcast by each picture are consistent with your teaching philosophy and brand. Are you smiling or serious? Performing in a tux for the masses or working side by side with a student?

Teacher Tools

Think of a website as the online hub for your studio. Build in functionality that facilitates communication, addresses logistical concerns, and makes life easier for both you and your community. For example, Music Teacher's Helper (www.musicteachershelper.com) offers wonderfully designed templates with features like:

- **Automatic birthday greeter.** Generates e-cards for students on their special day.
- **Automatic invoicing.** Input amounts and let the site do the rest.
- **Automatic lesson reminders.** Helps reduce missed lessons.
- **Calendar.** Displays teaching schedule for easy studio viewing.
- **Credit card payments.** Allows processing through companies like PayPal.
- **Email.** Facilitates communication between individuals or the whole class.
- **Lending library.** Tracks who has borrowed what so your collection isn't depleted.
- **Makeup lessons.** Tracks the number of makeup lessons for each student.
- **Mileage tracker.** Tabulates how many miles you have driven for professional purposes.
- **Repertoire tracker.** Catalogs literature each student has studied.
- **Studio announcements.** Post notices for your studio to view.
- **Track income and expenses.** Monitors all expenses from and payments to your studio.
- **Track lesson progress.** Input notes about each meeting so you remember what was covered and the student can't legitimately claim, "I forgot"!

Educational Tools

Continue education between lessons. Websites can showcase practice tips, composer information, music videos, instructional videos, podcasts, and learning games. If content is strong enough, students outside your studio may eagerly access this information as well.

Student Celebrations

Student/alumni profiles, photos, news, awards, recordings, and videos celebrate the lives and hard work of studio members. These inclusions also contribute to a sense of community.

Celebration Times

Members of Emily Fransen's piano studio (www.efransen.wordpress.com) who are awarded the proud designation of "Student of the Month" are featured on her webpage blog. In addition to a paragraph or two about their hobbies, school accomplishments, and distinctions, she uploads recordings of memorized pieces made during lessons. Outstanding renditions are also featured on a studio Facebook page.

Blog

Setting up a blog through wordpress.com or another server can be cheap (or free) and easy to customize. As with any public online activity, the benefits of contributing quality content expand beyond impacting students. It can serve as marketing, build reputation, and lead to gigs. Many artists featured in this book were "discovered" thanks to a compelling blog entry.

There are several ways for blogs to play an influential role in your studio:

- Posting articles, videos, and podcasts valuable to students
- Posting entries geared toward parents
- Having students post articles about musical experiences and challenges
- Requiring students to follow one or more music blogs

Many SMT blogs address readers beyond their students: local band directors, independent teachers, wind players. If this is the case, clearly identify your target audience, the focus of your platform, and how this positioning aligns with your brand and expertise. Also consider how it might help your own life/career. Will it open up doors to new opportunities or build your network? Creating this content takes time—be sure to spend life energy wisely.

One strategy for driving website traffic is offering information not readily available elsewhere. Perhaps you offer a list of iPad/Android apps, a downloadable practice card, an instrument buying guide, or helpful practice suggestions.

The Anti-Bot

"My studio consists of talented, devoted, conservatory-bound students. But churning out *violin-bots* is hardly my idea of success." Elizabeth Faidley (www.elizabethfaidley.com) insists on strong technique, to be sure, but she creates a learning environment that promotes curiosity, well-roundedness, and a sense of community.

Some of this activity occurs online. For one assignment on "mental practice," students were required to (1) read a practice blog, (2) schedule three practice sessions over two weeks focused on a given approach, (3) write and post about their own experience, and (4) comment on entries by peers. Another required learners to write a blog comparing and contrasting four recordings of the Fauré Sonata. Faidley also has them analyze literature from diverse genres, including repertoire with no connection to the violin.

Students communicate via a Facebook group focused specifically on practice frustrations. Within an hour of one commenting on the struggle to play octaves in tune without his pinky hurting, three colleagues offered advice and "secrets" they had discovered.

Faidley creates community in real space as well. In addition to retreats and camps, she hosts boot camp–like sleepovers at her house. Up to six girls can sleep in a row of bunk beds in the basement; boys stay upstairs. During these events, "practice buddies" coach one another.

While this multidimensional approach is a huge motivator for many to join her studio, it doesn't work for everyone. Some students have tunnel vision, resisting anything beyond the "essentials." Her response? "If you don't want to think outside the box, get another teacher."

Links

Carefully consider how many links to include on your site, and why visitors will care. An overwhelming, unfocused list just takes up space, diluting your message without benefiting anyone.

If you have a separate artist website, don't be shy about visibly sharing the address. It is fine to have a life beyond teaching, and maintaining two independent but linked sites gives the impression that both areas are taken seriously.

A Great Resource

The website of trombonist Brian Kay (www.brassstages.com) is loaded with information and links to helpful resources for various constituencies:

- **College and professional students.** Recommended recordings, performance tips, music stores, web resources, and a practice chart for advanced players
- **Adult avocational players.** Regional performing groups open to amateur trombonists
- **Middle/high school players.** Upcoming concerts, performance tips, and skill lists
- **Elementary school players.** CDs featuring your instrument, audio files, fun videos, position/fingering charts, and maintenance issues
- **Parents.** Kay's teaching philosophy, links for parents, and holiday gift ideas
- **Band directors.** Trombone teaching tips, pedagogy books, repertoire lists, and helpful handouts

Testimonials

When current or former students rave about your lessons, the message is significantly more credible than you saying the same thing.

Sincere Tributes

Student and parent testimonials featured on the webpage of Patty Sopita (www.pattythepianoteacher.weebly.com) do indeed argue the value of this teacher. One reads, "Dear Mrs. Patty, thank you for teaching me how to play the piano. It is very fun . . . especially when I play it with the CD because the CD goes really fast & I mess up & it is funny." In case there was any question, another explains the simple truth: "U are the best piano teacher EVER!"

But words are not the only compelling aspect here. Rather than typed text, this webpage cycles through photographs of notebook entries. Appearing in full color, many include heartfelt drawings and a variety of handwritten "fonts."

Strategy #5: Incentives

The hardest part of gaining new students is beginning the conversation. Once someone serious (or even quasi-serious) about lessons has taken the time to meet and experience your charismatic charm, chances are high he or she will join your roster. What is the most effective way to get someone through the door that first time? *Offer a no-risk incentive.* Give away something valuable for free, or at a steep discount.

Incentives work. Though just about every business type incorporates this tactic in some form, they are particularly effective for music lessons.

Types of Incentives

The most common SMT incentive is a free lesson for new students, though perhaps it's preferable to call this an "audition." True, the client gets to sample your approach to evaluate fit, but auditions go both ways. When you take on only the "right" students, those accepted into your "exclusive" studio may feel they've achieved an exciting accomplishment.

Other incentives exist as well: free 15-minute minisessions, free class enrollment for new lesson students, first year media fee waived, 10% to 20% first-semester discount, gifted books to new students. Try several offers to see what yields the highest success rate. As an added benefit at tax time, you can deduct these incentives from your bottom line.

Lessons from the Trenches

My personal favorite promotion is a trial lesson package of four consecutive weeks, where participants receive either a promotional price OR a monetary incentive if they continue further.

Rationale

This book stresses maximizing income, yet now you are asked to give things away. Doesn't that contradict your financial objective? As counterintuitive as it seems, it does not. Suppose you offer a free 45-minute, no-obligation introductory lesson to anyone who asks, rather than requiring your normal $40 fee. Three people sign up.

3 lessons × $40 = $120

In this hypothetical situation, just one of three joins your roster (though the success ratio for SMTs is typically higher). She remains a devoted student for five years, taking 40 lessons per year.

40 lessons per year × 5 years × $40 = $8,000

An investment of $120 led to $8,000. Your expense was just 1.5% of the ultimate yield. Tell that to any corporate marketing wing and watch their jaws drop. Many companies devote 20% of their budget to marketing!

$120 / $8,000 = 1.5%

However, the math is misleading. You didn't cancel work or suffer a $120 loss to facilitate these sessions. Marketing efforts are never compensated—they are a business investment. If your studio is not yet full, you have the time. Yet you did what you love for these 135 marketing minutes: teach music. In truth, it cost you $0 to return $8,000. Now *that* is savvy marketing.

Another concern about giveaways is whether people will take advantage of your generosity with no intent to continue. That is within the realm of possibility. Some freeloaders might do this, and you're out the better part of an hour. But most individuals who attend a free lesson have a sincere interest in continuing. After all, you can only get so far in one sitting. It takes time and repetition to improve musical abilities.

Promoting the Incentive

In addition to posting incentives online, consider ways to proactively promote your offer. One possibility is giving a free session or other benefit to current students who refer friends. This is comparable to an *affiliate program* (described in chapter 8).

Checking Your References

Violinist Linda Rodgers (www.violinqueen.com) offers a straightforward referral program. Bringing a new student to her studio gets you one free lesson.

Guitarist Leo Silva (www.silvaguitar.com) adds a slight twist with his Play It Forward Program. In lieu of the free lesson, referrers have the option of claiming a $25 iTunes gift card. For students whose parents pay for lessons, this prize is much more compelling.

Natalie-Anne Rutherford (www.natsmusicpath.com), who offers instruction in beginning piano, flute, and recorder, makes an even more generous offer. When students refer a new client and both parties continue at least four months, the referrer receives four free lessons. The newcomer also receives a session free of charge.

To encourage referrals, imagine what you might offer in return. A crisp $20 bill for each scheduled trial lesson? A local restaurant gift card? A free coaching? An advertisement in your studio recital program? Be creative, and offer true value in return.

Another technique is giving gift certificates for free lessons to the winner of a competition, raffle, or radio giveaway. Perhaps grade-school children write essays on the power of music, and the best "author" is rewarded three free half-hour sessions. Of course, they will likely get hooked and return for more.

To fill your studio, get people in the door. Then let outstanding teaching seal the deal.

Focus on the Right Marketing

Five savvy marketing strategies. That's what it takes to fill an SMT studio. Of course, there are many other tricks of the trade—try them if you like. But these five are winners.

12

TIME/LIFE MANAGEMENT

Money is not the only important resource to be managed in the life of a Savvy Music Teacher (SMT). Just as pressing a challenge, or maybe more, is time. Unlike income, which can always be increased with savvy strategies, the number of minutes in a day, week, or month is fixed and nonnegotiable.

Each week contains just 168 hours. After subtracting 6 to 8 per night for sleep, just 112 to 126 remain. That is the amount of time you have to work, eat, play, and accomplish all of life's other glorious adventures. Use it wisely!

Workload

Though full-time jobs traditionally require 40-hour workweeks, this number is trending upward in the United States. Fifty, 60-, or even 70-plus-hour commitments are increasingly the norm. (Whether that increases productivity is another question.)

What is a reasonable time commitment for *full-time* SMTs? Our blueprint suggests 30 to 45 hours per week. While your total depends on a number of variables, here is a typical breakdown:

Hours per Week	Paid?	Activity	Examples
20	Paid	Lessons	Teaching
2–3	Paid	Classes	Teaching
3–13	Paid	Additional income streams	Various
2–4	Nonpaid	Marketing	Website updates, networking, calls, promotional material design, etc.

(*continued*)

Hours per Week	Paid?	Activity	Examples
3–5	Nonpaid	Logistics and strategic planning	Student/parent communications; ordering music; planning for summer camp and concerts; processing payments, taxes, etc.
30–45	TOTAL		

In this model, two to four hours are allocated to marketing. For SMTs with a full studio, referrals alone (or a waitlist) may be sufficient to generate leads for new students when openings arise. Therefore, this time can be devoted to issues like generating gigs, recruiting for summer camp, or website editing. Before your roster is filled to capacity, however, more time and energy must be focused on studio promotion. If you have just 11 hours' worth of lessons but desire 20, change your fortunes by dedicating unfilled teaching slots to marketing, pursuing the savvy strategies from chapter 11.

Logistical and planning needs vary greatly throughout the year. Some periods require little work, while others overflow with urgency. Take advantage of lighter weeks, using them to get a head start on future projects. Though careful planning makes it possible to even out responsibilities to some degree, certain stretches will always be intense, particularly as a term begins and around events or camps.

The timetable shown previously does not account for practicing, doing passion projects, or commuting to gigs. If these things are part of your model, adjust workload calculations accordingly. Create a schedule that is ambitious but reasonable with your lifestyle.

Scheduling Life

In an average week, drummer Scott Strunk (www.scottstrunk.com) teaches 20 to 25 hours of lessons between Monday and Friday. Of those, around six hours of adult student lessons are scheduled late morning/early afternoon. The remainder comes between 3:30 and 9 PM, typically with a 30- to 60-minute dinner break. During summers, lesson scheduling is consolidated to a few days each week, though many students enroll in longer or more frequent "intensive" study.

Weekends are teaching free but often involve gigs at church and around town. Beyond reliable income, they provide opportunities to work alongside incredible musicians. Other regular activities include practicing daily, visiting the gym, and teaching business logistics.

For over a decade, Strunk worked on a book called *The Drum Lesson Manual* whenever he could, but it began feeling like this project was eternal. Determined to finish, he started scheduling "writing time" in iCal every day. This disciplined approach boosted efficiency, and the publication was finally released in 2012.

Balancing this busy schedule with family presents a challenge, but Strunk is careful to carve out time each day for his wife and two children. He and his oldest, also a drummer, bond when practicing together for 15 to 20 minutes each morning. His youngest returns from school around 2:30, giving them a full hour of playtime before lessons begin. Weekends present opportunities for full family outings.

The Master Grid

Because music teachers do not keep neat schedules akin to factory workers, poor planning results in wasted time and energy. Work strategically to build an efficient and manageable itinerary.

During the academic year, most students are unavailable Monday through Friday until at least 2:30 or 3 PM. Children are in school; professionals are at work. Therefore, most teaching occurs weekdays 3 to 9 PM and weekends 8 AM to 9 PM.

Some demographics are accessible during low-demand hours: homeschoolers, retirees, homemakers, evening employees, the unemployed, lottery winners, online students from distant time zones. Targeting these groups often makes scheduling, educational, and financial sense.

When plotting your master schedule, which includes times you are available for teaching, keep the following in mind:

- **Put it in writing.** No matter how impressive your photographic memory, avoid simply imagining the calendar. Use scheduling software, an app, or a large paper calendar with plenty of space to detail responsibilities.
- **Begin with external commitments.** Indicate regularly scheduled commitments you have at fixed and inflexible times: nonteaching employment, religious functions, regular obligations with your own kids, and so forth.
- **Map a dream schedule.** In an ideal world, what are the days/hours you hope to teach?

- **Block booking.** Seek chunks of two to three hours to schedule consecutive activities like lessons.
- **Periodic breaks.** Most teachers lack the endurance to operate at 100% for more than three hours. Schedule breaks appropriately. Even 10 minutes can make a difference.
- **Meals.** Obviously, you need to eat. Include time for meals at reasonable hours.
- **Behind the scenes.** The nice thing about marketing, logistic, and planning work is that it can be done during the day, late at night, in between lessons, or at other convenient times. Reserve times for these activities on the master calendar as well.
- **Free day.** Insist on keeping at least one to two days per week teaching free. Everyone deserves a "weekend" to recuperate and recharge, even if it occurs on Wednesdays.

Consider a few models following our blueprint. Low brass SMT Hugh Fonium schedules all lessons, classes, and studio-related work Monday through Friday. Though weekends are open, gigs and additional work typically take place then. Note that breaks are figured into longer teaching intervals. Therefore, the period from 4 to 9 PM is considered just 4 teaching hours, since it includes two 15-minute intermissions and a half hour for dinner.

Hugh Fonium's Schedule						
Mon	Tue	Wed	Thu	Fri	Sat	Sun
9–11 (2 hours) planning			9–12 (3 hours) marketing	9–12 (3 hours) logistics	Gigs/ free	Gigs/ free
3–4 (1 hour) class 1	3–4 (1 hour) class 2	3–4 (1 hour) class 3				
4–9 (4 hours) lessons	4–9 (4 hours) lessons	4–9 (4 hours) lessons	4–9 (4 hours) lessons	4–9 (4 hours) lessons		
7 hours	5 hours	5 hours	7 hours	7 hours	Variable	Variable

TOTAL TIME	31 hours + gigs

Woodwind SMT Al Tofloot schedules all lessons Friday through Sunday, with classes on Thursday. Eleven hours of part-time (PT) work occur Wednesday and Thursday; most behind-the-scenes duties happen early Friday; and Monday and Tuesday are free. Note how he specifically denotes blocks of sacred time for family each day.

Al Tofloot's Schedule						
Mon	**Tue**	**Wed**	**Thu**	**Fri**	**Sat**	**Sun**
		8–12 (4 hours) PT work	8–12 (4 hours) PT work	9–2 (5 hours) marketing/ logistics	9–12 (3 hours) lessons	9–12 (3 hours) lessons
		1–3 (3 hours) PT work	3–6 (3 hours) classes	2–4 *relax, family*	1–4 (3 hours) lessons	1–4 (3 hours) lessons
					4–7 *family*	5–7 (2 hours) lessons
		3– *family, etc.*	6– *family, etc.*	4–9 (4 hours) lessons	7–9 (2 hours) lessons	7– *family*
Free	Free	7 hours	7 hours	9 hours	8 hours	8 hours

TOTAL TIME	**39 hours**

SMT Ly Gateau, known for her sultry voice and stylistic versatility, schedules a full day of lessons each Saturday. She also teaches a number of homeschoolers Tuesday through Thursday mornings. Her work as music director of a church occupies Wednesday nights and Sunday mornings, and her band is booked Friday nights. From time to time, she supplements with additional gigs on Sundays, late Saturday nights, and the occasional Monday.

Note that Gateau commits to at least one hour of practice six mornings per week. Placing this activity on the master calendar creates routine and ensures this vital aspect is not overlooked.

Ly Gateau's Schedule						
Mon	**Tue**	**Wed**	**Thu**	**Fri**	**Sat**	**Sun**
8–10 (2 hours) practice	**8–9** (1 hour) practice	**8–9** (1 hour) practice	**8–9** (1 hour) practice	**8–10** (2 hours) practice		**8–9** (1 hour) practice
	9–11 (2 hours) lessons	**9–11** (2 hours) lessons	**9–11** (2 hours) lessons		**9–12** (3 hours) lessons	**–12** (3 hours) church work
	11–12 (1 hour) planning	**11–12** (1 hour) planning	**11–12** (1 hour) planning		*lunch*	*lunch*
	3–6 (3 hours) lessons	**3–6** (3 hours) lessons	**1–4** (3 hours) marketing/ logistics		**1–4** (3 hours) lessons	
	7–8 (1 hour) class 1	**8–10** (2 hours) church work	**7–8** (1 hour) class 2	**8–11** (3 hours) gig	**5–8** (3 hours) lessons	
2 hour	8 hours	9 hours	8 hours	5 hours	9 hours	4 hours

TOTAL TIME	**44 hours** (including practice)

Scheduling Lessons

Organizing 20 hours of lessons that accommodate the busy lives of students while creating a tolerable schedule for you is no small feat. Try as you may, it is not always possible to make everyone happy. Some slots are coveted; others seem repellant. Parents with triplets sprint the activity obstacle course with little room for error. Seven families want their old times; eight others are itching to change. Feeding the complexity are lessons of varied lengths (30, 45, and 60 minutes), making interlocking puzzle pieces all the more complex. As maturing students request expanded meetings, one slight adjustment throws everything out of whack.

As tough as it seems, *there is always a solution.* You just have to find it. So concentrate, get creative, and use the exceptional problem-solving skills that music study has taught you.

There are several SMT approaches to booking lesson times. The first involves collecting schedules before the term begins. Ask for "ideal" and "impossible" windows rather than "possible" times, as some families are tempted to list only preferred options. Whether beginning with the busiest students or lowest-demand hours, lay out your time sheets and work through this riddle. Post-its are a lifesaver, easily shifted around a calendar until the right scheduling emerges.

Another possibility is using a first-come, first-served approach. Since scheduling conflicts seem to arise earlier every year, begin thinking about summer and fall times in early spring. You might even set aside an enrollment day (Saturday?) when parents can come in, claim a slot, and review the summer/fall calendar with you.

As the schedule fills, there will undoubtedly be students who cannot or will not agree to remaining times. Unless you're prepared to lose them, options are (1) asking previously committed students to swap or (2) adding new slots. Though you want to be accommodating, beware of committing to lessons outside your master grid that are disruptive or inconvenient, leave gaping holes, or take place on days off. SMTs are careful to design logical, reasonable schedules.

Lessons from the Trenches

In advance of each academic term, I designate available lesson slots on my Studio Helper calendar. Here, clients can secure last year's time or opt for something else on a first-come, first-served basis. This takes the scheduling burden off of my shoulders, placing responsibility instead on clients. Parents sign up from the comfort of their living room.

Studio Helper and SignUpGenius are lifesavers when it comes to group events. In addition to the initial scheduling, these platforms can send automated reminders.

Summer Scheduling

Student schedules are often inconsistent throughout the summer. Tuesdays through Thursdays typically work best, as the rate of cancellation surrounding weekends increases. Unlike the school year, mornings are just as likely to fill as afternoons and evenings.

As was suggested in chapter 3, unconventional summer strategies accommodate irregular student schedules while providing an intriguing change of pace: longer but less frequent lessons, multiple meetings per week, and so forth.

Scheduling Classes

One frustration expressed by music teachers is that students are involved in a zillion activities: soccer, chess club, debate team, scouting, cheerleading, rock climbing, turtle racing, pie eating, tornado chasing—you name it. Music is but another activity on a ballooning list. Scheduling lessons is difficult enough; setting class times seems impossible.

Since classes involve more participants than lessons, schedule them first. Weeks or months before the term starts, ask key participants to provide windows they are (or are not) likely available. Obtaining as complete a picture as possible, identify common slots that work for you and a critical mass, even if one or two prospective clients must be omitted. Secure a time and stick to it. If a conflict emerges, explain that scheduling impacts other students and is regrettably not changeable. In many cases, a "miracle" solution appears.

When possible, keep class times consistent from term to term. If people know your all-important technique workshop occurs Thursdays at 4, they will make arrangements accordingly.

As counterintuitive as it seems, extra obligations (like a class) often make students *more* available. Additional activities elevate music in the hierarchy of importance. People are accustomed to accommodating complex sports schedules. If you offer meaningful experiences, they will do this for music as well.

Weekday Classes

Singer Tim Evanicki (www.starvingartiststudios.com) had a hard time filling his Mondays; they were always the last lesson slots that students wanted. He tried something new and scheduled classes during this slow period:

- 11 AM—History of Western Music
- 12 PM—History of Rock
- 1 PM—Intro to Music Theory
- 2 PM—Group Singing

Evanicki posted an announcement describing his courses through an online community targeting parents of homeschoolers. Within an hour, at least three people had signed up for each option. Within weeks, all classes were maxed out. During the first term alone, 18 new students enrolled. Seven ultimately signed up for voice lessons.

Cancellation Policy

From time to time, students will miss lessons because of illness, family trips, conflicting events, and other reasons. Can they reschedule? From the client point of view, the request seems quite reasonable, particularly if providing plenty of advance warning. They paid for the service, after all, and are entitled to a meeting.

But reality is more complicated, particularly for instructors with a full load. A missed lesson in the middle of a teaching block costs you wasted minutes while waiting for the next appointment, or even money squandered if paying for a babysitter or room rental. Identifying a substitute window that works for both you and the student is often stressful and time consuming in itself. Solutions that fall outside your master grid may disrupt life, causing inconvenience while stealing valuable family or personal time. The busier your schedule, the more problematic rescheduling becomes.

A clear and strict cancellation policy, articulated in your student contract, reduces missed meetings. Explain that tuition pays for your experience and a time slot, rather than the lesson itself. Limit makeups to a maximum of one per term (with no "rollovers"), or prohibit this practice altogether. When people understand the rules upfront, most respectfully comply.

SMT Policy	Explanation
No makeups	The strictest and least obtrusive policy is prohibiting makeup lessons. This may seem harsh, but it works wonders to ensure consistent attendance.
Swap list	Create a "swap list" with names and contact information of families who wish to be included, placing the responsibility of rescheduling on clients.
Designated makeup slots	Commit an hour per week in your master grid for makeups when inevitable conflicts and emergencies arise.
Makeup class	Schedule one group lesson toward the end of each term, open to anyone who needs a makeup.
Forgotten lessons	Sometimes, students just forget to show up. Life gets crazy, and it slips their mind. While understandable, this costs you time, and no refund or makeup should be granted.

SMTs run a business, not a charity. Expect professional behavior and watch your community rise to the occasion.

Lessons from the Trenches

What works well for me is a policy stating that makeup lessons are not guaranteed, though I make every effort to place that student in another cancelled spot for absences caused by school band concerts, illness, or family emergencies. Soccer games and birthday parties do not count!

If a slot becomes available, I email or text the parent, offering him or her the first right of refusal. Toward the end of each term, students with missed lessons can attend a master class, providing a learning opportunity while psychologically helping parents feel money wasn't "lost."

Six Power Tips for Maximizing Efficiency

I have yet to meet a bored, full-time independent music teacher with simply too many hours in the day. They are juggling an endless array of personal and professional obligations, and life gets busy. SMTs must learn to manage time efficiently.

Tip #1: Understand the Time Paradox

Days are busy, but if something is important enough, there is almost always a way to get it done. Don't waste time on negative energy complaining how overworked you are. Instead, make a plan, focus, and take action. As challenging as it appears, there is a path to completing the essential work of your life. The secret to reaching personal, professional, financial, and artistic goals may not require working longer, but rather smarter.

There is never enough time, but there is always enough time.

Tip #2: Distinguish between Urgent and Important

In his classic book *The 7 Habits of Highly Effective People*, Stephen Covey describes the matrix that follows. *Important* activities help achieve life goals; *urgent* things demand immediate attention.

	low URGENCY	high
high IMPORTANCE	"important goals"	"critical activities"
low	"distractions"	"interruptions"

"Critical activities" are likely to get done. Scheduled lessons, gigs, or editing a recording project under label contract are completed because you care about these things and the clock is ticking. Failing to fulfill critical activities rarely happens. People make the time.

In the opposite quadrant are "distractions." Facebook addictions, video games, long coffee breaks, British miniseries, or conversations about the weather with people you don't particularly enjoy squander valuable minutes while providing little in return. While everyone needs mindless downtime on occasion, cut here when there isn't enough time to get it all done.

"Interruptions"—text messages, email, phone calls, laundry, knocks at the door, paperwork, day jobs, "necessary evils," unforeseen "emergencies"—invade our world from every direction. Recall a frantic day of errands when, despite constant activity, nothing significant got accomplished. Interruptions are the culprit here. Though these items don't help realize major life ambitions, their pressing nature convinces you to drop all else. There may in fact be negative consequences for failing to complete these tasks. Over time, however, too much energy in this category prevents people from reaching their dreams. Most music teachers with time management problems get bogged down here.

Often sacrificed are "important goals": passion projects, life aspirations, health concerns, marketing, networking, finally completing your method series that will change the world. Though these things really matter to long-term success, a lack of pressing deadlines with consequences often results in inaction. Too many people get stuck year after year, never seeming to advance life ambitions that matter most. Realizing important goals demands discipline.

Masters of time management carefully limit distractions and interruptions. When acting responsibly, they regulate the number of minutes devoted here. Conversely, each day begins with critical activities and important goals (rather than email checking). Thoughtfully scheduling windows for these tasks, successful people move life aspirations forward each and every day.

Tip #3: Write It Down

Study after study has proven that people who keep "to-do lists" have exponentially greater chances of getting things done than those who simply store items in their head. Whether using paper, smartphone, or tablet, keep this checklist in an accessible place and refer to it often, ensuring that items aren't forgotten or ignored.

Rather than compiling an endless list of activities competing for attention, prioritize. Use numbers to show what should be addressed first, second, and so on. Rank by importance and urgency, possibly creating separate headers for these rival categories.

The best entries are specific and measurable. "Marketing" is simply too broad. How will you know when that objective has been accomplished? "Create 350-word bio," on the other hand, is clear and quantifiable. Though I ultimately need to complete this book, my goal for today is writing time management tip #3.

Cross off entries as they are completed. A great sense of satisfaction and accomplishment accompanies this ritual.

> ### Efficient Juggling
>
> Like many music teachers, guitarist Geoffrey Keith (www. successmusicstudio.com) finds himself juggling multiple income streams and a family. Achieving a balanced life where everything gets done requires a proactive, strategic approach to time management.

Keith is a devoted list maker. He inventories long-term (one to three years) and medium-term (one to three months) goals on lined paper, as well as daily to-do items on sticky notes. As soon as an idea or need emerges, he documents it *somewhere* (often using Dunkin Donuts napkins). Items are then consolidated, categorized, and clearly posted in his office. "While many people use technology for organizing their life, I prefer the visceral feeling of paper." Crossing completed entries off the list is empowering, providing a sense of accomplishment and forward motion.

Because there is always more to achieve than time in a day, Keith prioritizes tomorrow's activities each evening, including both urgent and important items. Estimating how many minutes are required for various actions, he officially schedules many tasks in a calendar to ensure they do not go overlooked.

Keith is mindful about managing disruptive activities. He hires an answering service to handle phone communications when unavailable and limits the number of times email messages are checked each day. To reply efficiently, a series of stored announcements and boilerplate responses to common questions can easily be pasted into messages.

Keith, a believer in routines, maintains steady meal and bed times when possible. He is strict about keeping weekends open for family time with the exception of one Saturday per month, reserved for makeup lessons.

"Working efficiently boosts my morale. The act of getting things done is motivating in itself and feeds me with energy."

Tip #4: Schedule Your Schedule

Beyond booking appointments such as lessons and classes, the best SMT time managers meticulously reserve time for other activities: marketing, logistics, planning, practicing, eating, errands, family, socializing, to-do list items, even downtime. Investing a half hour at the beginning of each week to strategize a detailed plan clarifies priorities and increases the likelihood that important but nonurgent tasks are not lost in the shuffle. If you want to get more done, determine how and when.

This approach only works when matched with resolute commitment. Don't allow yourself to procrastinate or get distracted—start and end on time. Working within constraints, as opposed to drowning in a single activity for hours on end, often boosts productivity.

When possible, schedule comparable tasks at consistent times. Human beings respond well to routines. Whether your best practicing is done before sunrise or after midnight, block out a consistent window. Conversely, negative habits wreak havoc. Throwing an hour away on video games or tabloids one Thursday afternoon won't cause much harm. But as that phenomenon transforms into a ritual, wasted time is etched into your existence.

Tip #5: Learn to Say "No"

Students will undoubtedly invite you to attend performances by school/community ensembles. They want you, the beloved music teacher, to partake. No doubt, you enjoy supporting them as well. But with 30 students in 14 groups, is this time commitment prudent? Similarly, as reputation and reach expand, you will be asked to serve on boards, help with causes, and participate in numerous initiatives. What should you do?

SMTs are nice, generous people, with a sincere desire to support others. Unfortunately, there are not enough hours in the day to pursue every worthwhile endeavor. Caring does not require forfeiting all personal time. Recognize the difference between opportunities and distractions, considering the full ramifications of participation. Without becoming a Scrooge, learn the difficult but crucial art of when and how to say "no."

Tip #6: Outsource and Automate

At the beginning of their career, SMTs often have lots of time (few students) and little income. At this point, they are solely responsible for addressing all career aspects, ensuring that steps are taken to solidify a positive future trajectory. But as the studio fills, responsibilities multiply, and scheduling overflows, consider what is more valuable, your money or your time?

Musicians are typically self-sufficient, hard workers. Asking for help can feel like a copout, accompanied by a sense of inadequacy or guilt. Yet outsourcing is more than acceptable—it may also be necessary for keeping your sanity.

Which aspects of work and life might others help accomplish? Typing a program? Updating the website? Cleaning your office? Helping with bookkeeping? Whether asking your niece, hiring a high school intern, bartering with parents, or employing a virtual assistant, farming out work in exchange for peace of mind may be one of the best decisions you make.

Unless tasks are exceedingly enjoyable, automate whenever possible. Automatically pay bills online. Save shopping time by shipping necessities like diapers, detergent, and dog food to your home through programs like Amazon's Subscribe & Save. Create computer *macros* (shortcuts) for repetitive tasks, and organize files electronically so time isn't wasted searching for "that one scribbled sheet of paper."

In other words, build a life that allows you to focus on what matters most.

Lessons from the Trenches

Life is too short to waste on uninteresting tasks that zap energy and time. Some people consider my teaching load of approximately 40 students (30 hours weekly) extreme, but this business model generates enough cash flow to hire others for less desirable activities.

The three main aspects I outsource are accounting, design, and cleaning. Data entry, graphic design, and dusting are not for me. Of course, I must still do some work related to these things. For example, I jot down notes on all business receipts describing each purchase in case I get audited. It is my responsibility to compile content for programs, posters, and websites, and to take out the trash. But for more in-depth attention, these tasks are handed over to professionals possessing far greater talent, interest, and efficiency than I.

I also automate whenever possible. Invoicing, tuition collection, bill payment, and scheduling essentially take care of themselves online, freeing up time for teaching and living.

Work and Life
Take a Break

Everybody needs a break from time to time. Just as SMTs should avoid seven-day teaching regimens, 52-week schedules are strongly discouraged. Whether or not you travel, take at least several weeks off from teaching each year to rest and recalibrate. Because of career demands, the most likely vacation periods occur close to holidays or during the summer.

> **Lessons from the Trenches**
>
> While I love teaching, vacation time throughout the year is nonnegotiable. During this "downtime," I often travel, work on passion projects, and spend uninterrupted time with loved ones. These activities fill me with physical and mental energy.
>
> In a given year, I typically take off three weeks around Christmas, six scattered throughout the summer, two weeks during spring break, and the days around Thanksgiving. That leaves 40 weeks for my intensive teaching regimen.

Teachers with Kids

For individuals so inclined, raising children may be one of the most important things you do. Kids bring joy, laughter, companionship, Harry Potter, pride, identity, potty humor, and meaning. Despite many challenges, I have yet to meet a parent who regrets this decision.

From a time management perspective, SMTs with kids are faced with at least three major challenges. First, children cost a lot of money. According to a 2012 study by the US Department of Agriculture, husband-and-wife families earning a combined income of $60,640 to $105,000 before taxes spend an average of $12,600 to $14,700 per child (ages 0 to 17) per year. (And then there's college!) Earning enough to support a family requires working more.

Second is the puzzle of carving out quality time to spend with your bundles of joy, particularly as they get older. If you teach weekday afternoons/evenings and they have school in the morning, when do you have family time?

Third, there is the question of what to do with youngsters during lessons. Teaching while simultaneously providing child care is not recommended. A crying baby, clingy toddler, or overexcited kindergartener is distracting to both teacher and student. Therefore, responsibility must be passed to a spouse, relative, or paid babysitter. Choosing the latter diminishes hourly income, and breaks between lessons cause expenses to pile up even when no tuition is generated.

Of course, these challenges are not unique to SMTs. Parents from all professions must discover creative time management solutions. It is indeed possible to become both a great parent and a great teacher. In fact, these aspirations benefit from many of the same qualities: love, passion, discipline, patience, planning, flexibility, creativity, and the relentless drive to make a difference.

Maternity Leave and Sick Days

Wendy Stevens (www.composecreate.com) is a composer, music teacher, and mother of three. "My husband and I could easily work all the time, but we choose not to. Instead, we are purposeful with scheduling, careful to leave time where family reigns supreme."

Stevens is among the highest-paid teachers locally, though some income is immediately rerouted to a babysitter. Composing, marketing, producing, and other career activities occur during naptimes and an additional three-hour weekly block with a sitter. Beyond that, she has become an expert at taking advantage of small chunks of time. Even five-minute windows add up.

Stevens's tuition structure works particularly well for teachers with kids. Her annual rate, divided over 12 equal monthly installments, covers a combination of 38 private and group lessons. Typically, she takes off Labor Day (one week), Thanksgiving (one week), Christmas (two weeks), spring break (one week), end of spring semester (two weeks), and end of summer semester (two weeks). That leaves five *flex weeks,* or lessons that can be cancelled when kids get sick, the weather is disastrous, jury duty summons, or she just needs a break.

One challenge for independent teachers is taking maternity/paternity leave without losing income or students. The 38-lessons policy also solved this issue. During her childbearing years, Stevens arranged the full number of sessions even after taking eight weeks when the baby was born. Though this redistribution required some explanation ("We're paying tuition for two months when no lessons are offered?"), just about all families agreed, and her income remained steady. That's valuable when growing a family!

Work/Life Balance

In his book *Off Balance*, Matthew Kelly argues that the notion of "work/life balance" is a myth. Few people, if any, create an existence perfectly combining these elements 50/50. Instead, we are always to one side or the other of equilibrium. Furthermore, he insists that balance is an unworthy aspiration. Aim instead to reach a high level of "personal and professional satisfaction," regardless of how many minutes are devoted to each. Great work environments positively impact nonwork events, and vice versa.

While symmetry may not be the answer, neither is sacrificing either of these aspects. Eighty-hour workweeks at the expense of family, friends, hobbies, and health is no solution. Nurture professional *and* personal segments of your life so they intersect and benefit one another.

Life Design

Like so many music teachers, vocalist Sarah Luebke (www.slvstudio.com) has a lot on her plate. Juggling 45 students, she teaches adjunct at two colleges and runs an independent studio. She also has a 9-month-old son. Balancing this heavy workload with family is tricky, but Luebke is discovering solutions that work for her.

All teaching is arranged Mondays through Thursdays, 8:30 AM to 5:30 PM. College responsibilities are scheduled mornings and early afternoons, followed by younger students after school. Just two half-hour breaks occur most days, but because "time is money and time away from family is hard," compact scheduling presents the best option. Since her husband also works, baby Christopher attends day care.

Part of Luebke's "secret" to creating work/life satisfaction is maintaining routines. Each weeknight at 7 PM she prepares for the next day: making lunch, packing diapers, laying out clothes. Fridays offer alone time with her son, though she also cleans, runs errands, and sets menus for the week. Sundays involve filling the gas tank. Each night before bed, she reviews the to-do list, identifying three top items to accomplish the following day.

To preserve family time, work is strictly prohibited during weekends. Once a month, she and her husband schedule date night. They also designate "no-screen nights," where TV, iPad, and other contraptions are forbidden.

While Luebke's schedule is undeniably full, one principle stands above all. "I don't bring my work home. Even thinking about work is banned during family hours."

13 WINNING THE MONEY GAME

The financial model employed by many independent music teachers looks something like this:

Earn what you can. Give lessons to existing students and pray for more. Take gigs that pop up. Add together earnings around tax time to discover last year's salary. Or, if thorough records weren't kept, report a number pulled out of the sky.

Spend what you need. Things are expensive, but you have to eat, live, and play a bit. In all honesty, the amount contributed to the economy each year is a mystery, with no formal budget or mechanism for tracking expenses.

Save what you can, though that may have to wait. Unfortunately, saving is next to impossible when living paycheck to paycheck. College funds for the kids? Retirement accounts? Investing in those faraway dreams is unfortunately impractical at the moment, as most financial energy must focus on the here and now.

This is no plan. It is chaos, denial, and surrender flirting with disaster. No small business, individual, or family can thrive financially with such an accidental and passive paradigm! You can do better. In fact, you *must* do better. Savvy Music Teachers (SMTs) engage in a four-step process:

1. Develop financial literacy
2. Architect an ambitious but feasible plan
3. Execute with vigor and commitment
4. Assess and modify regularly

This book makes no attempt to singlehandedly teach all you need to know about financial literacy. I am not a financial advisor or accountant, and many points that follow are simplified to provide a basic overview without getting bogged down in details. The hope is to provide enough information for SMTs to start thinking and acting with economic prudence while encouraging them to research further. See the chapter, Further Reading, which lists additional resources worthy of study.

The Financial Obstacle Course

Maximizing earnings is indeed beneficial, but a robust income is not the ultimate financial goal of this book. We have all heard stories of high-income individuals—even corporate CEOs or lottery winners—who struggle financially. These characters miserably fail the money game despite obscenely generous compensation packages.

Consider "King of Pop" Michael Jackson. Selling hundreds of millions of records, he should easily have amassed one of the fattest fortunes in show biz history. Yet upon his death, he was on the verge of bankruptcy, thanks to irresponsible spending, bad financial management, and exorbitant legal bills. Jackson lived beyond his means. That is always a losing formula.

Start with the Endgame

SMTs begin with long-term educational objectives and then determine specific steps likely to get there, rather than the other way around. The same principle applies to personal/business finance. While every individual has unique dreams, start by asking, "How can I reach *financial independence*?" Getting there requires three conditions:

1. **Debt-free living.** Liabilities need to be paid off entirely, including credit cards, automobiles, instruments, and student loans. (Paying off a home mortgage is even better, but that is not required for this definition of debt-free living.)
2. **Reasonable standard of living.** Though not exorbitant, living conditions are at least satisfactory.
3. **Retirement potential.** Ensure comfortable retirement is possible at the appropriate age. (Whether you actually retire is another story!)

Unless you were born or marry into wealth, financial independence will not occur overnight. Like Aesop's Fable *The Tortoise and the Hare*, winners tend to be masters of the long game. Make great choices today for the supreme prize down the road.

The Three Directions of Your Money

It is difficult to attain financial independence without reaching certain income thresholds (hence so much focus on earning in earlier chapters). However, what happens with this capital once it's in your hands is just as important. There are three directions this money can be directed:

1. **Past expenses.** Debt owed for things purchased earlier
2. **Present expenses.** Facilitating short-term living, business, insurance, and tax costs
3. **Future investments.** Savings for later

Interestingly, these directions are closely correlated to the three requirements of financial independence. Debt-free living means eliminating past encumbrances. A reasonable standard of living requires the ability to afford present expenses. And retirement potential only becomes possible through disciplined and adequate future investment.

Past Expenses

Start with the obvious: *debt is not desirable.* In fact, it is the opposite of freedom.

There are many reasons music teachers go into debt: college loans, career investments, overconsumption of consumer goods, health care bills, and unforeseen emergencies. When taking on debt, you are responsible for paying back principal plus interest (unless securing a no-interest loan or the financier is your generous grandmother) in exchange for the privilege of borrowing. Explained another way, cost is more than the sticker price, often significantly. Interest rates and terms vary depending on loan type, your credit score, your relation with the lender, and economic conditions at large.

While debt is never desirable, it is sometimes necessary. Buying a house, attending college, or purchasing a better instrument may in fact be essential to your well-being, career plan, and life plan even if you can't initially pay for them in full. Just consider the consequences, positive and negative. Something may seem like a good idea at the time, but will you still feel the same way 10 years down the road?

Common Types of Debt		
• Business loans • Car loans • Cash advances	• Credit card • Home equity lines of credit • Home equity loans	• Home mortgages • Personal loans • Student loans

The True Cost of Debt

What is the actual cost, in dollars, of a debt?

Consider credit cards. There are many good reasons for using this payment method. Charging helps establish credit history. Many cards come with benefits, such as cash back or frequent flyer miles. They allow you to easily purchase online and are more convenient than carrying currency.

Credit card companies make money in a number of ways, including annual fees, vendor fees, and late fees (when minimum payments are not made on time). But their biggest source of income is through interest charged when users pay less than the full balance.

Credit card interest rates are often higher than any other loan type. In the United States, charges typically range from 7% to 30+%. But what do these percentages mean? A number of online credit card calculators compute the total cost of loans over time. (The following figures were calculated through a credit card debt calculator by Bankrate.com.)

$5,000 Credit Card Debt							
Interest rate (APR)	8%	8%	12%	12%	18%	23%	28%
Payback length	3 years	5 years	3 years	5 years	3 years	5 years	7 years
Monthly payment	$156.68	$101.38	$166.07	$111.22	$180.67	$126.97	$136.30
TOTAL COST	$5,641	$6,083	$5,979	$6,674	$6,508	$8,457	$11,450
Cost of debt (%)	12.82%	21.66%	19.58%	33.48%	30.16%	69.14%	129%

The previous table shows the impact of various rates and payback lengths. It also demonstrates how the cost of borrowing can be significantly more than the *annual percentage rate (APR)*. The APR is the proportion of interest charged in one year. If you take longer, expect to pay more. In the examples in the table, it costs up to an astounding 129% of the original amount!

This chart considers a loan of $5,000. However, the US Federal Reserve estimates that the average July 2013 household with credit card debt owes $15,325. Some families carry $30,000, $40,000, or even $50,000+ balances. You do the math.

According to the same study, two sources of household indebtedness are even greater. In second place are student loans, averaging $32,041, beaten only by mortgages, at $147,924. What is their financial toll?

Student loans typically carry lower interest rates than credit cards, ranging from 4% to 9%. After graduation, alumni may defer payment for a certain period (typically less than a year), though interest continues to accrue. Since APRs are lower, borrowers often approach these loans with less urgency, stretching them out as far as 20 years. Consider the implications.

Student Loan Debt							
Loan amount	$10,000	$10,000	$20,000	$20,000	$30,000	$30,000	$40,000
Interest rate	5%	5%	7%	8%	6%	9%	5%
Payback length	5 years	10 years	7 years	15 years	10 years	20 years	12 years
Monthly payment	$188.71	$106.07	$301.85	$191.13	$333.06	$269.92	$369.96
TOTAL COST	$11,323	$12,729	$25,356	$34,404	$39,968	$64,781	$53,275
Cost of debt (%)	13.23%	27.29%	26.78%	72.02%	33.22%	115.93%	33.18%

Purchasing property typically requires a 20% down payment. When that is impossible, borrowers are charged *private mortgage insurance*. This option protects the lender, adding 0.5% to 2% to the loan amount annually.

There are many varieties of home loans, including *fixed interest mortgages* (typically for 30 years, also in 10-, 15-, and 20-year increments) and *ARMs* (*adjustable-rate mortgages*, where the interest rate changes after a given period, resetting each month either upward or downward). APRs for mortgages are less than most other loan types, and charges as of this writing are at historic lows. With a great credit score, rates can be locked in at 4% or less.

$100,000 Mortgage Debt	
Purchase price	$125,000
Down payment	$25,000 (20%)
Loan amount	$100,000
Interest rate	4%
Loan type	30-year fixed
Payback length	30 years (360 months)
Monthly payment	$477.42
TOTAL COST	**$171,872**
Cost of debt (%)	**71.88%**

Four percent is an astonishing rate if you can get it, and $478 per month for a house may be a steal. But to be clear, you will pay 72% in interest over the full life of this loan.

Before moving on, consider the cost of debt from one final perspective. Because money earned travels in three directions, we can derive the following:

$ earnings – $ past expenses (debt) – $ present expenses (living) = $ left for future investments (savings)

Imagine for a moment how things change without the burden of debt. Suddenly, the dollars previously sunk into this liability can be flipped to the other side.

$ earnings – $ living expenses = $ previous savings + $ previous debt

In other words, money formerly gobbled up by debt can now be applied toward savings, generating interest rather than paying it and advancing your journey toward financial independence. Alternatively, a portion can be directed to living expenses.

In this section, no fiery judgments were made. There is no suggestion that college debt or home mortgages are inherently wrong. However, you now have a more realistic understanding of their true cost. Next, consider value.

The True Value of Debt

Much more difficult to quantify is the *value* of debt. How much does a financed item contribute to your present or future quality of life? Do benefits outweigh the cost?

The answer is obvious in certain cases. Financing designer leather pants, a large-screen TV, or the latest fad in video game consoles is unwise. Borrowing for anything short of a true necessity is never a good idea. If you can't afford it outright, don't buy it at all.

Other dilemmas are more complex. For example, many musicians require student loans to attend college. If that describes you, I hope the experience was (or is) one of the best times of your life, providing an opportunity to grow, improve, and build community within a spectacular environment. College is an investment in the future both personally and professionally, and it is difficult to place a dollar sign on its true value.

But school is a choice. Programs come in all shapes and sizes, ranging from affordable junior colleges to extravagant Ivy Leagues. There are surely differences in quality, resources, curriculum, and opportunity (though not necessarily in proportion with price tag). Do you get what you pay for? Is it worth the price of debt? These questions are complex.

What about property? Everyone needs a place to live. If you can't purchase outright (and few citizens can), should you rent or buy? How does that change when the mortgage is also viewed as an investment, an opportunity to build *equity*? What about financing a nice(r) home with beautiful teaching space that strengthens earning capacity? Is debt worthwhile then?

Debt and investment often intersect. Few entrepreneurs enter the marketplace without loans. "No risk, no reward," as the saying goes. "You have to spend money to make money." If independent teaching is to be your livelihood, essential purchases may include instruments, technology, and additional equipment. What if you don't have the cash on hand? Is it better to invest in yourself today (through debt) or tomorrow (through lack of debt and savings)? When do liabilities become assets?

These questions should not be taken lightly. The money game is a mysterious roller coaster, filled with challenging intersections and paradoxical quagmires. Most situations are complex, and you may not know the true verdict until years down the line. Few music teachers enjoy a lifelong debt-free existence. Many wrestle with damaging loans for years before pulling themselves out; others never succeed.

Yet there is much you can do. Make getting out of debt a priority. Avoid impulsiveness. Become literate by pursuing the teachings of financial gurus who offer detailed advice on escaping the clutches of this demon. Weigh true cost against true value. And do not allow debt to crush your insistence on long-term financial independence.

Freedom

Life rarely works according to plan. When her daughter was just 18 months old, flutist Noelle Perrin (www.flutestars.com) found herself going through a divorce.

Determined to provide the best of everything despite being a single mom, Perrin and her daughter moved to an affluent area with outstanding public schools. While this saved the expense of private education, it also meant that rent was exorbitantly high. Adding to this burden was "keeping up with the Joneses": music lessons, sports coaching, academic tutoring, and designer clothes. By the time her daughter graduated high school, Perrin had accumulated $30,000 of credit card debt.

There was some good news. "The smartest thing I did was to give my daughter the education and skills necessary to get a college scholarship. Though majoring in education, she received a full ride for her flute playing, keeping her out of debt."

Determined to regain financial control, Perrin made significant life changes. Moving to a one-bedroom apartment, she adopted a simpler existence, boosted teaching to seven days weekly, and added new income streams (teacher training and a second book).

Perrin was shocked to learn it would take 40 years to eliminate her debt if paying monthly minimums. Using credit card calculators, she computed what was required to cover the full amount within five years. Disbursements were automated from her checking account each month, and she moved debt from card to card securing the lowest possible interest rate.

In August 2013, Perrin finally became debt free. The amount used to previously pay off her liabilities is now invested into a retirement account.

"And it feels fantastic! Being in debt is such a burden. Financial freedom allows me to choose projects I love the most. Ironically, pursuing what I'm best at enables me to earn more as well."

Present Expenses

Life is expensive. There's no way around it short of selling all earthly possessions and becoming a hermit in the desert (not ideal for SMTs!). Many households today require two breadwinners just to make ends meet, and even then, consumer debt still rears its ugly head. Expenses can be managed, however, with discipline and savvy.

Living

The Millionaire Next Door, by Thomas Stanley and William Danko, explains—perhaps counterintuitively—that most people who reach financial independence do not lead extravagant lives. They don't live in Beverly Hills or fit stereotypes typically associated with wealth. Instead, these individuals live well below their means, make budgets, buy used cars, and invest from an early age. They also choose the right occupation. "Self-employed people are four times more likely to be millionaires than those who work for others," the authors claim, an affirmation that should provide comfort to SMTs!

One of our criteria for reaching financial independence is achieving a "reasonable" standard of living. But what does that mean exactly, and how much does it cost? The SMT definition is influenced by a book called *Your Money or Your Life*, by Joe Dominguez and Vicki Robin: *a reasonable standard of living permits consumption of all necessities, some comforts, and occasional luxuries*:

- **Necessities.** At the least, this means basic sustenance, shelter, utilities, and clothing. You may need a basic phone, simple transportation, and home maintenance work that prevents larger expenses down the road. In addition, insurance and taxes are included here.
- **Comforts.** These include upgraded necessities and additional discretionary expenses that make life more convenient or enjoyable.
- **Luxuries.** Luxuries are fancy items, even verging on indulgence, that add *extreme* fulfillment and richness to your existence.

This formula can be applied across the board or to a particular spending category. For food, perhaps it means eating three home-cooked meals most days (necessities), visiting moderately priced restaurants a couple times per month (comforts), and splurging on The Melting Pot (a lovely fondue restaurant, but count on $100+ per couple) for special occasions once per year. Your challenge is finding the right balance, spending just enough and not a penny more.

There are mountains of savvy strategies for reducing living expenses: unsubscribe to cable, clip coupons, make rather than buy gifts, conserve energy, choose your zip code carefully, stop trying to impress, make tough choices.

The Frugal Girl

As a piano teacher with four kids, pennywise living was not a choice for Kristen Cross. Refusing to go into debt beyond mortgage, she got creative. Encouraged by friends to share her disciplined financial approach, she developed her blog *The Frugal Girl: Cheerfully Living on Less* (www.thefrugalgirl.com), which is currently among the most popular resources on this topic.

Cross dropped out of college and used her savings to buy a grand piano outright, an investment that has paid itself off many times. She offers slightly discounted lessons when parents agree to watch her kids, saving the expense of a babysitter. Five additional financial strategies of hers that may be of interest to prudent SMTs include:

1. **Eat at home.** Cooking meals is cheaper and healthier than the alternative. This single lifestyle choice saves her thousands each year.
2. **Lower your phone bills.** It may sound impossible, but Cross is living proof that $80 monthly cell phone bills are avoidable. She did buy a used iPhone but prepays for texts, data, and phone minutes used rather than keeping an expensive subscription. Of course, Wi-Fi usage costs nothing. Her average monthly bill runs $15.
3. **Get it used.** Cross regularly shops at Goodwill, Craigslist, and Freecycle (a grassroots organization for people giving things away) for used clothes, bikes, furniture, toys, books, and more. "One great aspect of buying used is that when you're done with it, you can often resell at the same price. In other words, you borrow for free."
4. **Get creative with entertainment.** Fun is possible without breaking the bank. Potluck dinners, Netflix viewings, and game nights top her entertainment choices.
5. **Reuse, refresh, repurpose.** Before throwing away anything, Cross asks whether it can be repaired or transformed. She repaints furniture for a new look and has altered dresses, shirts, and pants into skirts for her daughters. "I love to breathe new life into old things."

Business

One challenge for SMTs is that business and living finance are intertwined. What percentage of income should be apportioned to career costs? Are instruments/concert tickets professional or personal expenditures? When times get tough, do you sacrifice living expenses for business, or vice versa? (This prioritizing tug of war is often present with another valuable resource: time.)

There are three large-scale categories of business expenses:

1. **Startup.** Startup expenses are purchases that must be made before you can begin attracting customers.
2. **Cost of goods sold (COGS).** COGS are expenses directly related to a service or product. In the SMT blueprint, COGS are deducted upfront, allowing us to track income after these fees.
3. **Operations/overhead.** This category includes general expenses related to your business. In the SMT blueprint, operations/overhead are paid on the back end, after calculating your net salary.

The following chart categorizes expenses. Of course, it is possible for some items to appear in multiple columns or shift classifications, depending on how they are used.

Startup	COGS	Overhead
• Computer • Decorations • House down payment (for home studio) • Instrument (yours) • Keyboard • Metronome • Music library (basic) • Music stand • Seating/furniture • Technology (basic)	• Babysitter • Class/camp supplies • Employees (e.g., camp instructor) • Event expenses • Paraphernalia production • Room rental (hourly)	• Computer • Employees (e.g., general assistant) • Instrument repair • Home studio/room rental (monthly) • Music library (expansion) • Technology • Utilities • Website

Start-Over Startup

When piano teacher Carly Seifert (www.misscarly.musicteachershelper.com) decided to adopt a child from the Congo, she realized her career model would have to change. With a 4-year-old daughter and no family in the area, the notion of continuing private lessons five days weekly felt unmanageable. She ultimately opted to teach group lessons and classes only, two long days per week, engaging more students while earning comparably in less time.

Making this happen required startup investment. The first issue was one of space. With a living room too small for groups, she spent $2,000 converting part of a three-car garage into a classroom, erecting a wall, adding a door, paving a sidewalk, and carpeting. Another $3,000 purchased six weighted keyboards, making piano classes of up to six participants possible.

Seifert expanded her offerings, becoming a certified Music for Young Children (www.myc.com) teacher. Beyond the $700 training, this required $200 for instruction manuals, $150 for percussion instruments, and $50 for recordings.

To market these new services, Seifert revamped her website and ran an ad in a local parenting magazine, costing $400. This brought "start-over startup" expenses to $6,500. Coming up with this capital was a tall order, particularly when combined with the $35,000 required for the adoption. For the first time in years, she took on credit card debt.

Though the uncertain transition felt scary at the time, it turned out to be a wise decision. Within a year, enrollment was booming. Startup debt was paid off within the semester. More important, Seifert loves the dynamics of her groups and has ample time to be a mom.

Insurance

SMTs consider insurance to be a necessity, though some musicians don't see it that way. They view this protection as a desirable but expendable comfort. When finances get tight, this is where they cut. After all, no emergencies are anticipated. Beware—the decision to skimp here can uproot your entire existence if a crisis does occur.

Health insurance is particularly expensive for the self-employed (despite 100% of these payments being tax deductible). Yet going without coverage is one gamble nobody should take. The uninsured are just one car accident or airborne illness away from losing everything. In fact, more than half of all personal bankruptcies stem from unpaid medical bills.

If a spouse's job contributes to health care, the best solution is joining that policy. People under 26 can remain on their parents' plan even if married, living elsewhere, or attending school. Several associations offer group rate plans to members, including the Music Teachers National Association, American String Teachers Association, and American Federation of Musicians.

Of course, there are many types of insurance in addition to health care. All require capital, and all are a gamble: invaluable when needed, a nuisance expense when not.

The following chart describes major categories of insurance. To learn more, contact insurance agents, ask lots of questions, and shop around. When choosing any policy, consider *premiums* (policy cost), *copays* (fixed amount you are charged for particular services such as visiting a clinic or emergency room), *deductibles* (amount you must pay before insurance money kicks in), *limits* (maximum amount a policy pays), and other conditions.

Types of Insurance	
Health	
Health care	While policies vary greatly, plans may cover (to varying degrees) appointments with primary care providers and specialists, emergency room visits, prescription drugs, routine vaccinations, checkups, maternity care, mental health care, hospital room and board, physical therapy, and other services. Be sure you understand the costs associated with each plan, as well as which providers may participate (local network or national/international hospitals).
Catastrophic	These policies, meant for disaster relief only, have low premiums and high deductibles. They do not typically cover shots or drugs and frequently have an age limit of around 30. If you can't afford full heath care, at least buy catastrophic coverage (or another *high-deductible health plan*).
Dental	Dental benefits cover general/preventive dental care and a percentage of maintenance/cleaning visits, fillings, root canals, and oral surgery. They rarely contribute to orthodontics, meaning that braces for the kids are usually on you.
Vision	Benefits apply to eye exams, contact lenses, lenses for glasses, and frames.

(continued)

Types of Insurance
Health

Disability	Disability insurance pays your bills when an injury or disability makes doing your job impossible for an extended period. Since musicians are unable to work when certain injuries occur (carpal tunnel, vocal nodes), this insurance is worth consideration.
Long-term care	Long-term care insurance subsidizes services supporting individuals who can no longer take care of themselves (bathing, dressing, eating, etc.). This is important for people with families who want to protect against the possibility of long-term care needs draining all wealth.
Life	Life insurance pays a *beneficiary* a fixed amount when you die for any reason. Without this, how will your family get by if anything happens to you? Who takes care of expenses for your kids? Policies are often for $500,000, $1 million, or more. Some experts recommend securing 8 to 10 times your annual salary, but every circumstance is different.
Home	
Homeowner's	Most policies cover damage to the house, damage to other structures (e.g., detached garage), personal property (when lost, stolen, or damaged), loss of use (lodging if your residence become uninhabitable), and medical expenses due to home damage.
Flood, etc.	Additional insurance is typically needed to cover items like floods, hurricanes, and acts of war. (Unfortunately, this does not include belligerent students!)
Renter's	When renting, the landlord's homeowner's policy does NOT protect your possessions if something happens to their property. Therefore, renter's insurance may be helpful.
Vehicle	
Unlike health care, various types of vehicle insurance are wrapped into a single policy.	
Liability	This pays when you are responsible for the accident. Two types are bodily injury and property damage.
Personal injury protection	This pays for medical expenses, rehabilitation, lost earnings, and funeral expenses caused by an accident.

(continued)

Types of Insurance	
Health	
Collision	This is for damage resulting from collision with another vehicle or object.
Comprehensive	This is for damage not caused by collision (e.g., theft, vandalism, weather).
Uninsured/ underinsured	This covers damage when the person who caused the accident is uninsured or underinsured.
Rental reimbursement	This disburses rental car expenses when your vehicle is out of commission due to an accident.
Emergency road service	This is for towing after a breakdown or accident.
Business	
Commercial general liability	When income is earned through a home-based business, you should have this insurance, which covers accidents during private lessons, classes, and camps. The premium likely costs $300 to $500 annually if working with your home insurance company, but more with other providers.
Instrument	Instruments can be insured as part of your homeowner's/renter's insurance or separately. One company charges $2.40 for every $100 of the instrument's value for professional musicians (or $.58 per $100 for amateurs).
Workers' compensation	This pays wages and medical benefits to employees who are injured while working. You do not need this insurance unless providing full-time income to employees.

A Healthy Investment

Though completely self-employed, New York–based flutist Karen Bogardus (www.thumbtack.com/ny/new-york/piano-lessons/flute-piano-instructor) was fortunate to receive health insurance through the musician's union. In exchange for just $25 monthly, the union provides a basic plan covering sick visits and doctor fees, but little else (no checkups, prescriptions, or hospital stays). In addition, she bought hospitalization coverage through another company, costing $165 per month. "A vegetarian since age 20, I was extremely fit and health conscious. I certainly never expected health problems but made the investment just in case."

Years later, during an appointment with her gynecologist, the doctor shockingly spotted two huge tumors. An ultrasound pointed to cancer, though there was no way to be certain without surgery. A hysterectomy showed them to be slow-growing ovarian cancer.

Following four days in the hospital, the recovery process took time, requiring her to miss a full month of music making and income. But there was good news. "Though the medical bills topped $50,000, insurance paid for everything minus a few small copays. Luckily, I didn't require prescriptions, which were not covered by any of my plans. Miraculously, my expenses totaled just $100." Without the extra policy, her financial fate would have evolved quite differently.

More important, the operation was successful. Bogardus rebounded to complete health and continues to enjoy work as a performer and teacher. Though she has no plans to look illness in the face again any time soon, her coverage today is comprehensive. "You just never know."

Income Taxes

Like it or not, a good chunk of earnings must be paid through some form of income taxes: federal, state, local, Social Security, Medicare. For most SMTs, this falls between 25% and 33% of gross taxable income. That's a lot of money! Consider what is left after taxes have been paid.

- $50,000 nets $33,500 to $37,500
- $55,000 nets $36,850 to $41,250
- $60,000 nets $40,200 to $45,000
- $65,000 nets $43,550 to $48,750
- $70,000 nets $46,900 to $52,500
- $75,000 nets $50,250 to $56,250
- $80,000 nets $53,600 to $60,000
- $85,000 nets $56,950 to $63,750
- $90,000 nets $60,300 to $67,500
- $95,000 nets $63,650 to $71,250
- $100,000 nets $67,000 to $75,000

Employers are required to withhold a certain amount from each employee's paycheck. Without that structure in place, self-employed music teachers must be vigilant about setting aside this money, ensuring they don't run short when it's time to pay.

Self-employed individuals must file a *Schedule C* tax return by April 15 each year (unless requesting an extension, making October 15 the new deadline). In addition, each state and municipality has its own unique tax form. You must fill out multiples if receiving income in more than one state.

Self-employed workers are required to make quarterly estimated tax payments to the federal government, and often their state. Failure to do this, or underpaying drastically, results in fines. When the amount due is overpaid, a *tax refund* is issued.

Determining your exact tax rate is complicated, as laws can be confusing and change regularly. But a basic, oversimplified primer follows, using unmarried SMT Jess Improff as an example. In 2013, Jess's various income streams generated a *gross income* of $75,000. This includes all money paid to her through lessons, classes, camps, and other income streams.

People often talk about their federal tax bracket as if this is the percentage they owe. In reality, we have a progressive system where taxpayers are charged different rates for different levels of income. The chart that follows shows 2013 rates for various dollar amounts. (Our chart only goes to 28% since few SMTs pay more.)

Tax Rate	Single	Married	Head of Household
10%	$0–$8,925	$0–$17,850	$0–$12,750
15%	$8,926–$36,250	$17,851–$72,500	$12,751–$48,600
25%	$36,251–$87,850	$72,501–$146,400	$48,601–$125,450
28%	$87,851–$183,250	$146,401–$223,050	$125,451–$203,150

With $75,000 of earnings, Jess's top dollars (from $36,251-$75,000) are taxed at the 25% level. This highest percentage charged is known as her *marginal tax rate*. The average percentage actually paid is her *effective tax rate*. Based on this information alone, Jess's marginal tax rate is 25% and effective tax rate is 19.57%.

$ Range	$ Affected	Tax Rate	Charge
$0–$8,925	$8,925	10%	$893
$8,926–$36,250	$27,325	15%	$4,099
$36,251–$75,000	$38,750	25%	$9,688
TOTAL	$75,000	19.57% average	$14,680

However, Jess does not owe this much to the federal government thanks to some great news for self-employed music teachers. *Tax deductions*, or payments that are "ordinary and necessary" for your line of business (including startup, COGS, and overhead expenses), are not considered taxable income. In addition, deductions for certain health care costs, state and local income taxes, property taxes, home mortgage interest, charitable giving, and tax preparation fees all reduce taxable income. Appendix A has a worksheet listing common deductions for music teachers.

To take full advantage, however, Jess must *itemize* deductions on a *Schedule A* form. Over the year, she keeps careful records of relevant expenses, ensuring nothing gets overlooked. As it turns out, Jess has $20,000 of deductions this year resulting from a home studio, new equipment, music, instrument repair, hired camp counselors, driving to gigs, retirement savings, and other things. Therefore, her taxable income—or *adjusted gross income*—is just $55,000.

$75,000 gross income – $20,000 in deductions = $55,000 adjusted gross income

Tax Issues

Proof. "Proof" means clear record keeping through spreadsheets or electronic programs such as Mint.com, copies of receipts, credit card statements, bank statements, and/or check stubs.

Contract work. *You must mail a 1099-MISC form to any independent contractor who was paid over $600 by you* in a calendar year by the following January 31 to claim the deduction. Additionally, a copy must be sent to the IRS by the last date in February. This document shows how much was paid and allows you to deduct 100% from taxable income. Conversely, if you do contract work, employers are responsible for sending this form to you. Many freelance SMTs receive piles of 1099s each Fall!

Be accurate, thorough, and honest. Expensive though it may be, resist the temptation to underreport earnings. Beyond being unethical, it can haunt you in costly penalties if audited by the IRS.

Keep Track and Win

Hornist Jay Hanselman never misses a tax write-off. Why would he? Failure to do so is throwing money away, and expenses can be documented with minimal effort.

A special credit card is devoted to anything remotely related to his business: performance clothing, eating out on the way to gigs, postconcert "hangs" (since networking is a marketing expense), the 35,000 business-related miles he drives each year. For vendors that do not accept plastic, payment is made from a separate business checking account. All charges are entered into a Quicken account, so Hanselman can immediately det0ermine how much was spent on food, gas, clothing, hotels, and other items each year.

Another way to lower taxable income is through *tax credits*. These are given for things like education, child care, and first-time homebuyer expenses, as well as contributions to certain retirement accounts. For the sake of simplicity, Jess has none of these. But don't forget to report them when applicable, as they can save big money!

Consider how itemized deductions impact Jess's tax burden.

$ Range	$ Affected	Tax Rate	Charge
$0–8,925	$8,925	10%	$893
$8,926–$36,250	$27,325	15%	$4,099
$36,251–$55,000	$18,750	25%	$4,688
TOTAL	$55,000	12.9% average	$9,680

As you can see, her effective federal rate drops to just 12.9%.

However, these are not the only taxes due. In addition, Jess must pay into Social Security and Medicare. While this investment helps her in the long run when benefits kick in, there is some tough news here. Traditional employees split this amount 50/50 with their employer. But since sole proprietors play both roles, they bear full responsibility. In 2013, the so-called *self-employment tax* required 15.3% of taxable income.

$55,000 taxable income × 15.3% self-employment tax rate = $8,415

Finally, Jess must pay state and local taxes. These rates vary greatly depending on geography, so we won't get bogged down with specifics. Suppose her combined effective rate is 5%.

$55,000 × 5% state + local effective tax rate = $2,750

Let's add up the numbers to see how much Jess owes in taxes.

Type	$ Owed	% of $75,000
Federal taxes	$9,680	12.91%
Self-employed taxes	$8,415	11.22%
State and local taxes	$2,750	3.67%
TOTAL	**$20,845**	**27.79%**

In 2013, Jess owes $20,845 in income-related taxes. That is 27.79% of her gross $75,000 income.

As you can see, taxes are complicated, particularly for self-employed workers with multiple income streams. Though programs like TurboTax help individuals complete requisite documents, working with a good accountant or certified public accountant—particularly those specializing in musicians—may ultimately save more money and headache than they cost.

Future Investment
Profitability

Three companies manufacturing musical widgets release their annual sales numbers for the previous fiscal year. Business A reports $10,000, Business B shows $100,000, and Business C boasts an impressive $1,000,000. From a purely financial perspective, who did the best?

You may be tempted to answer Business C, since it sold 10 times as much as Business B and a hundredfold more than Business A. But, as it turns out, that speculation is incorrect. In fact, Business C is a catastrophe. It spent $1.4 million on product development, marketing, salaries, operations, and other expenses to make the seven figures. In other words, it lost money despite impressive sales figures. In contrast, Business B spent the same amount it earned and essentially broke even. It cost Business A just $8,000 to generate its $10,000. It turned a 20% profit.

Businesses love to focus on *gross earnings*, or how much capital they acquire. Of course, this figure does mean something, but it tells an incomplete story. How much did they spend? What was left over? Though the money game is complicated, the formula for financial success is not. *It's not how much you make that counts, but how much you keep.*

earnings – expenses = profit

Many financially conscious music teachers make the same mistake when approaching their financial life. They maximize earnings yet fail to generate profit. A salary of $90,000 is not nearly enough when expenses topple $100,000. On the other hand, $50,000 is stunning if costs are just $35,000. Once expenses have been paid, profit can be invested in savings.

profit = savings

Investing

The capital required to reach major life goals like retirement seems astronomical. Even if earning a respectable living, how can you possibly save enough? A healthy income helps, but *investing* is critical to this aim, providing passive income where money can literally grow as you sleep.

Four independent music teachers are committed to saving for retirement, religiously investing a given amount each day. However, their quests begin at different ages. Assuming they all generate an average return of 10% compounded annually, let's see how they do by age 65.

AGE	Trey Bull $5 per day $150 per month Total $ Invested	Ending $ Balance	Sarah Nade $10 per day $300 per month Total $ Invested	Ending $ Balance	Axel Rondo $20 per day $600 per month Total $ Invested	Ending $ Balance	Anne Dentino $50 per day $1500 per month Total $ Invested	Ending $ Balance
25	1,800	1,896						
26	3,600	3,982						
27	5,400	6,276						
30	9,000	11,576						
35	18,000	30,219	3,600	3,792				
40	27,000	60,243	18,000	23,152				
44	36,000	108,598	36,000	60,437	7,200	7,584		
50	45,000	186,474	54,000	120,486	36,000	46,303		
55	54,000	311,894	72,000	217,196	72,000	120,875	18,000	18,967
60	63,000	513,884	90,000	372,948	108,000	240,974	90,000	115,758
65	72,000	839,191	108,000	623,788	144,000	434,392	180,000	302,186

Trey is the big winner. He committed the least actual dollars, yet because capital was invested over such a long period, more than $800,000 accrued by age 65. Anne, on the other hand, contributed the most. Shelling out two and a half times more than Trey, she nonetheless emerged with less than half his total, with funds growing over a much shorter window.

This chart demonstrates one of the great principles of economics. *Money grows exponentially over time, thanks to compound interest.* In other words, when you invest money and it earns interest, future growth is applied to both your investment and the interest. The bottom line—start early, enabling the snowball effect of compound interest.

It does not require great fortunes to make investing worthwhile. Small, regular savings quickly add up (as do small expenses). Many musicians mistakenly believe they simply don't have enough to invest yet squander funds on nonessential, superfluous items like coffee, cigarettes, or eating out. All it takes is a few dollars per day. Hopefully the chart provides the evidence and inspiration you need!

Putting money aside can be difficult when juggling a fledgling career, student loans, living expenses, and raising a family. Many 20- or 30-something music teachers do not even begin thinking about retirement planning, but they usually come to regret this oversight. Are you sure you can afford to wait until age 30, 40, or 50?

The cardinal rule of investing is that there is no free lunch—*the greater the potential return, the larger the risk.* Safe investments, like Certificates of Deposit (CDs) and bonds, have guaranteed predetermined rates but low yields. Individual stocks, mutual/index funds, and real estate can earn considerably more, but with inherent risks. They can also lose money.

The previous chart assumed steady annual growth at 10%. Of course, there is no guarantee that investments consistently multiply at that pace. For example, 2008 was dismal for investors. At its lowest point, the market dipped almost 45% from its zenith a year earlier. However, if the possibility of losing money through the stock market makes you nervous, consider this: from 1926 to 1999, the average annual return was 11% even with the Great Depression and many short-term recessions. From 1990 to 1999, it was 18%. Chances are in your favor when investing for the long haul. While past performance is no guarantee of the future, the stock market has a long, proven history of growth. (On the day I wrote this paragraph, the Dow Jones Industrial Average, a major stock market index, reached a new all-time high.)

Since there is no crystal ball, it is essential to evaluate your tolerance for risk, diversify your portfolio, and invest wisely. Stock investing is not an adrenaline rush or spectator sport, but a means to achieving a less stressful, financially independent future. Do not obsess about daily, weekly, monthly, or even yearly fluctuations in the market. Investing for the long haul is a far better strategy than micromanaging day to day. The younger you are, the more risk you can afford (but don't be a fool!). As you approach retirement, conventional wisdom suggests shifting into more conservative asset classes with less potential for a large swing in either direction.

Enabling Retirement

The final of our three conditions for financial independence is the potential to comfortably retire. Without enough savings, this will be impossible. As we've seen, the earlier you start, the better.

How large your nest egg grows depends primarily on (1) the number of years until retirement, (2) contribution amounts (rate of saving), and (3) growth (rate of return). Of these, the only variable you control totally is how much and how regularly you save, since it's impossible to predict interest rates or turn back the clock 20 years.

Obviously, money from any source can be used during your golden years, but special *individual retirement accounts* (IRAs) offer compelling tax benefits. The catch is that penalties are assessed when making withdrawals before age 59½.

- **Roth IRAs** allow income that has already been taxed to grow tax free, meaning you are not charged additional tolls on even the interest when money is withdrawn. A maximum investment of $5,500 per year was allowed in 2014.
- **Traditional IRAs** are the opposite. Income invested is not taxed upfront, allowing you to invest more and see greater levels of return. Taxes are charged when money is withdrawn, however. As with Roth IRAs, $5,500 was the maximum contribution in 2014.
- **SEP-IRAs** are popular with sole proprietors. Fees are low, and up to 25% of net income may be invested. Like traditional IRAs, money is taxed later, lowering tax burden now.

Before leaving the topic of retirement, there is some good news. Remember the self-employment tax? At a certain point, you start to see dividends. Unless rules change, Americans are eligible for Medicare at age 65 and can begin collecting Social Security checks as early as age 62.

Savings Plan

Guitarist and SMT Phil Johnson (www.bigwhizbang.com) is insistent upon disciplined financial management and long-term planning. Because his self-employed income fluctuates significantly from month to month, he commits 20% to savings rather than a fixed dollar amount.

On the fifth of each month, his bank automatically transfers $458.33 into a Roth IRA account (totaling the $5,500 annual maximum).

Johnson also invests through Lending Club (www.lendingclub.com), a peer-to-peer lending institution. Individuals seeking credit for any reason may apply to this company rather than going through a bank. Those who pass the thorough vetting process are eligible for three- or five-year loans, with interest rates determined by their credit score. Minifinancers like Johnson fund loans by contributing as little as $25 apiece in exchange for interest payments. To date, the 25 loans Johnson has helped finance averaged a yield of 9%.

Additionally, he purchases stocks directly from companies like Coca-Cola and General Electric through *dividend reinvestment programs*. Interest generated is automatically reinvested, which drives compound interest. Buying directly from companies avoids broker fees.

Johnson is equally careful with daily expenses. Beyond his primary checking account, which pays for items like utilities and food, he compartmentalizes money in online interest-bearing savings accounts specifically designated for various things: mortgage payments, income taxes, property taxes, new car down payment (his current vehicle has 200,000 miles!), gifts, a trip to Europe, other travel, and "stupid things." "This is like sorting money into various envelopes, except that my system generates a little return through interest."

Other Considerations

Rainy Day Fund

If you don't already have one, a critical short-term savings goal should be building up a *rainy day fund*. Many experts recommend that these accounts hold three to eight months of income. This *liquid asset*, or cash holding that can be readily accessed, is stored in case you suddenly lose income, need a new roof, or experience another unforeseen crisis. When an emergency occurs, it prevents dipping into other savings or financing the charge.

College Funds

Beyond retirement, there are other large-scale goals in life. One major expense is college education for your children. We already considered the high cost of student debt. If you hope to help the kids, there are investments for just that. A *529 plan* works like a Roth IRA, taxed on the front end only. When money is withdrawn for college-related activities (tuition, room and board, books), no additional taxes are assessed. Each state offers unique 529 plans, and it is not necessary to choose states where you live or your children will go to college.

Protecting Your Legacy

As morbid as it sounds, protect assets after you die. This is particularly vital if you have a family. In addition to carrying life insurance, it is critical to make a will. Without one, property, possessions, and savings may not be allocated according to your wishes. In some cases, the government may even seize assets. You might also consider a *living trust*, which offers certain advantages such as the avoidance of *probate*.

Crafting this document with a lawyer costs less than $500, though you can generate one on your own. If you do so, it must be notarized and signed by two witnesses. Wills indicate assets you possess, specify how they are to be distributed, name an *executor* (appointed to carry out terms of the will), and clarify who will care for minors under age 18.

Checkmate

Like chess, winning the money game requires mastery of the rules, discipline, strategy, and long-term vision. (A little luck never hurts, either!) The choices you make each move have immense consequences. Though the match may not be easy, victory is possible for SMTs with acute determination and discipline.

Previous chapters have addressed earning, spending, and saving strategies, but all this knowledge is essentially meaningless unless matched with committed and resolute action. With that in mind, please welcome a very special protagonist: a Savvy Music Teacher (SMT) named *you*.

Reading this chapter with a highlighter is not enough. Reflection, research, and the completion of worksheets are required. Going through this process allows you to develop a fairly nuanced understanding of your financial picture in just five steps!

Step 1: Define Current Situation

Are you on track to reach financial independence or falling further behind by the day? Before making choices about the future, realistically assess current circumstances.

Net Worth

Calculating a human being's worth in dollars is ludicrous. No amount of money can replace a parent, child, friend, or SMT. However, from a financial perspective, everyone has a net worth. This is like a panoramic snapshot of a person's financial wealth at a given time.

assets – liabilities = net worth

Complete the Net Worth Worksheet on page 332 by inputting dollar amounts for current *assets* and *liabilities*. There are two categories of assets: *liquid* (cash or anything that can easily be converted to cash, such as CDs, stocks, bonds, mutual funds, and savings) and *fixed* (things you own that can be sold, like instruments or real estate). Liabilities include everything that you owe, from credit card debt to student loans to home mortgage. Be comprehensive and ensure entries are as accurate as possible.

Determining the value of liquid assets and liabilities is fairly easy. Check online or contact your bank/financial institution to learn the current balances. Fixed assets require more research, but there are helpful methods for estimating their cash price. What is the blue book value on your car? How much would your furniture generate if sold through Craig's list? What is today's market value of your instrument, or the appraised value of your home?

Some readers may discover that liabilities are greater than assets, thus indicating a *negative net worth*. While that can be a humbling realization, it does not forecast eternal financial gloom. Many SMTs find themselves "in the red" at some point yet make strategic, long-term decisions that ultimately help them thrive and win the money game. Rather than getting discouraged, use this opportunity to focus, make a plan, and get to work.

Credit Score

Another important number is your credit (FICO) score. This mysterious but critical figure has a direct impact on interest rates for all sorts of loans (a lower score triggers a higher percentage, and vice versa). Banks, landlords, employers, and other businesses evaluate this score when determining whether to get involved with you in the first place.

FICO scores are influenced by factors such as overall debt balance, debt-to-credit-limit ratio, payment history, length of credit history, and the number/mix of credit cards in your name. Ranging from 300 to 850, most scores fall between 600 and 750, with anything over 700 considered strong. Because this number influences so many aspects of financial life, make sure yours is desirable. If not, take steps to remedy this obstacle.

There are many ways to obtain a credit score. One easy and free method is through Credit Karma (www.creditkarma.com), which allows you to create an account and follow instructions until your score is provided. The site also displays a rating (e.g., "excellent") and explanation, along with tips for improvement. Write your credit score on the top of page 333.

If you are over 18 but don't yet have a score, beware. This means you have no credit history. As a result, banks, renters, utility companies, and others may be wary of working with you. Apply for a credit card and start charging items you already plan to purchase. Then pay off the full balance every month to establish an official record of responsible financial behavior.

Debt/Investment Interest Rates

One additional aspect of your current standing deserves scrutiny. There is no neutral with money—people either move toward greater financial independence or veer further from this target. With that in mind, what are your debt/investment interest rates?

Interest rates on debt are determined by a number of variables, including loan type, lender, current economic conditions, negotiated terms, and your credit score. Enter debt amounts for everything you owe (mortgages, student loans, car loans, etc.) on the chart on page 333. In the right-hand column, add the interest rate connected to each obligation.

On the next page, list investments. While it is impossible to accurately forecast growth for all but the safest assets (e.g., savings account with set rate), you can gain perspective on how these holdings have performed historically. Insert their rate of return over the past 1, 5, and 10 years. If you can't easily find this information on statements, contact your financial advisor, bank, or investment firm. Morningstar (www.morningstar.com) is an excellent resource.

These charts tell a story about your future. Because compounding impacts both sides of the equation, does the current trajectory have you positioned to pay or earn more in interest? Consider the implications when establishing goals in step 2.

While life is much more than dollars and cents, your current financial health has wide-reaching implications. What's the diagnosis?

Determined to Get Ahead

Just one year into her professional career, violinist Claire Allen (www.claireallenviolin.com) is excited about the future. Despite challenges ahead, she is driven with a passion for teaching, music making, and impacting the world.

Allen was fortunate to complete her undergraduate degree debt free, thanks to scholarships and parental assistance. Graduate school, on the other hand, required five student loans topping $87,000 with interest rates from 6.8% to 7.9%. Following school, she moved home with mom and dad. While she loves them dearly, "I wouldn't have done this without loans."

Now 25, Allen is well aware that getting ahead requires financial literacy, discipline, and a savvy career approach. Having read many personal finance books, she lives frugally and with intention. Teaching independently and through an academy, she hopes to eliminate student loans within five years and devotes a large percentage of her income accordingly. She also invests in herself, building an emergency fund and placing at least $100 monthly into a Roth IRA.

Does Allen regret her decisions? "While the price was high, I loved studying at a major conservatory and will always be grateful for that period of my life. My teacher was amazing, my quartet was coached by iconic figures, and I blossomed as a player while developing a solid foundation in pedagogy. If given the choice, I would do it again." Determined to get ahead, she exhibits all the SMT characteristics that will likely help her to do just that.

Step 2: Articulate Goals

Whether the picture is rosy or bleak, where do you go from here? While we never know what tomorrow will hold, defining and prioritizing ambitions helps SMTs forge a meaningful route forward. Brainstorm a list of short- and long-term spending/saving ambitions.

Break down huge dreams into attainable chunks. For example, trying to generate $1 million-plus over decades for retirement feels abstract and overwhelming. Smaller, manageable milestones such as "save $7,000 this year" are concrete, actionable, and realistic, allowing you to feel good about hitting targets in even the short term.

Common Spending/Savings Goals		
Pay down/off: • Car loan • Credit card debt • Mortgage • Other debt • Personal loan • Student loan	**Savings goals:** • Business/career • College/private school (for you or family) • Health related • Home improvement • House down payment • Investments	• Parent care • Passion project • Rainy day fund (build) • Retirement • Vacation • Vehicle (new/used) • Wedding/party

As is often the case, brainstorming is the easy part. Prioritizing, on the other hand, can be excruciating. Because something always comes at the expense of something else, this is when you evaluate what matters most.

The worksheet on page 335 has space for entering five short- (under one year), medium- (one to three years), and long-term (more than three years) goals in order of importance. For each entry, record the objective, price tag, and target date. For example, a short-term goal might be saving $3,000 for a new car down payment by one year from today. Some items, such as investing for retirement, are likely to appear on more than one chart. Key questions to consider are as follows:

• What priority should you assign to past expenses (debt), present expenses (living and business), or future investment (savings)?
• Which debts have the highest interest rates (and should be paid off first)?
• What is the true cost of these debts?
• Are items on your list necessities, comforts, or luxuries?
• How much financial benefit will a business investment realistically bring?
• How much financial security or personal fulfillment does each item offer?
• Which goals have the biggest impact?
• Which goals benefit the most people?
• Which goals cause the greatest harm if delayed?
• Are there ways to curb estimated costs?

Prioritizing forces difficult decisions, each with significant ramifications. For example, suppose 40-year-old SMT Al Feenay believes he can devote $10,000 next year to financial goals. This may sound like a lot, but it is also just a drop in the bucket. What is the best use of this money?

Tough Decisions for Al Feenay	
Rainy day fund	Al currently has just $1,000 in emergency savings. In a pinch, credit cards are his only option.
Credit card debt	Al carries a debt of $8,500 on one card with a 15% APR. Stretching this over five years ultimately costs $12,132 (around 42% interest or $203 per month). He could speed up payments to three years, requiring a total of $10,608 (24% interest or $295 per month), or pay it off now.
Vacation	Al hasn't taken a vacation for two years. He'd like to travel with his wife to Hawaii for one week, requiring around $6,000.

Tough Decisions for Al Feenay	
Business investment	Al's website needs an extreme makeover, estimated at $3,500. The investment has potential to attract more students.
College savings	A one-time investment of $10,000 placed in a 529 college fund for 11 years—until his daughter starts college—yields $18,983 at 6% growth compounded annually; $23,317 with 8% growth; $28,532 with 10% growth; or $34,786 with 12% growth. This money grows tax free.
Retirement savings	A one-time investment of $10,000 invested in a SEP-IRA over 25 years—until Al reaches age 65—yields $42,919 at 6% growth compounded annually; $68,485 with 8% growth; $108,348 with 10% growth; or $170,000 with 12% growth.

What recommendations would you make? Should Al divide the capital over several categories or focus on just one or two? Clearly, these are tough choices, with each decision having significant consequences on other areas. For example, paying off his debt eliminates this expense in the future, allowing more money to go elsewhere. The 15% interest rate is more than he can realistically expect to earn in the stock market. On the other hand, this choice provides no new savings, forcing him to use credit cards in case of emergency (driving up the balance again).

Weigh that against the extreme impact of compound interest on an investment. Capital grows exponentially over time. Al can never reclaim his relative youth (from an investing standpoint). Should he take advantage of time when it's still on his side?

Updating the website seems like a valuable investment since it may lead to new students and income. However, there are ways to curb this expense. Many free or inexpensive templates are satisfactory, and developing compelling *content* only costs time and imagination.

Of these options, one thing is clear: Al cannot afford Hawaii. With credit card debt and underfunded emergency savings, this luxury is off limits. True, everyone needs a break from time to time, but perhaps he and his wife can have just as lovely an adventure camping an hour from home at a fraction of the price.

Many people believe that earning is the most important financial consideration. It is not. That designation goes to *choices*. Make them wisely.

Accountability

Some people stockpile goals in their mind, others on paper. But pianist Ashley Danyew (www.ashleydanyew.com) ups her accountability by publically sharing aspirations on her blog. Though the process continually evolves, she establishes annual goals each January divided into four categories: (1) smarter business, (2) better teaching, (3) professional, and (4) living. Then, each month, specific action-oriented tasks are articulated.

For example, a "professional" entry one year was to develop and present two workshops. Related monthly tasks included researching opportunities, filling out applications, writing abstracts, digging into content, creating handouts, and booking travel.

One danger faced by SMTs is that work becomes all-consuming. "I love teaching and freelancing, but at one point, all my non-music-related activities completely evaporated. Music is my life, but not all my life." Determined to create balance, she has created short-term rules like never checking email after 5 PM, mandatory Sunday time off, and 90 minutes of intentional weekly exercise. Other items in the "living" category have involved reading, going skiing, and sending "just because" gifts to friends.

Danyew is also strategic about finance. After determining earning goals, she carefully calculates the number of students needed, which rates to charge, and the amount of time required. To achieve five-year ambitions of buying a house, piano, and car, she and her husband set annual savings goals. Money is automatically transferred into designated bank accounts each month.

Step 3: Calculate Spending Projection

From a purely financial perspective, what is the cost of being alive? How much do you pump into the economy each year? Though most people have no idea, identifying this number is paramount for several reasons. First, individuals are often alarmed to learn how much they spend. Discovering this amount is eye opening, shocking them into a more frugal existence. Second, personal finance is a lot like business finance, and you can't successfully run a company without understanding expenditures. Hopefully your life is at least as important as a business! Finally, an accurate spending projection is crucial to determining your *earning target* in step 5.

Tracking Spending

One of the most helpful things you can do to understand and control spending is tracking every penny over a given period of time. Doing this for just three months can transform your relationship with money, though some SMTs find it so beneficial that they adopt the habit for life. Beyond providing accurate data, this exercise encourages people to act prudently, since all expenditures are "on the books."

The moment an expense occurs, record it. Include everything from point-of-purchase sales to automatically withdrawn bank payments, overlooking nothing. Indicate the date and category of each entry, clarifying precisely where your money goes.

Though possible with pencil and paper, platforms like Mint.com or iXpenseit offer invaluable features. They can link directly to bank accounts and allow you to easily analyze spending habits by isolating a given time period or expense category.

Budgeting

Budgeting is an SMT annual ritual. Personal budgets predict the amount of money needed to run your life while suggesting spending limits.

The Annual Budget Worksheet on page 336 breaks down expenses into large-scale categories: debt, home, utilities, transportation, family, food, health, career/music, education, entertainment, business, insurance, miscellaneous, and "other." These classifications are further divided into specific line items. For each entry, set the amount allocated during a given year. Add category totals to determine your annual *expense projection*.

In your budget, be sure to account for debt payments, living expenses, insurance, and business overhead. Do not include taxes and saving (addressed later) or cost of goods sold (since they are paid before something is considered income in the SMT blueprint).

How can you forecast numbers with any semblance of accuracy? If life next year looks a lot like last year's, review bank statements, credit card bills, receipts, and tax returns for clues. When a major change is on the horizon (getting married, having a baby, moving across country), more research is necessary. Here are some pointers:

- **Over and under.** It is a good idea to overestimate expenses and underestimate income. If you can make finances work with this kind of caution, you'll consistently exceed goals.

- **Debt.** Minimum payments can be provided by the lender(s). If planning to exceed that threshold (a good idea!), set realistic but proactive allocations.
- **Fixed expenses.** Because items like mortgage, health insurance, and membership dues are set and predetermined, they are easy to predict.
- **Recurring expenses.** For recurring but fluctuating bills like utilities, take cues from the past while accounting for inflation. Find the monthly average and multiply by 12. If moving, ask tenants or real estate agents for assistance.
- **Major expenses.** When contemplating major product purchases (computer, furniture, instrument, etc.), research pricing online. Remember to account for supplementary costs such as sales tax, shipping, and accessories. For service-related items, such as remodeling the kitchen, obtain estimates from local contractors (and add a 20% buffer).
- **Lifestyle expenses.** There are two approaches for regular but variable charges like eating out, gas, or Starbucks. One is forecasting future actions based on past behavior (easier to do after tracking expenses). The other is setting a line-item budget and sticking to it.
- **Unforeseen expenses.** There *will* be unanticipated costs. Perhaps your car breaks down, the basement floods, or you get sick. One option is budgeting a certain amount for the "unexpected." Another possibility is overestimating several expense items, leaving leftovers to apply elsewhere. Or, you might decide that emergencies are paid from your rainy day fund, without counting toward this year's budget. Just be sure to replenish.
- **Multiple incomes.** If your household contains two working adults, determine the total family budget and then decide which items or percentage your income will fund.

Determining a realistic budget for the first time can be time consuming (if you do it right) and frustrating—the reality being that life is expensive. But rather than crossing your fingers and hoping for a miracle, be prudent and take control.

Budgeting with Pride

Trombonist and teacher Philip Brown (www.brownmusicstudio.com) makes separate budgets for personal and business expenses. He creates them in Quicken at the end of each summer, and revisits calculations in December and May to analyze and reflect. As each fiscal year draws to a close, projections are compared with actual expenditures, overall and by category.

An early and important step is determining estimated tax payments. Studying the last tax return, he considers this year's projected difference.

Brown contributes monthly to a SEP-IRA. When opening this account, just 8% of annual income was invested here, but he now devotes 15% of a steadily growing income.

Hoping to cover eight semesters of undergraduate tuition for his son (now in grade school), he also invests in a 529 college fund that locks in today's tuition rate at a specific university. Additional savings are directed to paying down the mortgage.

Also projected meticulously are present-day expenses like utilities, home repair, transportation, health care, groceries, and eating out. Business costs include marketing, subscriptions, music, union dues, studio furniture/equipment, and room rentals.

Brown has experimented with placing cash budgeted for various expense categories into envelopes. When one is emptied, he must either borrow from another "fund" or discontinue this expense for the remainder of the month. "Some musicians have the reputation of being financially illiterate or undisciplined. I take great pride in not being one of those people."

Step 4: Calculate Savings Target

With financial independence a priority, how much should SMTs save each month/year? Many experts recommend funneling 15% to 25% of gross income into retirement funds. When that is impossible, deposit what you can. Ten percent is preferable to 5%, and something is always better than nothing. The important thing is to start early and contribute regularly.

While designating a fixed percentage of your salary is the easiest solution to calculate, another possibility entails working backward. How large must your nest egg ultimately be to constitute financial independence? Many free, online calculators help pinpoint your "magic" number. After inputting a few variables, the vital statistics appear:

- **Desired retirement age.** You must be 59½ to withdraw from most retirement accounts without penalty. Many people consider 65 the target.
- **Life expectancy.** The difference between retirement age and life expectancy determines how long this money must last. According to the World Health Organization, average life expectancy is 79 years in the United

States (with Japan, the world leader, at 83). Of course, we never know our own number. Money left over can be willed or gifted, but you don't want to run out with 10 years to go!

- **Current age.** Calculators use this to determine years to retirement and project inflation.
- **Desired retirement income.** Though many experts recommend around 70% to 80% of preretirement working salary, this varies greatly depending on lifestyle choices. The retirement savings chart that follows uses 80% to predict conservatively high numbers.
- **Additional income sources.** What additional revenues will you have?

Conclusions are far from gospel, as equations incorporate impossible-to-predict assumptions. For example, nobody knows how long you will live, how much you will spend, future investment return, or inflation over time. However, it is helpful to have a specific savings goal. (Projections here use a calculator available through CNN Money.)

Retirement Savings Goals					
Current age	30	30	40	40	50
Current annual income	$50,000	$75,000	$50,000	$85,000	$75,000
Desired retirement age	65	65	65	65	65
Desired retirement $ (% of current)	80%	80%	80%	80%	80%
Life expectancy	85	85	85	85	85
Social security income	$18,000	$21,500	$15,000	$20,000	$15,000
TOTAL NEEDED	**$918,160**	**$1.6 M**	**$776,360**	**$1.5 M**	**$1.0 M**
(Total in today's dollars)	$316,176	$553,308	$362,540	$696,077	$658,473

A million plus dollars sounds like a mountain of money! But there is a way to get there, particularly for SMTs who make sound financial decisions. Calculators determining how much must be saved on a monthly/annual basis require the following:

- **Retirement savings goal.** This is determined through the previous step.
- **Current savings.** How much have you already accumulated?

- **Annual percentage growth rate.** Input an educated guess. Factors include how aggressively funds are invested, the specific performance of investments, general economic trends, and associated taxes, expenses, and fees.
- **Number of years until retirement.** How much time does your money have to grow?

In the examples that follow, retirement age is set to 65, but other aspects are varied.

Monthly/Annual Retirement Savings Required*					
Name	Tim Panny	Barry Tone	Dell Kapo	O. Peretta	Bay Soon
Savings goal	$1.5 M	$1.5 M	$1.0 M	$1.75 M	$1.5 M
Current age	25	35	35	45	45
Years until retirement	40	30	30	20	20
Current savings balance	$0	$100,000	$50,000	$250,000	$5,000
Annual % growth rate	8%	7%	6%	9%	8%
Monthly savings	$430	$606	$710	$523	$2,507
Annual savings	$5,160	$7,272	$8,520	$6,276	$30,084

* Projections use a calculator developed by FinancialMentor (www.financialmentor.com/calculator/savings-goal-calculator).

Note that Tim has no savings at age 25. However, because he starts young, contributions can be relatively low. Just $5,160 per year generates $1.5 million by retirement age, assuming an 8% rate of return. If he currently earns $50,000 annually (the minimum salary described in this book), just 10% of income is directed toward retirement. His earnings will undoubtedly rise over time, increasing the level of investment even if maintaining an identical percentage. Said another way, Tim will be just fine. He is beautifully positioned to exceed his saving goal.

Bay has the same retirement aspiration and rate of return, but with essentially no reserve by age 45, six times as much must be socked away. Even if she earns $100,000 annually (the top-level salary described in this book), getting on track requires 30% of her income. While all hope is not lost, Bay will have to adjust expectations or make significant sacrifices to achieve her goal—a final reminder to *start saving early* (though it is never too late to get proactive).

Retirement is probably not your only savings goal. For other long-term objectives such as college funds, employ a similar process. With short-term aspirations, determine the full or down payment price and divide by the number of months you plan to save. For example, if you hope to buy a $5,000 instrument a year from now, reserve an average of $417 each month.

The Annual Savings Chart Worksheet on page 340 allows you to input savings goals. When necessary, use online calculators to help determine appropriate amounts.

The Path to Retirement

Passionate about his livelihood, Perry Long (not his real name) finds it difficult to imagine voluntarily giving up teaching. But a chill ran down his spine when a famous pedagogue confided, "Independent music teachers don't retire, honey. We just die." Life is uncertain. You never know how long health will last or what unexpected expenses might arise during our golden years. Therefore, retirement saving is too important an issue to overlook.

Graduating with a doctorate at age 28, Long saved minimally during his 20s. Founding a teaching studio required considerable startup investment, and it took several years to reach a desirable income level. (That said, Long is certainly savvy. Consider his gross income trajectory: year 1, $10,000; year 2, $20,000; year 3, $55,000; year 4, $70,000; year 5, $82,000). In other words, investing wasn't a serious pursuit until his mid-30s. He got a late start.

Determined to reach financial independence by age 65, Long directs 15% of income to retirement savings. Over time, he hopes to raise that percentage, as well as overall earnings. "In addition to work I currently do, my goal is adding one new income stream for the next several years." Regardless of what the future brings, he insists on having options.

Step 5: Calculate Earning Goal

This book unveils a blueprint for SMTs to generate $50,000 to $100,000 annually. But what kind of salary do *you* hope to earn? Or, more important, how much do you *need* to bring home?

A common but horribly inadequate response is "as much as possible." Why? For starters, this target cannot be measured. How is success substantiated? Since there are always paths to earning more, your actual figure comes up short every time, even if you do become the Donald Trump of SMTs. There must be a clear metric. If the goal is $65,000, but actual income is just $64,000, the verdict is clear—you underperformed (though not embarrassingly). On the other hand, $68,000 is a triumph, surpassing all expectations.

Second, people use this "fuzzy goal" as an excuse to justify low earnings ("well, I guess $24,000 was all that was possible . . ."), rather than beginning with a plan.

Finally, it's not true. If earning gobs of cash had been your primary consideration, you would not have chosen music teaching. There are plenty of more lucrative paths. You picked this career because chasing a passion while doing meaningful work was more important than getting rich quickly. So rather than getting greedy, determine what is "enough."

You are finally prepared to derive a specific, measurable *earning goal*. An ideal salary covers expenses, savings, and taxes. In addition, I recommend adding a 10% cushion to accommodate unforeseen costs that inevitably arise.

expense projection + savings target + 10% buffer + taxes due = earning goal

Use the worksheet on page 343 to determine your annual earning target.

1. Add annual spending projection to savings goal.

   $_____ spending projection + $_____ savings target = financial obligation

2. Multiply your financial obligation by 1.1 to add the 10% buffer and come up with a "safety number."

   $_____ financial obligation × 1.1 buffer = safety number

3. Indicate what percentage of income will be kept after taxes. To do this, subtract your estimated income tax rate for federal, state, and local sources from 100 (e.g., 30% tax rate means you keep 70% of income after taxes).

100 total income – _____% tax rate = _____% income after taxes

4. Divide your safety number by the percentage of income after taxes to determine an earning target.

$_____ safety number ÷ _____% income after taxes = $_____ earning target

Let's plug in some numbers. Suppose you project expenses at $38,000 and hope to save $12,000, with a tax rate averaging 30%.

Item	Annual	Monthly Average
Expenses	$38,000	$3,167
± Savings goal	$12,000	$1,000
Financial obligation	**$50,000**	**$4,167**
+ 10% Buffer (× 0.1)	$5,000	$417
Safety number	**$55,000**	**$4,584**
Taxes = 30% (0.3); income after taxes = 70% (0.7)		
EARNING TARGET (÷ 0.7)	**$78,572**	**$6,549**

Safely meeting these aims requires around $78,500 annually, or $6,550 per month. If this number seems unattainable, adjustments must be made to spending or saving expectations. But perhaps there is a way to reach this aspiration. The final chapter ties together our seven SMT impact/income streams, illuminating a path to your earning goal.

Bundles of Joy (and Implications)

By his mid-20s, clarinetist and saxophonist Scott Moore (www.woodwindscott.com) and his wife had racked up $70,000 in student and credit card debt. Determined to get ahead, they followed "baby steps" recommended in Dave Ramsey's program Financial Peace University, eventually paying off the entire amount. "Eliminating debt greatly increased the flexibility of our career decisions. My wife was able to quit her job and start an independent psychotherapy practice loaded with potential, despite income dropping in the short term. Similarly, it allowed me to make smart strategic decisions about the future."

Moore is now in his mid-30, and his life has taken a wonderful but unexpected turn. The couple has two babies under the age of 7 months: one biological, the other adopted. Though this is a blessing, it has significant economic consequences, causing Moore to rethink his business model. "Reaching my earning goals requires a strategic approach. As an independent teacher, you only get paid when working. But it is important for me to spend time with the kids as well."

Several years ago, he started a chamber program for wind quartets and quintets. Beyond its profound educational impact, this "product" generates a higher wage. Lessons currently cost $60 per hour, whereas ensembles deliver $90 to $110 for the same period. Moving forward, he hopes to increase this aspect of his profile. In fact, hiring colleagues to direct some of the groups has allowed him to earn money when *not* working.

Moore has another opportunity to increase passive income through his websites NCMusicLessons.com and USAMusicLessons.com, which allow independent music teachers to advertise their studios for $50 to $75 per year.

Reflecting on the Process

By completing these five steps, you now have a clearer idea about your financial picture and future, with specific data about your:

- Net worth
- Debt and investment interest rates
- Credit score
- Prioritized short-, medium-, and long-term financial objectives
- Spending projections
- Annual earning goal

All of this was done with deliberation, research, and old-fashioned math. Just going through the worksheets places you ahead of the pack. How do things look? Removing the mystery around finance can be both humbling and liberating. Though the path to financial independence may not be easy, knowledge and literacy are far superior to ignorance. They will serve you well.

The SMT controls finances, rather than the other way around. Understanding how money works in your life is the first step toward mastering it.

15 THE SAVVY MUSIC TEACHER CAREER BLUEPRINT

The Savvy Music Teacher began with a promise to deliver a career model that generates $50,000 to $100,000 annually while increasing impact. The preceding chapters examined financial and value-creating elements under a microscope, often moving seamlessly between the two to emphasize their connectivity. Finally, we are ready to assemble the Savvy Music Teacher (SMT) income and impact puzzles.

Piecing Together the Earnings Puzzle

In the abstract, the notion of generating your target salary can feel overwhelming. Yet by breaking things down and articulating specific manageable goals for each stream, it is possible to envision multiple realistic scenarios for realizing most earning aspirations. Energy spent here becomes well worth the investment when implementing this plan and watching income rise.

Annual Income

Chapters 3 through 9 described seven income streams typical in the life of an SMT, along with low and high projected earnings. The following chart combines them to forecast a yearly total.

Income Stream	Annual Income (Low)	Annual Income (High)
1. Lessons	$32,000	$52,000
2. Classes	$6,300	$20,250
3. Camp	$3,425	$7,100

(*continued*)

Income Stream	Annual Income (Low)	Annual Income (High)
4. Events	$1,000	$1,750
5. Media	$1,000	$2,000
6. Products	$1,000	$5,000
7. Additional	$6,000	$12,000
TOTAL	$50,725	$100,100

From this career blueprint, the SMT earns between $50,725 and $100,100 per year. Of course, every situation is different. Consider some hypothetical but instructive models.

Variation #1

SMT Aria Singer is a voice teacher who also gigs with a wedding band. She has no trouble attracting students and consistently maintains a waitlist. The challenge, however, is that her hourly rate of $36 per hour ($18 per half hour) is already more than most of the local competition. Her annual income goal is $60,000 per year.

1. **Lessons.** Aria isn't comfortable charging more than $36 per hour. To reach her income goal, she decides to (a) boost teaching to 22 hours per week and (b) offer only half-hour lessons, giving her a larger client base for augmenting additional streams.

    $36 fee × 22 hours per week × 40 lessons per year = $33,120

2. **Classes.** Aria offers six singing-related classes (three per semester) to high school students, charging $300 tuition. Her room rental is $15 per hour ($1,350 per year), and she averages eight students per class.

    ($300 tuition × 6 classes × 8 students each) – $1,350 rental = $13,050

3. **Camp.** Aria does not host a summer camp.

4. **Events.** In addition to tuition, Aria charges an annual event/media fee of $100 to offset costs and compensate her time (shown in stream 5). This

contributes to four cool studio events per year, each with a different theme. Expenses involve an accompanist ($500 total), rental space for two of the shows ($200), and food and supplies ($300).

see stream 5

5. **Technology.** Aria regularly records lessons. Expenses for camera upkeep, memory cards, and other technology run $600, covered by the event/media fee.

($100 event/media fee × 44 students [$4,400]) –
$500 accompanist – $200 venues – $300 food/supplies – $600 technology = $2,700

6. **Products.** Aria wrote an e-book on vocal technique a few years back, available only through her website, which lists for $15. It is selling modestly, and 110 downloads have been purchased by voice students and teachers this year.

$15 e-book × 110 sales = $1,650

7. **Additional.** Aria sings an average of one gig per week with a wedding band, though some periods are busier than others. Paychecks average $200 per event or $800 per month.

$800 income per month × 12 months = $9,600

Lessons	Classes	Camp	Events		Tech	Products	Additional
$33,120	$13,050	$0	→		$2,700	$1,650	$9,600
		TOTAL		$60,120			

Variation #2

SMT Reid Dubbler teaches saxophone, flute, and clarinet. He also owns a home recording studio. Though offering lessons in person and online, he has a hard time attracting more than 20 students. The majority take

45-minute or hour lessons, providing 15 teaching hours per week. Reid's acclaimed Recording for Performers camp has grown over time, with three back-to-back sessions this summer. His annual income goal is $55,000.

1. **Lessons.** Reid averages $50 per hour for his 15 hours of private lessons.

   $50 fee × 15 hours per week × 40 lessons per year = $30,000

2. **Classes.** In the past, Reid tried organizing performance classes, but his woodwind students simply weren't interested. This year, he created a music technology course that was met with enthusiasm, enrolling five students per semester at $300 apiece. The classes are taught in his home studio, so there is no additional rental expense.

   $300 tuition × 2 classes × 5 students each = $3,000

3. **Camps.** His three summer camps ($400 tuition) accommodate 12 students apiece. During the course of each week, participants learn studio techniques, rehearse with chamber groups, and record/edit one piece. Total expenses are $2,500.

   ($400 tuition × 36 students [$14,400]) – $2,500 expenses = $11,900

4. **Events.** Reid throws a traditional recital in the fall, with no expenses or revenue. The spring event, held in a donated church space, is more of a spectacle. A professional guitarist and drummer accompany students on the first half and then perform as a trio with Reid after intermission. Fifty-five family members and other guests purchase $10 tickets. Hired musicians receive $125, and $80 is spent on a reception.

   ($12 × 55 tickets [$660]) – $250 to musicians – $80 reception = $330

5. **Technology.** In addition to lessons, Reid has his students record at least one piece per year in his recording studio. This package, which averages one hour of studio time and 75 minutes of editing, costs $125.

   $125 recording package fee × 20 students = $2,500

6. **Products.** Reid has two student model saxophones, rented for $40 per month ($480 per year), and one flute and one clarinet that each rent for $20 monthly ($240 per year). He also does some minor instrument repair work, bringing in an extra $500.

($480 × 2 saxophones [$960]) + ($240 × 2 flute/clarinet [$480]) + $500 repairs = $1,940

7. **Additional.** Reid drums up a bit of business recording in his home studio. He also does some computer notation copy work. These activities return about $500 per month.

$500 per month × 12 months = $6,000

Lessons	Classes	Camp	Events	Tech	Products	Additional
$30,000	$3,000	$11,900	$330	$2,500	$1,940	$6,000
		TOTAL		$55,670		

Variation #3

SMT Phil Harmonik is a violinist specializing in classical violin and fiddling. He teaches advanced violinists and beginners on all bowed string instruments. His annual income goal is $80,000.

1. **Lessons.** Phil teaches a total of 30 students for 20 hours per week. His annual tuition model includes 38 meetings, valued at $62 per hour.

$62 fee × 20 hours per week × 38 lessons per year = $47,120

2. **Classes.** Each semester, Phil teaches a fiddle class to 6 students ($500 tuition) and an early childhood class to 10 youngsters and their families ($250 tuition). Room rentals are $25 per hour ($1,500 per year).

($500 tuition × 6 students × 2 semesters [$6,000]) + ($250 tuition × 10 students × 2 semesters [$5,000]) – $1,500 room rental = $9,500

3. **Camps.** His weeklong fiddle camp is an annual highlight, attracting 25 students ($500 each). He hires three assistant teachers, including the often imitated but rarely duplicated SMT Viola Fidler. Salaries and expenses run $5,000.

   ($500 tuition × 25 students [$12,500]) – $5,000 expenses = $7,500

4. **Events.** Phil hosts three fun recitals and organizes a field trip to hear an Irish group. Doing this costs him $250. He does not charge a recital fee, instead covering expenses through his tuition package.

   – $250 in recital expenses

5. **Technology.** Phil recently added the option of a technology lab for younger students. Instead of half-hour lessons, they can pay $8 more and stay for a full hour, working on theory apps for part of the time (during the school year only). Twelve students have opted in. Already owning an iPad, he spends $220 on new programs.

   ($8 lab × 12 students × 30 lessons [$2,880]) – $220 apps = $2,660

6. **Products.** Products are not a part of Phil's income.
7. **Additional.** Phil is an active freelancer. He plays with regional orchestras, gigs with a string quartet, fiddles with an Irish group, and arranges fiddle music for various ensembles and educational groups. He averages $1,100 per month.

   $1,100 per month × 12 months = $13,200

Lessons	Classes	Camp	Events	Tech	Products	Additional
$47,120	$9,500	$7,500	($250)	$2,660	$0	$13,200
			TOTAL	$79,730		

The Portfolio Life

Jess Allured (www.alluredmusicstudio.com) had worked for seven years as a middle school music teacher when her program was defunded. Rather than seeking another job, she began building a self-employed SMT career.

1. **Lessons.** Allured teaches flute, piano, and voice lessons. At its peak, her studio reached 30 students, totaling 20 hours per week. She also offers isolated instrumental and vocal coaching sessions at a higher hourly rate.
2. **Classes.** Though she advertises classes in music theory, note reading, and music history, none have come to fruition as of yet. This is a goal for the near future, however, and theory inquiries have led to private students. She works with up to three voice lesson groups per semester (two students for 45 minutes weekly; three for an hour) and leads a handful of choral and cantor workshops.
3. **Camp.** This summer, she will direct two weeklong day camps (divided third to fifth grade and sixth to eighth grade).
4. **Events.** Allured schedules two studio recitals annually, charging a $10 participation fee for each. After accounting for venue and food, generated revenue is marginal.
5. **Technology.** This stream does not play a role in Allured's economic model.
6. **Products.** Allured's duo The Chickadees is in the process of recording a CD of original religious music. Published compositions, sold online and at performances, are marketed to church communities.
7. **Additional.** Allured works with several bands and is a first-call musician for many organizations. She regularly plays or conducts church services, musicals, funerals, weddings, and bar gigs and also accompanies solo ensemble competitions.

Your Savvy Music Teacher Income Blueprint

It is finally time to architect your very own SMT Income Blueprint. This tool, found in Appendix B, helps you design a realistic, manageable, and fulfilling career model that generates your desired level of income. Completing multiple versions allows you to imagine a variety of viable pathways.

First Steps

After entering your name, write start and end dates considered by the blueprint. Because this is a planning document, when do you hope to realistically execute this strategy? In the coming year? Three years from now? Pick a time frame that is feasible yet ambitious.

This document addresses income over a *fiscal year*, the period that a company or individual calculates finances for planning, accounting, and tax purposes. Though often corresponding to the calendar year (January 1 to December 31), many SMTs find it more logical to begin mid-August and follow the academic calendar. Choose dates that make sense to you.

Next, enter the earning goal determined last chapter where it says *desired annual income*. Your objective is to find a realistic formula for reaching that magical number.

Streams and Substreams

The SMT Income Blueprint is for a *portfolio*—rather than a single-income-source—*career*. Write down large-scale streams that will likely play a role in your model in the indicated spaces. Most SMTs incorporate four to seven streams.

This document is not meant to be prescriptive, but rather a flexible tool. It is not necessary for your headings to match those described in chapters 3 to 9. For example, feel free to omit some categories (perhaps *camps* play no role) or divide up large classifications (i.e., *additional* might be split into separate *performance* and *composing/arranging* streams). The important thing is to organize in ways logical to you.

This blueprint provides space for dividing each stream into up to four substreams (labeled A, B, C, and D) to help you more accurately predict income while clarifying where energy must be spent. Once again, choose logical designations relevant to your model. For example, in the *lessons* stream, you could:

- Calculate all lesson income together under (A)
- Break things down by term, separating (A) *fall,* (B) *spring,* and (C) *summer*
- Distinguish lesson durations, particularly if using scaled pricing: (A) *30 minutes,* (B) *45 minutes*, and (C) *60 minutes*
- Differentiate between (A) *online* and (B) *in person*, particularly if charging different rates
- Separate teaching locations, such as (A) *independent studio*, (B) *music store X*, (C) *music store Y*, and (D) *house calls*
- List both (A) *private lessons* and (B) *group lessons* as substreams here, rather than considering the latter a subcategory of classes

The following chart outlines streams and substreams discussed throughout this book.

Stream 1—Lessons	Stream 2—Classes	Stream 3—Camps	Stream 4—Events
Independent lesson tuition Teaching in another program House calls A la carte lessons Supplemental/ sporadic lessons Online lessons Additional fees	Group lessons Enrichment classes Chamber music Early childhood Presentations and workshops Online courses	Day camp tuition Sleep-away camp tuition	Recital fees Ticket sales Built-in fees

Stream 5—Technology	Stream 6—Products	Stream 7—Additional
Technology products/ services Passive technology income Technology fees Technology "labs"	Dealership Buying and selling Manufacturing Instructional materials Merchandizing Instrument rentals Affinity/affiliate programs	Running a music school Classroom music teaching Assistant teaching/coaching Adjunct college professor Performance Composing/arranging Other musical activities Nonmusical possibilities

Data

The chart that follows clarifies other categories of data needed for the SMT Income Blueprint.

Item	Description	Example	#
A	Variable A (whatever makes sense)	Hours per week	20
B	Variable B (second number, when helpful)	Lessons per year	40

(*continued*)

Item	Description	Example	#
$	Cost (per term, session, unit, etc.)	Hourly rate	$55
Gross	Gross income (multiply first three columns)	20 × 40 × $55	$44,000
(COGS)	Cost of goods sold (expenses that wouldn't exist if you didn't have the offering)	Rental room ($5/hour) ($5 × 20 × 40)	($4,000)
Net	Net annual income (gross – net)	$44,000 – $4,000	$40,000
Notes	Short explanations clarifying variables and how figures were derived	A = hours per week; B = lessons per year; $ = hourly rate	
Stream total	After completing data for substreams in a given category, add them together to compute each stream total.		
Annual income	Re-enter *stream totals* at the bottom of page 348 adding them together to determine your projected annual income.		

Working Inward

There are two approaches for inputting data. Working inward starts with large-scale goals and then determines the best way to get there. For example, suppose your earning target is **$75,000**, generated through five major income streams. Begin by estimating stream totals that equal or exceed your annual goal when added together. Multiple solutions are compared here (something you may want to try).

Stream	Solution A	Solution B	Solution C
1—Lessons	$30,000	$40,000	$50,000
2—Classes	$18,000	$10,500	$5,000
3—Camps	$7,000	$15,000	$3,000
4—Technology	$2,000	$1,500	$5,000
5—Gigging	$18,000	$8,000	$12,000
TOTAL	$75,000	$75,000	$75,000

While each profile shown in the chart incorporates the same streams and annual total, they represent vastly different career models. Lesson income increases with each subsequent solution. Solution A places high emphasis on classes, while solution B generates sizable revenue from summer camps (probably two or three separate events). Solutions A and C require significant gigging ($1,500 and $1,000 per month, respectively) compared to solution B ($666 per month). Solution C generates a good deal through "technology," perhaps as the result of labs or a home recording studio.

Once you are satisfied with a particular distribution, divide the numbers further. Apply a similar process to substreams, clarifying what it will actually take to achieve projections. For example, solution B suggests that $10,500 must be generated from classes. How many courses will that require? What average enrollment is needed per class? Where is tuition set? If no reasonable, achievable solution emerges, look to absorb the difference elsewhere on the worksheet.

Working Outward

Working outward is the opposite process, beginning with small scale details and then computing totals. In order to demonstrate how flexible the SMT Income Blueprint can be, I will use different kinds of variables for each line in the chart that follows describing *stream 1: lessons*.

For sub-stream (A), suppose you hope to attract 20 students who take an average of 40 half hour lessons per year at $30 per meeting.

For sub-stream (B), let's calculate things differently. In this case, you aspire to recruit five additional studio members who enroll in hour-long lessons. Their fall/spring tuition of $1,800 is divided into nine equal installments of $200 apiece.

All 25 students are required to pay an annual fee of $65 to help fund administrative efforts and events (which cost you $800 per year). See how this is indicated in sub-stream (C).

Additionally, you offer music theory tutoring, shown in sub-stream (D). This work is sporadic and meeting lengths vary. Rather than breaking things down by the hour or client, you simply estimate that $1800 will be generated. However, evening sessions typically require you to hire a babysitter, eating up around $200 (COGS) over the year.

In the "notes" section, variables are clarified as needed.

Sub-Streams	Stream 1: Lessons					
	A	B	$	Gross $	(COGS)	Net $
A) 30-minute slots	20	40	$30	$24,000	—	$24,000
B) 60-minute	5	9	$200	$9,000	—	$9,000
9-month tuition	25	—	$65	$1,625	($800)	$825
C) Annual fee	1	—	$1,800	$1,800	($300)	$1,500
D) Online a la carte lessons						
Stream 1 TOTAL						**$35,325**

<table>
<tr><td rowspan="2">NOTES</td><td>

1A *A = # of students*
    B=lessons per year
    $ 30-minute lesson rate

</td><td>

1C *A = # of clients*
    $ = annual fee
    COGS = recital expenses

</td><td rowspan="2">NOTES</td></tr>
<tr><td>

1B *A = # of students*
    B = # of installment payments
    C = monthly tuition

</td><td>

1D *1 x typical amount earned here*
    COGS = babysitting

</td></tr>
</table>

According to this model, *stream 1: lessons* generate $35,425. Apply a similar process to other streams and add totals to determine the *projected annual earnings*. Ultimately, one of three scenarios will become evident:

1. **Projected earnings exceed desired income.** This means you have a solid strategy, with wiggle room in case some aspects don't pan out according to plan. (Count on this!)
2. **Projected earnings equal desired income.** This is a good plan, though you will need to be particularly disciplined, prepared to make adjustments if and when something goes awry.
3. **Projected earnings are less than desired income.** In this case, adjust earning expectations to derive a more realistic number or find a solution that increases revenue.

Whether working inward or outward, double-check your math. Don't let a sloppy adding mistake leave you $10,000 short at year's end!

Augmenting Income

If projected earnings are not enough, there are several strategies for augmenting income:

1. **Raise your rate.** This option doesn't require additional time on your part, and clients might not mind. Even small increases add up.
2. **Work more hours.** Increase the number of lessons, classes, or other services offered.
3. **Add income streams or substreams.** For best results, identify activities that generate significant financial yield and impact.
4. **Become more efficient.** Group lessons pay more than individual lessons. Classes pay more than group lessons. A class of 15 pays more than a class of 5. Favor settings that generate more per hour.
5. **Develop passive streams.** Find ways to get paid when *not* working. One possibility is creating products that sell on their own, like a book, CD, or instructional video. While these take time to produce on the front end, the investment becomes worthwhile when in-demand products generate income and impact down the road.
6. **Found a music academy.** This is the most common way SMTs exceed the $100,000 goal. When hiring other teachers, *you* earn a commission every time *they* work!

The Salaried Savvy Music Teacher

Even SMTs who realize their earning objectives may face a challenge when it comes to *cash flow*, thanks to the sporadic nature of income. Unlike traditional employees, who receive regular paychecks, music teachers are compensated unevenly throughout the year. Additionally, without an employer to deduct taxes, insurance benefits, and retirement savings, these professionals must be particularly disciplined.

When studio members pay by the semester, September and January (or whenever your terms begin) can feel like winning the jackpot. Twenty teaching hours times four months of lessons adds up to a considerable sum. But months later, with limited new dollars in the bank, the tide turns. Finances appear bleak.

This constant cycling through feast and famine is tough for all but the most methodical SMTs. Without a consistent paycheck, managing finances becomes a challenge in the short term, even if annual income is sufficient.

Here's a radical idea: pay yourself a regular salary, such as 26 biweekly installments per year, similar to a company employee. This option only becomes feasible when you have an accurate picture of how much is earned:

1. **Business account.** Deposit any and all earnings into an interest-bearing, low-expense business account. Cash here is used only to pay expenses directly related to the business and to comply with the following steps.
2. **Annual income projection.** Realistically predict how much will be generated using the SMT Income Blueprint. Suppose your projection is $75,000.
3. **Eliminate buffer.** Recall that when calculating your desired income last chapter, a 10% buffer was added. Temporarily eliminate the safety net, multiplying by 90%.

   $75,000 × 90% of income after buffer = $67,500 safety income

4. **Determine tax burden.** If estimated income taxes are 27%, store that money in the business account until it is time to pay or open a separate savings account.

   $67,500 safety income × 27% tax burden = $18,225 in taxes
   $67,500 safe income − $18,225 in taxes = $49,275 after-tax income

5. **Pay yourself first.** Don't make the mistake of so many teachers who wait for the end of the year to see how much is available for retirement and other savings goals. Instead, ensure success by paying yourself first. Direct a certain amount (i.e., $10,000, or 13.3% of gross income here) into Roth IRAs and other investment mechanisms.

   $49,275 after-tax income − $10,000 investments = $39,275 salary

6. **Determine biweekly payments.** Divide the remainder by 26 for your biweekly salary. While this number may not be huge, you have already accounted for taxes and savings. This total shows how much you can afford for living, business, and debt expenses.

   $39,275 salary ÷ 26 installments = $1,511 per pay period

7. **Automate.** Set up your business account so that the bank automatically generates a check or transfers payment every second Friday (or other day of choice). Work with the financial institution to find a no-cost solution. Obviously, be sure there is enough cash on reserve to avoid the expense and inconvenience of overdrawing.
8. **Give yourself a bonus!** Remember the 10% buffer deducted in step three? If earnings equal or exceed projections, you have cash in retainer. At the fiscal year's end, give yourself a bonus! Buy a treat, add to savings, make home improvements, or invest this capital back into the business.

Self-Employed, but with a Salary

Flutist Kim Lorimier (www.bostonsuzukiflute.com) confronted a situation known to many independent teachers. Income was steady throughout the school year but dried up during summers. How could she experience relative financial stability? The solution evolved over time with the guidance of a great accountant.

Lorimier currently accepts tuition in three ways: (1) a single lump sum covering nine months; (2) nine automated PayPal payments, due the first of each month; or (3) nine installment checks written by the beginning of the year but postdated for each month (i.e., September 1, October 1, guaranteeing this income). These payments, along with additional predictable income (i.e., annual teacher training institutes), are deposited into a business checking account. As each month between September and May begins, she makes three transfers:

1. **Taxes.** Fifteen to 20% is directed to a money market designated specifically for quarterly estimated taxes.
2. **Summer.** One ninth of the amount budgeted to cover expenses from June to August is placed in a "summer account."
3. **Salary.** She pays herself a fixed salary, enough to cover mortgage, utilities, insurance, and other personal expenses.

Undispersed money remains in the checking account until it is used for business expenses: new computers, instrument repair, work-related travel. "Think of it as a bucket account for all things business." Surpluses are typically left here for future expenses.

Less predictable freelance income, viewed as a separate stream, is placed in a "rainy day" account. Typically, $5,000 to $7,000 lives here, accessible in case of emergency. When the balance grows larger, extra cash is placed in retirement savings, college funds for her daughters, or other investments.

"Few independent teachers have a clear financial strategy, which I fear puts them at a disadvantage. I cannot overemphasize the importance of an economic blueprint." What SMT could disagree?

Your Savvy Music Teacher Impact Blueprint
Completing the Success Equation

Impact makes up the other side of our success equation. While studying music with any competent instructor offers intrinsic reward, the truly extraordinary is achievable in the hands of a master SMT.

Beyond tallying up the number of names that appear on a studio roster or the percentage that continue lessons for a given period of time, impact is difficult to measure quantitatively. How can we possibly know which off-the-cuff comments ultimately resonate for years, or how many memories or life takeaways each student internalizes?

Assessing achievement (e.g., Matthew is now comfortable with scales in all 12 keys) or improvement over time (e.g., Suzy completed level 2 of her method book in just nine months) is both possible and valuable. But these metrics can mean many things (what if tone got better but rhythm got worse?) and are not necessarily synonymous with meaning (the most advanced student may be bored with lessons, while a less gifted one finds her calling). Achievement and impact can certainly be related, but that is not an automatic law of nature.

Impact—that which makes a meaningful impression or difference—comes in many forms. To follow is an incomplete list of issues that can affect the impact music study has on students. While some items are impossible for music teachers to control, others are directly connected to studio curriculum and culture.

- Amount of time spent practicing music
- Artistic achievement
- Connection made between music and other areas of life
- Curricular priorities, values, and learning objectives
- "Extracurricular" studio offerings

- Friends and their attitudes
- General student/teacher relationship
- Number of activities pursued beyond music
- Parents' view of music
- Pedagogy/methodology employed
- Personal student connection to repertoire
- Reward incentives
- Role of family in the music learning process
- Skills and perspectives emphasized
- Specific student/teacher interactions
- Studio activities and traditions
- Studio community
- Studio dynamic
- Summer requirements
- Teacher expectations
- Time of day lessons are scheduled
- Variety and quality of musical encounters

The impact of a music studio expands beyond enrolled clients. SMTs also directly influence the lives of families and audience members. When people from any of these groups are touched by your work (in ways big or small), the ripple effect can be substantial.

Using This Document

Understanding the fuzzy nature of *impact*, I have built the SMT Impact Blueprint (Appendix C) around words and concepts rather than numbers. It also stresses studio traditions and large-scale biases that can be easily explained in an elevator pitch or online, rather than items of nuance just as likely to make a difference. However, if something is important to you, make sure to include it.

As with the Income Blueprint, commit by writing things down rather than simply considering points in your head. The act of doing this prompts you to discover new solutions likely to increase value and demand for your studio. It also highlights which aspects of your business currently shine, along with those that might benefit from evolution and redesign. This document is meant as a guide; you decide how literally to follow the format.

A single SMT Impact Blueprint applicable to your entire studio is a great starting point. Because specific activities are likely to vary from student to student depending on age, experience, and interest, some teachers fill out parts of multiple forms for various categories of learners, or even a customized worksheet per student. Use this tool in personalized ways, clarifying your brand while imagining ways to continually expand *impact*.

Priorities and Positioning

Refer to chapter 1 when completing the first page of this blueprint. Enter your essential question, top five learning objectives *in order of importance*, and up to four specific activities that emphasize each value and play a role in your curriculum.

The next page allows you to address studio specifics. For each of the eight boxes, list up to five elements critical to your brand:

1. **Who you teach.** Young children, retirees, business professionals, homeschoolers, special needs learners, advanced performers. While most teachers won't turn away students, focusing on certain groups helps build community and reputation.
2. **What you teach.** Trumpet, Baroque trumpet, theory, yoga for musicians. Offering instruction in more than one specialty increases demand while providing you variety.
3. **Repertoire you teach.** Classical, jazz, blues, popular, fiddling. Though incorporating genres that are less familiar can understandably feel intimidating, doing so has potential to ignite enthusiasm while allowing the teacher and student to grow side by side.
4. **Approaches you use.** Suzuki, Eurhythmics, Alfred, Breathing Gym. List books or methods that play a role. While some purists stick entirely to a single approach, most SMTs are constantly on the lookout for new inspiration.
5. **Technologies you integrate.** Specific apps, notation software, recording opportunities, blogs, hardware. All else being equal, the SMT who effectively integrates technology offers a superior experience to those who don't.
6. **Interesting studio traditions.** Incentive programs, practice competitions, candy bar parties, newsletters, composer of the month, jam sessions. What fun, quirky, interesting customs separate your studio from the others?
7. **Teaching space features.** Go beyond the obvious—creative decor, purple piano, waiting area with home-baked cookies, student photo albums, public music journal. What does your teaching space say about you, and how does it benefit clients?

8. **Notable teaching/studio strengths.** Positive environment, personalized instruction, community feel, high artistic standards, great alumni. Last but not least, list additional attributes that are special to your studio.

The impact potential of SMT events is enormous. In 10 years' time, students may not remember specifics of last Thursday's meeting, but they are unlikely to forget a blockbuster studio show. As we have seen, studio events come in a thousand flavors. The best ones foster commitment, promote hard work, build community, and provide a great time for participant and observer alike. Variety is key.

The SMT Impact Blueprint provides space to describe up to four events. For each, add the date, title, and unique features that make it unforgettable.

Tuition Packages

SMTs charge tuition by the term. Beyond ensuring revenue, reducing cancellations, and increasing likeliness that students continue throughout the period, this structure encourages teachers to imagine comprehensive educational packages rather than an endless stream of one-on-one meetings.

In a given term, what does tuition include? How many private lessons, group classes, and events? What kind of technological access? On the blueprint, indicate if each listed feature plays a role in your instructional model in the Y/N column. In the # column, indicate the amount (e.g., if there are 15 lessons per term, write "15").

The final page of the SMT Impact Blueprint allows you to consider three separate packages. The most common solution is detailing fall (term A), spring (term B), and summer (term C). Another possibility is showing different tracks you offer, such as "in-studio," "online," and "in-home" options. A third is dividing by ability level: "beginner," "intermediate," and "advanced." Once again, choose designations that make sense for you.

Enter tuition rates for various-length lessons toward the bottom of the page. SMTs with interesting and varied curricula often command more than the competition, and for good reason. *The more you give, the more you receive.*

Vision to Reality
Take Action

The act of completing the SMT Income and Impact Blueprints is an accomplishment in itself. Doing so requires commitment, strategic planning, research, and creative thinking. Bringing proposals to fruition, however, requires another layer of action. Growing a business demands determination, persistence, and blistering hard work. Full realization will not occur overnight, though many resolute SMTs achieve success within a few years.

Fortunately, things get easier over time. Once your studio reaches capacity, maintaining those numbers and growing a waitlist almost happen automatically. Planning a class or summer camp is most challenging the first time around. Designing a website is more laborious than updating it. Time and energy strategically spent now is an investment in the future.

Whatever your circumstance today, how should you move forward? Brainstorm challenges that need to be met. How can I increase enrollment? Where will classes be held? With whom must I network? How many income-producing activities can I realistically add next year? Identify obstacles within each stream, and prioritize a to-do list. Be precise, just as you were with the blueprints, implementing what are commonly known as SMART goals:

- **Specific.** What exactly do you hope to accomplish? Address the six "Ws": who, what, where, when, which, and why?
- **Measurable.** What conditions must be met to constitute success? (For example, in your Income Blueprint, all financial data is measurable.)
- **Actions.** What precise steps must be taken to make specific, measurable goals happen?
- **Resources.** What resources are required? Money? Partnerships? An assistant? A computer? Post-it notes?
- **Timeline.** By what date do you hope to successfully reach this goal? Placing time restrictions creates a sense of urgency, increasing the likelihood that tasks get completed. Deadlines with consequences (real or imagined) are an important part of the process.

Now there's just one thing left . . . get to work! Transform your plan into reality.

Lessons from the Trenches

After graduating from college, many questions surrounded my future, but one thing was certain: I did not want to move back home with my parents (though I love them dearly). So I drafted a business plan and began taking action.

Step 1 was finding the right location. Following months of detective work, I settled on Frisco, TX, in December. Using a combination of careful research and rough guestimates, I began calculating how much it would take to comfortably live there and ultimately determined that landing in the black required at least 25 students by August. Though that goal seemed daunting, it was nice to have a specific target.

With zero leads and no friends in town, I pursued the first two agenda items: (1) find a house/studio and (2) build a website. Because few local competitors were online at the time, I actually got some nibbles early on and lined up six students before moving.

After relocating in April, I committed to marketing daily: contributing actively to a local website on education, joining a big band for fun and networking, placing myself in social settings. Each morning began with the question: "What can I do to get the word out today?" Some days were easy; others proved frustrating.

The efforts worked, and my roster grew. I threw a party when enlisting my 25th client, but the phone kept ringing. By my August deadline, the studio was more than 40 strong, allowing me to exceed income and impact goals in even the first year.

Assess and Modify

No matter how much preplanning, research, and diligent commitment are involved, it is impossible to precisely predict an SMT's career trajectory. There are simply too many unknowns.

At least once a year, assess your progress and revisit the blueprints. On the financial side, did you meet large-scale earning goals? Which streams/substreams exceeded targets, and which ones underperformed? Do parts of the master plan require revamping? Even if there were no major disappointments, does the future require revision? Page 349 contains a worksheet for comparing projected versus actual earnings.

Approach issues of impact with similar scrutiny. Did you stay true to your essential question? Have students devoted ample time to vital learning objectives? Which innovations were introduced? Did they work? What modifications should be incorporated? Like learning an instrument, SMTs recognize the infinite growth potential when it comes to *impact*. There is always more we can do to increase the value of musical engagement and instruction.

The Real Win

You have just read a manual for maximizing income and impact within the field of independent music teaching. I sincerely hope this content was thought provoking, relevant, and beneficial. But after all has been said and done, it is just a book. The vital work is up to you.

SMTs are proactive entrepreneurs and devout educators. Your "company" may have just one "employee" (you!), but careful and regular strategic planning, assessment, and change are every bit as crucial as they are for multibillion-dollar corporations. In fact, these things are more important, because this is your life.

Savvy means wise. Clever SMTs carefully design multifaceted careers that value impact, financial independence, and self-actualization. *Music teacher* is not merely a job description, but a title bestowed upon bold leaders who change lives and impact the world.

Thank you for your valuable contributions as a musician and an educator. SMTs are very, very, *very* important professionals, as there is so much work to do. Make your minutes count!

CODA

STAYING INSPIRED

At the outset of their career, most music teachers radiate passion. Eagerly anticipating each lesson, they have a brimming enthusiasm that transmits contagious energy.

Over the years, one of two phenomena occurs. Savvy Music Teachers (SMTs) maintain their level of gusto, or even see it grow. They're just as madly in love with music and education at their retirement party as they were decades earlier. In fact, many of these special individuals never give up teaching. Why sacrifice such a rewarding passion?

With time, however, less savvy teachers lose that spark. Sure, they continue delivering acceptable exchanges, walking through the motions. But the *je ne sais quoi* that once permeated their essence has vanished. Teaching is no longer a thrilling, paid "hobby." Instead, it becomes a chore, or even (yikes!) a "job."

Why do some educators stay inspired yet others become disenchanted? This is certainly not controlled by the random whims of life's roulette wheel; savvy decisions ensure the fire stays lit, benefiting master and apprentice alike.

Workload

Among the top reasons for burnout is overteaching. Though your students may be sweet, few teachers stay enthusiastic when juggling 30- to 40-plus-hour rosters each week, year after year. Our blueprint suggests 20 hours of lessons weekly. In reality, some teachers can handle more, while others feel overwhelmed with fewer. If students ever begin to morph from individuals to numbers in your mind, reassess workload.

Some teachers argue they need the money, providing no choice but to teach ridiculous hours, despite the toll. I respectfully disagree. As this book has demonstrated, there are many paths to generating a desired level of income. Overteaching serves no one in the long run.

A related issue entails downtime. Ten-hour lesson blocks without a break, seven-day teaching weeks, or years on end without vacation are detrimental to mental and physical health. Few music teachers are lazy, but choosing this profession mustn't mean sacrificing all personal time. Strategic scheduling is more than logistical—it keeps you motivated.

Lessons from the Trenches

To describe my first work year as a whirlwind is an understatement. Beyond teaching during traditional after-school hours (3 to 6:30 PM weekdays), I also gave lessons before school started, as late as 10 PM, and both Saturday and Sunday. With 70 students in total, the schedule was insane. I felt burned out after just one year.

I quickly wised up and implemented boundaries. Beyond reducing this load, I came up with the idea of setting up "office hours" for basic communication with parents. I began responding to emails, answering phone calls, and scheduling conferences only during designated windows. Though still a hard worker, I am careful to leave time for myself. Doing this makes me a sharper, better teacher when students arrive.

Varied Routine

Over the years, you will undoubtedly solidify effective ways to present material. These methods minimize preparation time and work well for students. We've all heard the saying, "If it ain't broke (or was it 'Baroque'?), don't fix it." After mastering such approaches, is it really necessary to continue exploring?

The answer for SMTs is a resounding "yes," and not just because the world is changing and music lessons must reflect that reality. No matter how effective the tactic, even the most jovial among us loses spunk when presenting a particular concept or piece the 163rd time. Everyone requires variety and fresh challenges.

Reinventing the wheel for every student or lesson is exhausting and unsustainable. But over the years, make a habit of incorporating new literature, method books, pedagogies, games, and learning objectives. There are thousands of ways to approach even a triad. Vary the recipe, stirring your teaching stew.

Continuous Reinvention

"I am always improving as a teacher," reflects pianist Jenny Boster (www.jenniferbosterpiano.blogspot.com). Since beginning this work as a teenager, she has consistently evolved her once traditional approach throughout the years.

Boster prefers her own pedagogical solutions to existing methods. She experiments in lessons and writes down successful strategies. "It is amazing when new approaches just click. Students get excited when they progress quickly, and I love creating an education that is uniquely mine." The decision to publish these ideas forced her to explore further. *My Muscle Builder Book*, currently in four graded volumes, features cutesy original clip art and a variety of engaging exercises.

One major development occurred when her oldest son was 3. Amazed by his deep connection to classical music, she began inventing musical games. His enthusiastic response gave her an idea: why not teach early childhood classes? Rather than training through an existing program, she and a friend designed original curricula where participants explore keyboard-based activities and sing original lyrics over classical masterpieces. Beyond engaging a new audience, she was able to have her son attend every class!

A few years later, now with a second child, Boster began targeting adult students primarily due to their availability mornings and after her kids went to bed. This demographic prompted new teaching priorities, allowing a greater focus on nuance and large-scale issues over the nitty-gritty of note reading, theory fundamentals, and basic technique.

Boster also manages a blog on issues related to piano teaching (www.theteachingstudio.blogspot.com). Guest contributors, polls on educational issues, and the need to consistently create valuable content challenge her to consider fresh perspectives and solutions. "Sometimes I stay up all night working on a lesson plan or blog post. I just get so excited by engaging in a creative and always evolving approach to teaching."

Musical Existence

Some independent teachers make the costly mistake of sacrificing an active musical life. Their entire artistic worldview is defined by student work. Let's face it: even the best pedagogue becomes jaded when this year's highlight is introducing *Für Elise* to a 10-year-old for the hundredth time. As a result, passion for this magical art form dwindles.

This book advocates a holistic approach to music education. Such a paradigm isn't just good for students. Teach by example and reap the rewards. True, life gets busy, and it may be tempting to forego superfluous experiences that don't pay the bills. But SMTs are careful not to surrender that which brought about their musical love affair in the first place.

An SMT Musical Existence	
Play/ sing	Being a virtuoso is not necessary, but you and your students should share the joy of music making. At a minimum, carve out an hour each week to practice, read new literature, or simply make music for fun.
Perform	Many SMTs maintain active gigging schedules. If that doesn't describe you, there are still plenty of opportunities. Join a community band. Sing with the church choir. Sight read music with fellow educators. Play at your studio recitals. Students love seeing their teachers perform, and that in turn motivates the teacher.
Train	You may have sufficient musical chops to instruct students, but there is always room for personal growth and exploration. Regardless of level or age, we all benefit from continued music study. Lessons are also reminders of what it's like to be on the other side, helping us relate to students.
Explore	Why not investigate a fresh artistic skill? Study improvisation, take up a new instrument, begin composing, or learn to dance. The arts span a vast universe, and as long as exploration and growth occur, you are likely to stay inspired.
Attend	Never forget the mystical power of live music. Whether buying season tickets to the opera or mixing and matching genres, regularly witness high-quality art.

Extreme Music Making

"What I care about is doing the thing that makes me happiest: being a working musician. The specifics—instrument, style, setting—are merely details. If music is involved, I'm in!" claims Ann Marlowe (www. annmarlowe.tripod.com).

There is perhaps no better word to describe Marlowe's musical engagement than *extreme*. A small sampling of her experiences include playing upright bass with The Strolling Strings, saxophone with a big band, tuba in community wind ensembles, flute (her original instrument) in wedding ceremonies, accordion for *Fiddler on the Roof*, woodwind doubles in countless musicals, electric bass in a Dixieland group, and cello in regional orchestras. Performing classical, jazz, country, Klezmer, rock, and "international," she has also dabbled with trumpet, trombone, violin, oboe, orchestral percussion, harmonica, guitar, ukulele, and—naturally—nose flute. Her current project is learning the drums.

With such a multitude of skills, Marlowe has plenty of professional opportunities even when the economy tanks and others struggle to obtain work. Beyond that, she finds great inspiration in the constant challenge of developing new aptitudes. Each endeavor seems to strengthen the others.

Learning a new instrument or style every few years also makes her a better teacher. "I constantly rediscover the joy, challenge, and excitement of developing new skills. Experiencing a process comparable to my students, though on a different instrument and level, helps us develop an empathetic relationship. Together we conquer and explore, side by side."

Lifelong Learning

Regular professional development in both music and teaching not only helps you stay up to date but also fuels continuous growth and passion. Take steps to continue your education each year.

Enrolling yourself in music lessons can be exhilarating, as SMTs rarely take this activity for granted. Other options include university/community college courses, weekend workshops, evening seminars, academic conferences, and summer training programs. These communal activities allow you to (re)connect with colleagues, discuss professional challenges, study current trends, and kindle inspiration.

Another helpful exercise is observing colleagues in action. Audit lessons to see what you can learn, and generously return the favor. Additionally, make a habit of reading relevant materials. Investigate books, scour blogs, and sub-scribe to at least a few trade journals.

In other words, don't lose sight of the most important student in your life: you!

Filling the Tank

At age 29, tenor Dan Callaway (www.lorimoranmusic.com/dancallaway.html) stopped taking music lessons. He was getting cast in Broadway musicals and national tours, and it was time to move on. Plus there was another problem—he could no longer afford them.

Despite wonderful opportunities along the way, the next seven years were a roller coaster, involving a divorce, cross-country move, and financial calamity. He buried many dreams and lost passion.

And then a solo cabaret performance proved life changing. While classical singing had always come less naturally than musical theater, a few audience members were impressed by his arias and encouraged him to resume voice lessons.

Formal study changed everything. "Lessons showed what a mess I was and helped rescue me from a tough time. Some people fear failing as a musician, but I had been terrified of success. When you get really good, after all, there are responsibilities. So I resisted, as if the stubborn 8-year-old Dan were trapped in the body of an adult."

The challenge of music study "fills my tank creatively." He now practices every morning, something that had not occurred regularly for years. Taking lessons also helps Callaway relate better to students. He now helps even pop-oriented students discover their "secret opera singer inside" and often shares stories from his own lesson that week. Being inspired makes him a better teacher and that, in turn, is inspiring.

Community

Music is a powerful tool for building community, yet ironically, many inde-pendent teachers experience loneliness and isolation. Though interactive communication with young students provides fulfillment, it is no substitute for discourse with friends, colleagues, and other adults. Avoid becoming a hermit and neglecting basic social needs. Social interaction rejuvenates the soul.

Building Community	
Chat	Though your relationship with parents of most students is professional, don't be shy about engaging them in conversation before or after lessons when time permits. Many are fascinating people.
Join	Become an active member of your state or local Music Teachers Association. Other music organizations, or societies built around a hobby (e.g., book clubs), provide great potential as well.
Work	This book argues the benefits of teaching for yourself. An advantage of working for a music academy (yours or someone else's), however, is the opportunity to walk among colleagues. Gigs, summer camps, and other professional engagements also foster social interaction with like-minded individuals.
Bond	Make a point to meet and mingle. Host dinner parties, attend house concerts, and seek additional situations that nurture relationships.
Schedule	The challenge is rarely a shortage of good people, but rather lack of minutes. Yet somehow, there is always enough time. Proactively schedule social engagements.

Being Present

What is the secret to remaining as inspired about music teaching into your 70s as you were 50 years prior? To solve this mystery, consider violinist Judy Silverman, 71 years young during our interview. "Why would I ever retire?" she asks rhetorically. "I never felt any burnout, even during the busiest periods. I would do this even if I didn't get paid."

Music has been an important force in Silverman's life from the start. The daughter of amateurs, she grew up performing with a family quartet. "Though music was always present, it was never considered a career path. My dad felt that amateurs loved music the most, since their motivation was pure passion rather than the need to make a living." But despite majoring in sociology and stints in various professions, a musical career was her destiny.

Beyond teaching and playing, Silverman has held official roles within leagues of organizations: the Johansen International Competition,

American String Teachers Association, Maryland State Music Teachers Association, Strings Plus Competition, Weaver Competition, Friday Morning Music Club Foundation, and National Philharmonic Orchestra, to name a few. She also cofounded a community orchestra and summer camp.

To be sure, her proactive involvement is a tremendous asset to these groups. But the gesture is not completely selfless, as Silverman finds this engagement thrilling. "Above all, my mission is igniting the love of music in others that I have always felt. At every level, being involved with music, kids, and communities is extremely fulfilling."

Silverman shares another secret. Throughout their marriage, she and her husband have played quartets with amateurs and professionals alike. These collaborators form the nucleus of her social circle. "Making music with friends—what could be more inspiring than that?"

Passion Projects, Hobbies, and Life beyond Music Teaching

As wonderful as music teaching can be, it is difficult to stay inspired when life centers exclusively on any one thing. Artistic *passion projects*, whether paid or not, are pursuits that generate excitement and stimulate personal growth. Recordings, concerts, benefits for worthwhile causes, outreach efforts, creative initiatives, collaborative ventures, and interdisciplinary explorations complement teaching, serving as powerful generators of positive energy.

In addition, create space for hobbies and interests beyond music: family, friends, traveling, sports, cuisine, reading, aeronautics, quilting. Music may represent life, but what is it that brings life to your music? Inspired teachers find inspiration all around them.

Get a Hobby

Violinist/violist Tasha Miner Salsido (www.minermusiclessons.com) grew up hearing sound career advice from her father: find something you love and get people to pay for it. Doing just that, she now earns the majority of her income teaching music.

But Salsido has other passions. For starters, she is an animal aficionado. She rode horses almost every day growing up, is currently the proud owner of three rescued greyhounds, and works as a certified dog trainer on the side. Beyond its own merits, this pastime helps her become a more patient music instructor and better break down tasks. "Teaching dogs to weave through your legs in a figure eight pattern is not so different from helping kids learn vibrato. At first, there must be several target points rehearsed independently. With time, steps are sped up until the action comes naturally."

Salsido's list of hobbies continues. A voracious reader, she divides time between fiction and books related to music, dogs, and horses. She is also a writer; her novel in progress tells the adventures of a girl and her canine, based loosely on Salsido's own childhood. A newer interest in photography has helped her recognize more beauty in all things. As a natural-born "techy," she likes building websites and has a slight obsession with downloading apps.

Like all SMTs, Salsido's plate is full. But she is sure to make time every day for enjoyable activities outside of music. "For every lesson, I seem to have a new analogy, story, or way of describing a phrase. Hobbies make me a better teacher!"

Economics

Financial well-being is a central theme of this text. Throughout, I have argued that income and impact should be linked. Do economics also influence inspiration? Once again, the answer is yes.

Obviously, an obsessive focus on getting rich is not the solution. But I have never met a music teacher with that inclination. People choosing this profession do so to follow a passion and make a difference. However, music teachers may struggle to meet basic financial thresholds. Beyond the direct challenge of making ends meet, economic hardship is often accompanied by negative energy and stress, sometimes even translating into bitterness. Such anxiety distracts teachers from the meaningful and important work they are meant to do.

The path to financial independence grants freedom to maintain a musical existence, engage in lifelong learning, tackle passion projects, pursue hobbies, sustain a social network, have a family (if that's in the cards), and preserve life beyond music teaching. Furthermore, meaningful lessons, classes, camps, events, technology, products, and additional activities benefit more than just students. When teachers feel good about their work, inspiration soars.

Solitary Retreat

In the weeks before each year draws to a close, jazz pianist, teacher, vocal coach, and composer Neeki Bey (www.neekibey.com) disappears from sight. During these "blackout days," he travels to an interesting location, takes long walks, reflects on the past, and contemplates the future. "It is critical that my life moves forward with fulfilling and challenging creative projects. This solitary retreat presents an opportunity to set out my intentions for the year."

Though getting rich is certainly not the point, financial freedom is crucial. "I believe my craft is every bit as valuable as the work of a doctor or architect. Raising my standard of living helps me feel better about work I pursue." He asks, "What can I do to make money that allows me to feel good about these contributions?" Beyond offering intriguing initiatives, this process has convinced him to drop activities or students unworthy of the life energy they zap.

Also considered are spending priorities. One year, he decided to pay off the car. Another was devoted to buying equipment for a high-quality home recording studio. International travel, recording, organizing concerts, and giving to meaningful charities are prioritized.

Rather than tempering dreams, he insists on financial solutions that facilitate a meaningful existence. For example, three rental properties generate enough revenue to cover his mortgage payments, leaving money on the table for passion projects.

The retreat itself, as well as the results of the process, helps keep Bey inspired. "I'm a very spiritual person. It is important to me that all these aspects of life match up."

Perspective

Let's face it: sometimes music teaching becomes frustrating. Students don't practice. They forget music at home or cancel *again* an hour before the lesson. You are forced to explain which note is F# for the 15th time, and then they disregard the profound message you poetically introduced last week. Are you talking to a wall? This could give a yoga instructor a heart attack!

If a student truly boils your blood no matter how hard you try, the best solution is referring them to another teacher. Life is too short and precious to waste negative energy on learners with whom you can't connect. Pessimism spreads quickly.

Beyond that, take a step back and keep things in perspective. Even at your worst lesson, you're not scrubbing toilets, performing hard manual labor, or fighting a world war. Music and teaching are passions! So stay positive, maintain humor, and count your blessings. Attitude makes a huge difference for both you and the student. Laugh about the tough moments.

Never forget this great news: you get to teach music!

Lessons from the Trenches

The way life looks is largely a mindset. Only I can control which thoughts enter my mind and where they ultimately go. I choose to make them positive.

Every morning when waking up, and then again before fading off to sleep, I read inspirational stories. Much of this is done through an app called Zite, which compiles newspaper and blog articles based on keywords inputted by the user. Some of mine are "happiness," "self-development," and "healthy living." I also watch *Super Soul Sunday* on the Oprah Winfrey Network, which profiles amazing individuals who have overcome adversity and struggle. These tales are constant reminders that all human beings face challenges, yet life is great. If I ever notice myself starting to get negative, such narratives help push the reset button.

I rarely experience anger but do get frustrated from time to time. When that happens, I take a walk, concentrate on the beauty around me, and come back later with a fresh perspective.

Mindset also impacts how I view students. All my clients are genuinely wonderful people. If they don't practice well one week, or struggle with a concept, I remind myself this is just one short moment in a long, complex journey. Luckily, my job is not to make virtuoso musicians, but rather to help students discover their own greatness. That process is truly awe inspiring.

FINANCIAL WORKSHEETS

The worksheets in Appendix A address various financial issues raised throughout this book. Instructions on several are contained within the text.

Worksheets are also available for download and completion on the website: www.oup.com/us/thesavvymusicteacher

Net Worth

This worksheet allows you to determine your net worth in dollars at a given point in time.

Name_____   Date_____   Age_____

Liquid Assets		Fixed Assets	
$_____	Cash in hand	$_____	Primary residence (owned)
$_____	Savings account(s)	$_____	Secondary properties
$_____	Checking account(s)	$_____	Vehicles (cars/boats/bikes)
$_____	Money market account(s)	$_____	Musical instruments
$_____	Certificates of deposit (CDs)	$_____	Other musical equipment
$_____	Savings bonds	$_____	Furniture
$_____	Investments	$_____	Technology/electronics
$_____	Retirement savings	$_____	Collectables (including art)
$_____	College investment savings	$_____	Clothing
$_____	Health savings account	$_____	Jewelry
$_____	Life insurance (cash value)	$_____	Assorted equipment
$_____	Other insurance (cash value)		(sports, home appliances, etc.)
$_____	Other investments	$_____	Debts owed to you
		$_____	Other assets
$_____	**TOTAL LIQUID ASSETS**	$_____	**TOTAL FIXED ASSETS**

$_____ **TOTAL ASSETS** (Liquid + Fixed)

Liabilities			
$_____	Mortgage amount owed	$_____	Personal loans
$_____	Equity lines of credit	$_____	Taxes due (income,
$_____	Car debt		property)
$_____	Credit card balance total	$_____	Other liability A
$_____	Unpaid bills (medical, etc.)	$_____	Other liability B

$_____ **TOTAL LIABILITIES**

$_____ Assets – $_____ Liabilities =
$_____ **NET WORTH**

Credit Score/Interest Rates

This worksheet allows you to consider interest rates on debt and investments.

CREDIT SCORE

The credit rating for _____ (your name) on _____
(MM/DD/YYYY) is ___ ___ ___.

DEBT

Debt		
Type of Loan	**$ Amount Owed**	**APR %**
Mortgage	$_____	_____%
Second mortgage	$_____	_____%
Equity line of credit	$_____	_____%
Car loan 1	$_____	_____%
Car loan 2	$_____	_____%
Credit card 1	$_____	_____%
Credit card 2	$_____	_____%
Credit card 3	$_____	_____%
Student loan 1	$_____	_____%
Student loan 2	$_____	_____%
Personal loan	$_____	_____%
Other loan 1	$_____	_____%
Other loan 2	$_____	_____%
Other loan 3	$_____	_____%

INVESTMENTS

Investments					
Investment Type	**Current Balance**	**Fixed %**	**1 year %**	**5 year %**	**10 year %**
Savings account	$_____	_____%			
Checking account	$_____	_____%			
Money market account	$_____	_____%			
Home equity	$_____	_____%			
CD 1	$_____	_____%			
CD 2	$_____	_____%			
Bond 1	$_____	_____%			
Bond 2	$_____	_____%			
Other fixed interest	$_____	_____%			
Home equity	$_____		_____%	_____%	_____%
Roth IRA	$_____		_____%	_____%	_____%
Traditional IRA	$_____		_____%	_____%	_____%
SEP-IRA	$_____		_____%	_____%	_____%
529 plan	$_____		_____%	_____%	_____%
Investment account	$_____		_____%	_____%	_____%
Other investment 1	$_____		_____%	_____%	_____%
Other investment 2	$_____		_____%	_____%	_____%

Financial Goals

This worksheet allows you prioritize short-, medium-, and long-term goals.

Short-Term Goals (under 1 year)	$ Amount	Target Date (MM/YY)
1.	$	__ __ / __ __
2.	$	__ __ / __ __
3.	$	__ __ / __ __
4.	$	__ __ / __ __
5.	$	__ __ / __ __

Medium-Term Goals (1–3 years)	$ Amount	Target Date (MM/YY)
1.	$	__ __ / __ __
2.	$	__ __ / __ __
3.	$	__ __ / __ __
4.	$	__ __ / __ __
5.	$	__ __ / __ __

Long-Term Goals (Over 3 years)	$ Amount	Target Date (MM/YY)
1.	$	__ __ / __ __
2.	$	__ __ / __ __
3.	$	__ __ / __ __
4.	$	__ __ / __ __
5.	$	__ __ / __ __

Annual Budget

This worksheet allows you to forecast expenses over the period of a year.

Spending projections for _____ (your name)

Proposed plan from _____, 20_____ (beginning date), to _____, 20_____ (end date)

Total annual spending projection $_____

Average monthly spending projection $_____ (Annual divided by 12)

Debt		Home (besides mortgage)	
$_____	Credit card	$_____	Rent
$_____	Student loans	$_____	Property taxes
$_____	Car loans	$_____	Home repair/
$_____	Home mortgage		maintenance
$_____	Home equity lines	$_____	Home items
	of credit	$_____	Other
$_____	Home equity loans		
$_____	Business loans		
$_____	Personal loans		
$_____	Cash advances		
$_____	Other		
$_____	**Debt Total**	$_____	**Home Total**

Utilities		Transportation	
$_____	Electric	$_____	Car purchase
$_____	Water and sewage	$_____	Auto repairs
$_____	Natural gas or oil	$_____	Gas
$_____	Phone (land and cell)	$_____	Parking
$_____	Internet	$_____	Other driving expenses
$_____	Cable		(tolls, tickets)
$_____	Other	$_____	Public transportation
		$_____	Rental cars
		$_____	Air transportation
		$_____	Other
$_____	**Utilities Total**	$_____	**Transportation Total**

Family		Food	
$_____	Day care/babysitting	$_____	Groceries
$_____	Child support/alimony	$_____	Alcohol
$_____	Education expenses	$_____	Restaurants
$_____	Activities (sports, music lessons, camps)	$_____	Coffee/snacks
$_____	Toys/things	$_____	Other
$_____	Child-related purchases		
$_____	Other		
$_____	**Family Total**	$_____	**Food Total**

Health		Career/Music	
$_____	Copays	$_____	Musical projects
$_____	Deductibles	$_____	Equipment/instruments
$_____	Prescriptions	$_____	Instrument maintenance
$_____	Noncovered medical	$_____	Accessories
$_____	Fitness (gym, yoga, etc.)	$_____	Scores/recordings
$_____	Leisure activities	$_____	School tuition
$_____	Other	$_____	Association dues
		$_____	Other
$_____	**Health Total**	$_____	**Career/Music Total**

Education		Entertainment	
$_____	College tuition	$_____	Concert tickets
$_____	Workshops/conferences	$_____	Movies
$_____	Lessons/continued education	$_____	Other arts events
$_____	Family education expenses	$_____	Hobbies
$_____	Other	$_____	Books and magazines
		$_____	Leisure travel
		$_____	Other
$_____	**Education Total**	$_____	**Entertainment Total**

Business		Miscellaneous	
$_____	Accountant	$_____	Toiletries
$_____	Lawyer	$_____	Grooming/beauty
$_____	Agent	$_____	Clothing
$_____	Business assistant	$_____	Computers/technology
$_____	Business supplies	$_____	Furniture and appliances
$_____	Rentals	$_____	Pets
$_____	Other	$_____	Gifts
		$_____	Emergency purchases
		$_____	Donations
		$_____	Other
$_____	**Business Total**	$_____	**Miscellaneous Total**

Insurance		Other Category	
$_____	Health care	$_____	_____
$_____	Dental	$_____	_____
$_____	Vision	$_____	_____
$_____	Life	$_____	_____
$_____	Homeowner's/renter's	$_____	_____
$_____	Instrument	$_____	_____
$_____	Vehicle	$_____	_____
$_____	Commercial general liability	$_____	_____
$_____	Travel	$_____	_____
$_____	Other	$_____	_____
$_____	**Insurance Total**	$_____	**Other Total**

Totals
$_____ Debt Total
$_____ Home Total
$_____ Utilities Total
$_____ Transportation Total
$_____ Family Total
$_____ Health Total
$_____ Food Total
$_____ Career/Music Total
$_____ Education Total
$_____ Entertainment Total
$_____ Miscellaneous Total
$_____ Business Total
$_____ Insurance Total
$_____ Other Total
$_____ **EXPENSE PROJECTION**

Annual Savings Target

This worksheet allows you to calculate your savings target for a given year.

Fill out only lines that you plan to address this year:

- Column 1: Indicate savings priority you plan to address this year.
- Column 2: What is the total (estimated) cost of this goal?
- Column 3: How much do you hope to contribute this year?
- Column 4: What does that mean per month (divide Annual $ by 12)?
- Column 5: What does that mean per week (divide Annual $ by 52)?

Proposed plan from _____, 20____ (beginning date), to _____, 20____ (end date)

Savings priority	Total $	Annual $	Monthly $	Weekly $
Business/career	$ _____	$ _____	$ _____	$ _____
College/private school	$ _____	$ _____	$ _____	$ _____
Health related	$ _____	$ _____	$ _____	$ _____
Home improvement	$ _____	$ _____	$ _____	$ _____
House down payment	$ _____	$ _____	$ _____	$ _____
Parent care	$ _____	$ _____	$ _____	$ _____
Passion project	$ _____	$ _____	$ _____	$ _____
Rainy day fund (build)	$ _____	$ _____	$ _____	$ _____
Retirement	$ _____	$ _____	$ _____	$ _____
Vacation	$ _____	$ _____	$ _____	$ _____
Vehicle (new/used)	$ _____	$ _____	$ _____	$ _____
Wedding/party	$ _____	$ _____	$ _____	$ _____
	$ _____	$ _____	$ _____	$ _____
	$ _____	$ _____	$ _____	$ _____
TOTAL ANNUAL SAVINGS TARGET	$ _____	$ _____	$ _____

Tax Deduction Worksheet

This worksheet allows you to itemize your tax deductions for a given year.

Tax deductions for calendar year 20 ___ ___

Totals	
$_____	Hired Help Total
$_____	Space Total
$_____	Marketing Total
$_____	Continued Education Total
$_____	Business-Related Travel Total
$_____	Taxes/Fees Total
$_____	Supplies and Expenses Total
$_____	**TAX DEDUCTIONS**

Hired Help		Space	
$_____	Accountant	$_____	Camp space rental
$_____	Administrative expenses	$_____	Class space rental
$_____	Agent/manager	$_____	Event hall rental
$_____	Cleaning expenses	$_____	Home studio
$_____	Contracted teachers	$_____	Lesson space rental
	(for lessons, classes,	$_____	Liability insurance
	or camps)	$_____	Security (alarm
$_____	Legal costs		system)
$_____	Other	$_____	Other
$_____	**Hired Help Total**	$_____	**Space Total**

Marketing		Continued Education	
$_____	Advertising	$_____	Coaching and lessons
$_____	Business cards	$_____	Conferences and
$_____	Printing		workshops
$_____	Professional photos	$_____	Journal subscriptions
$_____	Website design	$_____	Professional organization/
$_____	Website hosting		union dues
$_____	Other	$_____	Other
$_____	**Marketing Total**	$_____	**Continued Ed. Total**

Business Related Travel		Taxes/Fees	
$_____	Airfare	$_____	Bank fees/charges for
$_____	Car rental		credit card payments
$_____	Driving to gigs, teaching,	$_____	Business loan interest
	and business	$_____	Business taxes
$_____	Lodging	$_____	Personal taxes
$_____	Meals on	$_____	Property taxes
	business trips	$_____	Other
$_____	Parking		
$_____	Taxi, bus, train		
$_____	Tolls		
$_____	Other		
$_____	**Business Related Travel Total**	$_____	**Taxes/Fees Total**

Supplies and Expenses			
$_____	Accessories (strings, reeds, picks, cases, etc.)	$_____	Internet
		$_____	Musical supplies
		$_____	Office furniture/ decoration
$_____	Bookkeeping expenses	$_____	Office supplies
$_____	Business gifts ($25 max. each)	$_____	Phone
		$_____	Postage
$_____	Camp/class related	$_____	Printer
$_____	Computers/tablets	$_____	Recordings
$_____	Equipment rentals	$_____	Sheet music
$_____	Event tickets	$_____	Software and apps
$_____	Instrument insurance	$_____	Video equipment
$_____	Instrument repair	$_____	Other
$_____	Instruments		
$_____	**Supplies and Expenses**		

Earning Goal

This worksheet allows you to determine an income goal that works for your circumstances.

Earning goal for _____ (your name)

Proposed plan from _____, 20____ (beginning date), to _____,
20____ (end date)

Spending projection	$
+ Savings target	$
Financial obligation	$
× 10% buffer (× 1.1)	$
Safety number	$

Total Income	100%
– Estimated tax rate	___ ___ %
Income % after taxes	___ ___ %

Safety number	$
÷ Income % after taxes	___ ___ %
ANNUAL EARNING TARGET	$

SAVVY MUSIC TEACHER INCOME BLUEPRINT

This worksheet is designed to help you imagine income streams and earning amounts over the period of a fiscal year.

Worksheets are also available for download and completion on the website: www.oup.com/us/thesavvymusicteacher

Savvy Music Teacher Income Blueprint

Portfolio mix for _____ (your name)

Proposed plan from ____, 20____ (beginning date), to ____, 20____ (end date)

Desired annual income $____

Stream 1 _____						
Substreams	**A**	**B**	**$**	**Gross $**	**(COGS)**	**Net $**
A) ____	_____	_____	$____	$____	($____)	$____
B) ____	_____	_____	$____	$____	($____)	$____
C) ____	_____	_____	$____	$____	($____)	$____
D) ____			$____	$____	($____)	$____
Stream 1 TOTAL						$____

NOTES	1A	1C	NOTES
	1B	1D	

Stream 2 _____						
Substreams	**A**	**B**	**$**	**Gross $**	**(COGS)**	**Net $**
A) ____	_____	_____	$____	$____	($____)	$____
B) ____	_____	_____	$____	$____	($____)	$____
C) ____	_____	_____	$____	$____	($____)	$____
D) ____			$____	$____	($____)	$____
Stream 2 TOTAL						$____

NOTES	2A	2C	NOTES
	2B	2D	

Stream 3 _____

Substreams	A	B	$	Gross $	(COGS)	Net $
A) ____	_____	_____	$____	$____	($____)	$____
B) ____	_____	_____	$____	$____	($____)	$____
C) ____	_____	_____	$____	$____	($____)	$____
D) ____	_____	_____	$____	$____	($____)	$____
Stream 3 TOTAL						$____

NOTES	3A	3C	NOTES
	3B	3D	

Stream 4 _____

Substreams	A	B	$	Gross $	(COGS)	Net $
A) ____	_____	_____	$____	$____	($____)	$____
B) ____	_____	_____	$____	$____	($____)	$____
C) ____	_____	_____	$____	$____	($____)	$____
D) ____	_____	_____	$____	$____	($____)	$____
Stream 4 TOTAL						$____

NOTES	4A	4C	NOTES
	4B	4D	

Stream 5 _____

Substreams	A	B	$	Gross $	(COGS)	Net $
A) ____	_____	_____	$____	$____	($____)	$____
B) ____	_____	_____	$____	$____	($____)	$____
C) ____	_____	_____	$____	$____	($____)	$____
D) ____	_____	_____	$____	$____	($____)	$____
Stream 5 TOTAL						$____

NOTES	5A	5C	NOTES
	5B	5D	

Stream 6 _____

Substreams	A	B	$	Gross $	(COGS)	Net $
A) ____	_____	_____	$____	$____	($____)	$____
B) ____	_____	_____	$____	$____	($____)	$____
C) ____	_____	_____	$____	$____	($____)	$____
D) ____	_____	_____	$____	$____	($____)	$____
Stream 6 TOTAL						$____

NOTES			NOTES
	6A	6C	
	6B	6D	

Stream 7 _____

Substreams	A	B	$	Gross $	(COGS)	Net $
A) ____	_____	_____	$____	$____	($____)	$____
B) ____	_____	_____	$____	$____	($____)	$____
C) ____	_____	_____	$____	$____	($____)	$____
D) ____	_____	_____	$____	$____	($____)	$____
Stream 7 TOTAL						$____

NOTES			NOTES
	7A	7C	
	7B	7D	

STREAMS	PROJECTED $
Stream 1:____	$____
Stream 2:____	$____
Stream 3:____	$____
Stream 4:____	$____
Stream 5:____	$____
Stream 6:____	$____
Stream 7:____	$____
ANNUAL INCOME (Projected)	$____

Projected versus Actual Earnings

This worksheet allows you to compare projected income for a given period of time with actual earned income.

SOURCES	PROJECTED $	ACTUAL $
STREAM 1: _____		
➢ A. _____	$_____	$_____
➢ B. _____	$_____	$_____
➢ C. _____	$_____	$_____
➢ D. _____	$_____	$_____
Stream 1 TOTAL	$_____	$_____
STREAM 2: _____		
➢ A. _____	$_____	$_____
➢ B. _____	$_____	$_____
➢ C. _____	$_____	$_____
➢ D. _____	$_____	$_____
Stream 2 TOTAL	$_____	$_____
STREAM 3: _____		
➢ A. _____	$_____	$_____
➢ B. _____	$_____	$_____
➢ C. _____	$_____	$_____
➢ D. _____	$_____	$_____
Stream 3 TOTAL	$_____	$_____
STREAM 4: _____		
➢ A. _____	$_____	$_____
➢ B. _____	$_____	$_____
➢ C. _____	$_____	$_____
➢ D. _____	$_____	$_____
Stream 4 TOTAL	$_____	$_____

SOURCES	PROJECTED $	ACTUAL $
STREAM 5: _____		
➤ A. _____	$_____	$_____
➤ B. _____	$_____	$_____
➤ C. _____	$_____	$_____
➤ D. _____	$_____	$_____
Stream 5 TOTAL	$_____	$_____
STREAM 6: _____		
➤ A. _____	$_____	$_____
➤ B. _____	$_____	$_____
➤ C. _____	$_____	$_____
➤ D. _____	$_____	$_____
Stream 6 TOTAL	$_____	$_____
STREAM 7: _____		
➤ A. _____	$_____	$_____
➤ B. _____	$_____	$_____
➤ C. _____	$_____	$_____
➤ D. _____	$_____	$_____
Stream 7 TOTAL	$_____	$_____

STREAMS	PROJECTED $	ACTUAL
Stream 1:_____	$_____	$_____
Stream 2:_____	$_____	$_____
Stream 3:_____	$_____	$_____
Stream 4:_____	$_____	$_____
Stream 5:_____	$_____	$_____
Stream 6:_____	$_____	$_____
Stream 7:_____	$_____	$_____
TOTAL EARNINGS	$_____	$_____

APPENDIX C

SAVVY MUSIC TEACHER IMPACT BLUEPRINT

This worksheet allows you to organize your philosophy, core objectives, and what makes your studio unique.

Worksheets are also available for download and completion on the website: www.oup.com/us/thesavvymusicteacher

Savvy Music Teacher Impact Blueprint

Your name _____   Studio name _____

Studio address _____   Web address _____

Essential Question

Top Learning Objectives (ranked)	Activities
1.	a. b. c. d.
2.	a. b. c. d.
3.	a. b. c. d.
4.	a. b. c. d.
5.	a. b. c. d.

Studio Positioning

Who You Teach (Demographics)	What You Teach (Subjects)
1. _____	1. _____
2. _____	2. _____
3. _____	3. _____
4. _____	4. _____
5. _____	5. _____
Repertoire You Teach	Methods/Approaches You Use
1. _____	1. _____
2. _____	2. _____
3. _____	3. _____
4. _____	4. _____
5. _____	5. _____
Technologies You Integrate	Interesting Studio Traditions
1. _____	1. _____
2. _____	2. _____
3. _____	3. _____
4. _____	4. _____
5. _____	5. _____
Teaching Space Features	Notable Teaching/Studio Strengths
1. _____	1. _____
2. _____	2. _____
3. _____	3. _____
4. _____	4. _____
5. _____	5. _____

Events

Events	
Event/Activity #1 Date: __ __ / __ __ , 2 0 __ __ Title: _____ _____	**Interesting Features**
Event/Activity #2 Date: __ __ / __ __ , 2 0 __ __ Title: _____ _____	**Interesting Features**
Event/Activity #3 Date: __ __ / __ __ , 2 0 __ __ Title: _____ _____	**Interesting Features**
Event/Activity #4 Date: __ __ / __ __ , 2 0 __ __ Title: _____ _____	**Interesting Features**

Tuition Package

	Term A		Term B		Term C	
Term description	_____		_____		_____	
FEATURE	Y/N	#	Y/N	#	Y/N	#
Private Lessons						
Group Lessons						
Enrichment Classes/ Opportunities						
Performance Events						
Field Trips						
Ensemble Playing						
Other Collaborations						
Competitions						
Technology Access						
Recording						
Music and Supplies						
Other Feature 1: _____						
Other Feature 2: _____						

Term A Tuition Rate		
30-minute lessons	45-minute lessons	60-minute lessons
$	$	$

Term B Tuition Rate		
30-minute lessons	45-minute lessons	60-minute lessons
$	$	$

Term C Tuition Rate		
30-minute lessons	45-minute lessons	60-minute lessons
$	$	$

Compared to the competition, my rates are:

- ☐ The cheapest
- ☐ Below average
- ☐ Average
- ☐ Above average
- ☐ The most expensive

APPENDIX D

SAMPLE SAVVY MUSIC TEACHER DOCUMENTS

The following documents were created by Kristin Yost, founder of Centre for Musical Minds (www.centreformusicalminds.org) and the Savvy Music Teacher featured in "Lessons from the Trenches" throughout this book.

The Centre for Musical Minds
Financial Responsibility Contract
——— 2014-2015 ———

By signing this agreement, you acknowledge your financial responsibilities to the Centre for Musical Minds. You are acknowledging that you have read, understand and agree to our tuition handbook, including missed lesson and makeup policies, available at www.CentreforMusicalMinds.org.

All tuition is due on the 1st of each month, one month in advance. See detailed summary of tuition below. Commitment is for one semester at a time and unless we receive a 30-day notification of withdrawal, we assume you will be continuing your musical journey with us. A $15 late fee will be applied to your account if tuition payments are received after the 3rd of the month. Accounts past due after the 5th of the month will result in lesson cancellation. All past-due accounts receive a courtesy email and phone call before lesson termination occurs. Should something come up where you cannot financially fulfill your commitment to your child's piano lessons, we appreciate and encourage advanced notice and open, ongoing communication with our office.

SCHOOL - YEAR MONTHLY TUITION

Frisco Tuition*
Miss Kristin/Dr. Lin/Dr. Holland

30 min $147 / 45 min $207 / 60 min $284.75
30 min $157.25 / 45 min $217.25 / 60 min $304.75

Southlake Tuition*
Miss Kristin

30 min $140.75 / 45 min $198.75 / 60 min $274.25
30 min $147 / 45 min $207 / 60 min $284.75

*Additional Fee for Students taking the Royal Conservatory Exams: $120 total for the year which includes 4 Theory classes and 4 Master Classes

SUMMER 2015

Frisco Tuition
Southlake Tuition

No increase from 2014
No increase from 2014

PAYMENT CYCLE

*July 1..	Annual Enrollment Fee
August 1......................................	Fall Tuition Installment 1
September 1...............................	Fall Tuition Installment 2
October 1....................................	Fall Tuition Installment 3
*November 1...............................	Fall Tuition Installment 4
December	Spring Tuition Installment 1
January 1....................................	Spring Tuition Installment 2
February 1..................................	Spring Tuition Installment 3
*March 1.....................................	Spring Tuition Installment 4
April 1..	Summer Tuition Installment 1
May 1...	Summer Tuition Installment 2
June 1..	Summer Tuition Installment 3

*Denotes special pay-in-full discounts when tuition is paid in full for the upcoming semester.

For detailed billing instructions, and to view your invoices, please log into your www.StudioHelper.com account.

Parent Signature _____   Date _____ Email _____

Track Options

Please choose the track that best represents the goals of your family while enrolled in lessons at The Centre for Musical Minds.

Please initial at the selected track

RECREATIONAL/HOBBYIST _____

30 or 45-minute lessons
- Participation in one or two recitals throughout the year.
- Students are required to practice 15 minutes each day, 4 days per week.

SERIOUS HOBBY _____

45 or 60-minute lessons
- Participation in all recitals and judged events throughout the year. Consider a creative performance such as the Clavinova Festival or Roland Piano Idol.
- Students study a mix of classical repertoire, popular genres, some technique and theory.
- Students are required to practice 30 to 45 minutes each day, 5 days per week.
- Most recommended course of study at CMM.

Students who wish to participate in The Royal Conservatory Development Program are required to enroll in separate performance and theory classes. The goal of each student is to pass the exams with a score of 70 or above.
Teacher Recommendation: All

PRE-PROFESSIONAL _____

60 - minute lessons
- Participation in all recitals and judged events throughout the year,
  plus The Royal Conservatory Exams as well as extra adjudicated events.
- Students study a mix of classical repertoire, popular genres, extensive
  technique and collegiate level theory.
- Students are required to practice 60 to 90 minutes each day, 5/6 days per week.

All pre-professional students are required to enroll in a separate theory and performance classes. The goal of each student is to achieve a score in the upper 80's/low 90's.
Teacher Recommendation: Dr. Lin & Claudia Fuenmayor

Student Name _____

By signing this agreement, you acknowledge and understand what your tuition covers, as well as our attendance policy at the Centre for Musical Minds. By signing this document, you are acknowledging that you have read, understand and agree to our tuition handbook and absence policies available at www.CentreforMusicalMinds.org.

At the *Centre for Musical Minds*, we are all professional music teachers. Because we are experienced, degreed music professionals with full schedules, we do not schedule individual makeup lessons. Imagine what ten cancellations in one week would do! Please understand we do this to be fair to **all** of our students as well as to protect our personal time. If we do have a cancellation, we will contact you by the email address we have listed on file.

At the *Centre for Musical Minds*, we feel everyone deserves one makeup class per semester in the event of illness, family emergency or school event. Makeup classes are **not** for students who miss lessons due to play dates, games, non-emergency doctor appointments or family vacations. Our calendar is published well in advance so please make sure you check your personalized Studio Helper Calendar AND our website calendar for performance and vacation dates, locations and times. Makeup classes are in the form of small group performance classes and TBD; 3 students must sign up in order for the class to be held.

EVER WONDER WHERE YOUR TUITION DOLLARS GO?

We'd like to give you some insight on what your fees cover,
so you can better understand what we as a music school provide for you.

- Teacher Experience
  (Minimum 3 years)
- Teacher Formal Education (Mini
  mum B.A. and M.M. in Progress)
- Teacher connections with other
  professionals in the industry
- Time spent with student in lessons
- Time spent planning for student
  lessons
- Trips to music store

- Sales, Property and other taxes
- High quality Instruments
  Professional quality acoustic
  and digital instruments)
- Upkeep of instruments
- Teacher Accomplishments
- Teacher Publications
- Planning recitals
- Time spent at recitals
- Shipping costs associated with
  music

- Email/administrative time/paid
  staff to handle accounts and
  schedules
- Professional accountant to
  keep your account accurate
- Faculty Development
- Teacher salary
- Teacher retirement
- Office Supplies
- New Software to stay
  up-to-date

You get the idea...

Thank you for choosing the Centre for Musical Minds team of professionals to guide your child's musical journey!

Parent Signature _____ Parent Email _____

Mobile Phone _____ Date _____

August 2013

Su	M	Tu	W	Th	F	Sa
				1	2	3
4	5	6	7	8	9	10
11	12	13	14	15	16	17
18	19	20	21	22	23	24
25	26	27	28	29	30	31

September 2013

Su	M	Tu	W	Th	F	Sa
1	2	3	4	5	6	7
8	9	10	11	12	13	14
15	16	17	18	19	20	21
22	23	24	25	26	27	28
29	30					

October 2013

Su	M	Tu	W	Th	F	Sa
		1	2	3	4	5
6	7	8	9	10	11	12
13	14	15	16	17	18	19
20	21	22	23	24	25	26
27	28	29	30	31		

November 2013

Su	M	Tu	W	Th	F	Sa
					1	2
3	4	5	6	7	8	9
10	11	12	13	14	15	16
17	18	19	20	21	22	23
24	25	26	27	28	29	30

December 2013

Su	M	Tu	W	Th	F	Sa
1	2	3	4	5	6	7
8	9	10	11	12	13	14
15	16	17	18	19	20	21
22	23	24	25	26	27	28
29	30	31				

January 2014

Su	M	Tu	W	Th	F	Sa
			1	2	3	4
5	6	7	8	9	10	11
12	13	14	15	16	17	18
19	20	21	22	23	24	25
26	27	28	29	30	31	

February 2014

Su	M	Tu	W	Th	F	Sa
						1
2	3	4	5	6	7	8
9	10	11	12	13	14	15
16	17	18	19	20	21	22
23	24	25	26	27	28	

March 2014

Su	M	Tu	W	Th	F	Sa
						1
2	3	4	5	6	7	8
9	10	11	12	13	14	15
16	17	18	19	20	21	22
23	24	25	26	27	28	29

April 2014

Su	M	Tu	W	Th	F	Sa
		1	2	3	4	5
6	7	8	9	10	11	12
13	14	15	16	17	18	19
20	21	22	23	24	25	26
27	28	29	30			

May 2014

Su	M	Tu	W	Th	F	Sa
				1	2	3
4	5	6	7	8	9	10
11	12	13	14	15	16	17
18	19	20	21	22	23	24
25	26	27	28	29	30	31

Centre for Musical Minds
2013 - 2014 Calendar

August
26 Fall Classes begin

September
2 Labor Day - No Lessons

October
21-26 Fall Performance Classes
No Private Lessons; PPK classes are regularly scheduled

25-27 Clavinova Festival, Times TBA at Metroplex Pianos in Dallas

November
3 Fall Recitals; Location TBA

10 Fall Performance Evaluations 12:30 to 4:30 p.m. ($20 optional)

25-30 Thanksgiving Break
No Private Lessons; PPK classes are regularly scheduled

December
14-15 Holiday Recitals

23 Holiday Break Begins
No Lessons

January
12 Holiday Break ends

13 Spring Semester Begins

February
11 Royal Conservatory Exams Registration Deadline

17-22 Spring Performance Classes
No Private lessons; PPK classes are regularly scheduled

March
2 Pop Showcases at SMU

9-23 Spring Break (two weeks)

April
13 Achievement Auditions 12:30 to 5:30 p.m.

May
5-10 Piano Idol Week
No Private Lessons; PPK classes are regularly scheduled

11 Honors Recital

17 Final Day of Spring Classes

19 Summer Session Begins

For detailed location and time information of events, see the full calendar at www.CentreforMusicalMinds.org

The Centre for Musical Minds
POP SHOWCASE
——— March 2nd 2014 ———
2 pm

Taylor Badillo	Penguin Blues, Nancy Faber
Ellison Cushman	Hungry Herbie Hippo
Caitlin Badillo	Cups
Jack DeWeese	We Are the Champions, Queen
Madison Greene	Roar, Katy Perry
Connor Stimson	What does the Fox Say
Parker DeWeese	Let It Go, from Frozen
Caitlyn Wilson	Demons, Imagine Dragons
Anamika Suresh	Roar, Katy Perry
Elaine Zheng	Payphone, Maroon Five
Will Junkin	Skyfall, Adele
Ben Turner	Piano Man, Billy Joel
Adam Cordeiro	The Medallion Calls, from Pirates of the Caribbean
Kyler Kocher	Viva la Vida, Coldplay
Neebelle Khromachou	Radioactive, Imagine Dragons
Emily Palmer	Say Something, Christina Aguilera
Jessica Jennings	All I Ever Needed, AJ Michalka
Kaci Pelias	Let Her Go, Passenger
Sarah Hoving	Fields of Gold, Sting
Jordan Sado	Black Flag, Jordan Sado
Jacob Cordeiro	They Can't Take that Away from Me, Gershwin

SUMMER CLASSES 2014

Option A: Camp plus
three 45 minute private lessons

Centre for Musical Minds

Summer Camp for Elementary Students
(this is preferred for students in first 1-3 years of study - lays a more solid foundation, & the kids have fun!)
Monday-Thursday 9:30am to 12pm or 5: 30 to 8pm;

Dates: June 9-12 or August 11-14

Ages: 6 - 10, *limit 10 students* (sibling exceptions may be accepted upon request)

Teachers: Miss Lexi, Miss Kristin and Mrs. Susan

- Improvisation and composing
- Rhythm Reinforcement Activities
- Solfege/singing
- Theory Games
- Piano Safari/Keyboard ensemble
- Pop Play-A-Long each day featuring Way Cool Keyboarding and PianoPronto
- Fun Music History lessons

Option B: Five 45-minute
lessons plus 2 classes

Enrichment Classes; 90 min – CMM Factuly and Guests
(Enrichment classes may be substituted for any private lessons)

1. **History:** Music History from Beyoncé to Bach;
(choose one date) May 27th 5-6:30pm, June 3rd 5-6:30pm, August 5th 5-6:30pm

2. **Ensemble:** African Drumming with S'Ankh Rasa
May 31st 11-12:30pm

3. **Perspective:** Music Store Tour!
(meet at Penders for 1 hour);
Learn to navigate through the thousands of books available for young musicians.
May 24th 11am, June 13th 11am, July 16th 11am

Enrichment Classes Continued

4. **Perspective:** Classical Piano Concert/Piano Party
with classical pianist, Alex McDonald, Van Cliburn Competitor
July 1st 5:30-7pm

5. **Perspective:** Jazz Piano Concert/ Piano Party with
world-renowned jazz pianist, Fredrick Sanders
June 1st 5:30-7pm

6. **Ensemble 1 & 2: Series of two classes.** Keyboard Ensemble
(Preparation required!) This is a two-part class where Ensemble 2 must be
selected as the student's second enrichment class. Time TBD based on
student level and availability. We schedule around those interested!
(Choose your own schedule based on your ensemble partner(s)!)

7. **Accompanying 1 & 2: Make music with your peers! (Series of
two classes)** Perfect for the intermediate student to learn to play with
another musician. These classes will prepare students to play with another
instrumentalist enrolled in piano at CMM, but studies another instrument in
school. We will work directly with other private teachers and band directors
to ensure a successful first experience into accompanying. Don't play
another instrument but still want to take the class? No problem - we will make
sure we provide a young musician. Focus on how to have a productive
rehearsal or figure out what to do if one person gets "off" in the music. This is
a great first step in setting students up for a potentially lucrative and
rewarding part-time (or full-time) job! Students need to register for both
Accompanying 1 & 2 if choosing these classes.
(Choose your own schedule based on your ensemble partner(s)!)

8. **Recording Your Piano Performances:**
Learn how to record a great video for YouTube! This is a series of two-
classes and students must sign up for Recording 1 & 2 for both enrichment
classes.
May 19 and 20; 5:30 to 7pm OR July 21 and 22; 5:30 to 7pm

*Each session must have 5 students signed up for
the class to take, or other options will be provided.
If other options are not satisfactory, tuition will be
credited or refunded at the discretion of the family
and executive director.*

Summer 2014 Scheduler

PLEASE PRINT CLEARLY*

Student Name _____

Parent Name _____

Parent Email _____

Parent Mobile # _____

Teacher _____

Spring 2014 Lesson Day and Time _____

Do you want to change your Lesson Day/Time for Fall 2014?   Yes / No

If Yes, Day/Time Preference _____

Office Use Only:

Date & Time Received _____

Received by _____

Students will be scheduled for summer lessons in the order this completed form is received. Our preferred way of receiving this form is electronically, which you can do by scanning with a printer, or by using a free App on your iPads/Tablets. We recommend CamScanner, which is free. Alternatively, you can drop by CMM and have any teacher date and initial with time stamp, and place in the Tuition box.

Once schedules have been set, a confirmation email will be sent to the address you provide, and your schedule will be available to view on Studio Helper. It is your responsibility to write lesson dates and times down, though we do set up reminders through our scheduling system.

Once your schedule has been confirmed, please understand we cannot guarantee any schedule changes. Missed summer lessons will NOT have a reschedule option if you no-show. We understand things come up and schedules change. If you cannot make one of the confirmed lessons, please give your teacher, or Janna, at least 72-hours notice so that we can attempt (though not guaranteed) to reschedule your lesson.

Lastly, it is important to understand that not all teachers will be available all weeks. Therefore, you will be asked to indicate what is most important to you: 1) the ability to choose days/times to fit your schedule OR 2) scheduling lessons with your regular teacher. In either case, we will do our absolute best to keep your child scheduled with your regular teacher, but if the ability to choose day/time is most important to you, then your child/children may have a lesson or two that is with another qualified CMM instructor.

For questions, please contact Janna directly at accounts@centremm.org or by calling 214-586-4309.

Page 1 of 3

Step 1: Please indicate with an "X" the Summer Option you choose:

_____ Option A – Camp plus three (3) 45-min private lessons OR

_____ Option B – Five (5) 45-min private lessons and Two (2) classes

Step 2: Please indicate with an "X" what is most important to you:

_____ Lesson dates/times that fit our family's schedule OR

_____ Lesson dates/times with my child's/children's regular teacher

Step 3: Please indicate with an "X" the weeks and times you are available for your 45-minute private summer lessons. If you chose Option A above, you will choose at least three (3) lesson dates. If you choose Option B, you will choose at least five (5) lesson dates. If the dates/times you select are not available, we will select lesson times for you based on what was most important to you.

Morning = Before 12pm
Early Afternoon = 12pm-2pm
Late Afternoon = 2pm-5pm
Evening = After 5pm
■ = Day/Time Not Available

May 19-24

	Mon	Tues	Wed	Thur	Fri	Sat
Morning						
Early Afternoon						
Late Afternoon						
Evening						■

May 26-31

	Mon	Tues	Wed	Thur	Fri	Sat
Morning						
Early Afternoon						
Late Afternoon						
Evening						■

Morning = Before 12pm
Early Afternoon = 12pm-2pm
Late Afternoon = 2pm-5pm
Evening = After 5pm
■ = Day/Time Not Available

June 2-7

	Mon	Tues	Wed	Thur	Fri	Sat
Morning						
Early Afternoon						
Late Afternoon						
Evening						■

June 9-14

	Mon	Tues	Wed	Thur	Fri	Sat
Morning						
Early Afternoon						
Late Afternoon						
Evening						■

June 16-21

	Mon	Tues	Wed	Thur	Fri	Sat
Morning						
Early Afternoon						
Late Afternoon						
Evening						■

June 23-28

	Mon	Tues	Wed	Thur	Fri	Sat
Morning						
Early Afternoon						
Late Afternoon						
Evening						■

June 30-Jul 5

	Mon	Tues	Wed	Thur	Fri	Sat
Morning						■
Early Afternoon						■
Late Afternoon					■	■
Evening					■	■

July 7-12

	Mon	Tues	Wed	Thur	Fri	Sat
Morning						■
Early Afternoon						■
Late Afternoon						
Evening						

July 14-19

	Mon	Tues	Wed	Thur	Fri	Sat
Morning						■
Early Afternoon						■
Late Afternoon						
Evening						

July 21-26

	Mon	Tues	Wed	Thur	Fri	Sat
Morning						■
Early Afternoon						■
Late Afternoon						
Evening						

July 28-Aug2

	Mon	Tues	Wed	Thur	Fri	Sat
Morning						
Early Afternoon						
Late Afternoon						
Evening						

Aug4-9

	Mon	Tues	Wed	Thur	Fri	Sat
Morning						■
Early Afternoon						■
Late Afternoon						
Evening						

Aug 11-16

	Mon	Tues	Wed	Thur	Fri	Sat
Morning						■
Early Afternoon						■
Late Afternoon						
Evening						

Morning = Before 12pm
Early Afternoon = 12pm-2pm
Late Afternoon = 2pm-5pm
Evening = After 5pm
■ = Day Time Not available

Comments (other information you would like to provide that would help us with your summer schedule):

_____
_____
_____
_____
_____
_____
_____
_____
_____
_____
_____
_____

Step 4: Sign up ONLINE for your Camp week (Option A) or for your Two (2) 90-minute each enrichment classes (Option B). This year, parents will sign up for their camp week or their two (2) enrichment classes using SignUp Genius. See attached links. SignUp Genius links will be taken down May 1st and added to each child's schedule in StudioHelper at that time.

FURTHER READING

To follow is a list of books relevant to Savvy Music Teachers.

MUSIC TEACHING BUSINESS

- *The Complete Idiot's Guide to Teaching Music on Your Own*, by Karen Berger
- *The Dynamic Studio: How to Keep Students, Dazzle Parents, and Build the Music Studio Everyone Wants to Get Into*, by Philip Johnston
- *How I Made $100,000 My First Year as a Piano Teacher*, by Kristin Yost
- *The Independent Piano Teacher's Studio Handbook*, by Beth Gigante Klingenstein
- *Making Money Teaching Music*, by David Newsam
- *The PracticeSpot Guide to Promoting Your Teaching Studio: How to Make Your Phone Ring, Fill Your Schedule, and Build a Waiting List You Can't Jump Over*, by Philip Johnston
- *The Private Guitar Studio Handbook: Strategies & Policies for a Profitable Music Business*, by Mike McAdam
- *The Private Music Instruction Manual: A Guide for the Independent Music Educator*, by Rebecca Osborn
- *The Private Voice Studio Handbook: A Practical Guide to All Aspects of Teaching*, by Joan Frey Boytim

MUSIC CAREER GUIDES

- *Beyond Talent: Creating a Successful Career in Music*, by Angela Myles Beeching
- *Lessons from a Street-Wise Professor: What You Won't Learn at Most Music Schools*, by Ramon Ricker
- *The Musician's Journey: Crafting Your Career Vision and Plan*, by Jill Timmons
- *The Savvy Musician: Building a Career, Earning a Living, & Making a Difference*, by David Cutler

TECHNOLOGY IN MUSIC TEACHING

- *The iPad Piano Studio*, by Leila Viss
- *Making Music with GarageBand and Mixcraft*, by Robin Hodson, James Frankel, Richard McCready, and Michael Fein
- *Music Education with Digital Technology*, by Pamela Burnard and John Finney
- *Music Learning Today: Digital Pedagogy for Creating, Performing, and Responding to Music*, by William Bauer
- *Musical iPad: Creating, Performing, & Learning Music on Your iPad*, by Thomas Rudolph & Vincent Leonard
- *Teaching Music through Composition: A Curriculum Using Technology*, by Barbara Freedman
- *Technology Strategies for Music Education*, by Thomas Rudolph, Floyd Richmond, David Mash, Peter Webster, William Bauer, and Kim Walls
- *Using Technology to Unlock Musical Creativity*, by Scott Watson
- *YouTube in Music Education,* by Thomas Rudolph and James Frankel

PRACTICING

- *The Art of Practicing: A Guide to Making Music from the Heart*, by Madeline Bruser
- *How to Get Your Child to Practice . . . without Resorting to Violence!!* by Cynthia Richards
- *The Musician's Way: A Guide to Practice, Performance, and Wellness*, by Gerald Klickstein
- *Not until You've Done Your Practice: The Classic Survival Guide for Kids Who Are Learning a Musical Instrument, but Hate Practicing*, by Philip Johnston
- *The Practice Revolution: Getting Great Results from the Six Days between Lessons*, by Philip Johnston
- *Practiceopedia: The Music Student's Illustrated Guide to Practicing*, by Philip Johnston

PERFORMANCE ANXIETY AND MINDSET

- *Effortless Mastery: Liberating the Master Musician Within*, by Kenny Werner
- *Fight Your Fear and Win: At Work, in Sports, on Stage*, by Don Greene
- *Free Play: Improvisation in Life and Art*, by Stephen Nachmanovitch
- *The Inner Game of Music*, by Barry Green and Timothy Gallwey
- *The Mastery of Music: Ten Pathways to True Artistry*, by Barry Green
- *Perfect Wrong Note: Learning to Trust Your Musical Self*, by William Westney
- *Performance Success: Performing Your Best under Pressure*, by Don Greene
- *The Talent Code: Greatness Isn't Born. It's Grown. Here's How,* by Daniel Coyle
- *The War of Art: Break through the Blocks and Win Your Inner Creative Battles*, by Steven Pressfield

BUSINESS AND MARKETING

- *The $100 Startup: Reinvent the Way You Make a Living, Do What You Love, and Create a New Future*, by Chris Guillebeau
- *The Brand Called You: Make Your Business Stand Out in a Crowded Marketplace*, by Peter Montoya and Tim Vandehey
- *Business Model You: A One-Page Method for Reinventing Your Career*, by Tim Clark, Alexander Osterwalder, and Yves Pigneur
- *The E-Myth Revisited: Why Most Small Businesses Don't Work and What to Do about It*, by Michael Gerber
- *Guerilla Marketing: Easy and Inexpensive Strategies for Making Big Profits from Your Small Business*, by Jay Conrad Levinson
- *Infinite Possibilities: The Art of Living Your Dreams*, by Mike Dooley
- *The Small Business Bible: Everything You Need to Know to Succeed in Your Small Business*, by Steven Strauss
- *You, Inc: The Art of Selling Yourself*, by Harry Beckwith and Christine Clifford

WEBSITES AND SOCIAL MEDIA

- *Creating a Website That Sells Your Business: The Radical Blueprint to Turning Your Visitors into Buyers*, by J. R. See
- *Cyber PR for Musicians: Tools, Ticks, & Tactics for Building Your Social Media House*, by Ariel Hyatt
- *How to Create a Website: 7 Steps to the Best Website for Your Business*, by Jurgita Glodenyte
- *Make Money Blogging: The Ultimate Guide to Monetizing a Blog Website*, by Sarah Goldberg
- *The New Rules of Marketing & PR: How to Use Social Media, Online Video, Mobile Applications, Blogs, New Releases, and Viral Marketing to Reach Buyers Directly*, by David Meerman Scott
- *The Really, Really, Really Easy Step-by-Step Guide to Building Your Own Website: For Absolute Beginners of All Ages*, by Gavin Hoole
- *The Social Media Bible: Tactics, Tools, and Strategies for Business Success*, by Lon Safko
- *WordPress to Go: How to Build a WordPress Website on Your Own Domain, from Scratch, Even if You Are a Complete Beginner*, by Sarah McHarry

TIME MANAGEMENT

- *The 7 Habits of Highly Effective People: Powerful Lessons in Personal Change*, by Stephen R. Covey
- *The 25 Best Time Management Tools & Techniques: How to Get More Done without Driving Yourself Crazy*, by Pamela Dodd and Doug Sundheim
- *The Checklist Manifesto: How to Get Things Right*, by Atul Gawande

- *Getting Things Done: The Art of Stress-Free Productivity*, by David Allen
- *Life in Cut Time: Time Management for Music Teachers*, by Emily Schwartz
- *Pomodor Technique: Illustrated: The Easy Way to Do More in Less Time*, by Staffan Noteberg
- *The Skinny on Time Management: How to Maximize Your 24-Hour Gift*, by Jim Randel
- *Time Management from the Inside Out: The Foolproof System for Taking Control of Your Schedule—and Your Life*, by Julie Morgenstern

FINANCIAL MANAGEMENT

- *925 Ideas to Help You Save Money, Get out of Debt, and Retire a Millionaire so You Can Leave Your Mark on the World*, by Devin Thorpe
- *America's Cheapest Family Gets You Right on the Money: Your Guide to Living Better, Spending Less, and Cashing in on Your Dreams*, by Steve and Annette Economides.
- *The Automatic Millionaire: A Powerful One-Step Plan to Live and Finish Rich*, by David Bach
- *A Beginner's Guide to Investing: How to Grow Your Money the Smart and Easy Way*, by Alex Frey and Ivy Bytes
- *How to Get out of Debt, Stay out of Debt, and Live Prosperously*, by Jerrold Mundis
- *The Millionaire Next Door*, by Thomas Stanley
- *The Money Book for the Young, Fabulous, & Broke*, by Suze Orman
- *Rich Dad Poor Dad: What the Rich Teach Their Kids about Money that the Poor and Middle Class Do Not!* by Robert Kiyosaki
- *Saving for Retirement (without Living like a Pauper or Winning the Lottery*, by Gail Marks Jarvis
- *The Total Money Makeover: A Proven Plan for Financial Fitness*, by Dave Ramsey
- *Think and Grow Rich*, by Napoleon Hill

TEACHING PHILOSOPHY

- *Drive: The Surprising Truth about What Motivates Us*, by Daniel Pink
- *Intelligent Music Teaching: Essays on the Core Principles of Effective Instruction*, by Robert A. Duke
- *Making Musical Meaning: Unlocking the Value of Music Education in the Age of Innovation*, by Elizabeth Sokolowsky
- *Mindset: The New Psychology of Success*, by Carol Dweck
- *Music, Informal Learning and the School: A New Classroom Pedagogy*, by Lucy Green
- *The Music Teaching Artist's Bible: Becoming a Virtuoso Educator*, by Eric Booth
- *Start with Why: How Great Leaders Inspire Everyone to Take Action*, by Simon Sinek

FEATURED ARTIST INDEX

SUBJECT INDEX

CPSIA information can be obtained
at www.ICGtesting.com
Printed in the USA
BVOW03s0247141017
497334BV00005B/16/P